Cruise Of Miracles

Calvin F. Meyer

Cruise Of Miracles
ISBN: Softcover 978-1-955581-97-4
Copyright © 2022 by Cal Meyers

All rights reserved. No part of this book may be reproduced or transmitted in any form or by any means, electronic or mechanical, including photocopying, recording, or by any information storage and retrieval system, without permission in writing from the publisher.

Parson's Porch Books is an imprint of Parson's Porch & Company (PP&C) in Cleveland, Tennessee. PP&C is a self-funded charity which earns money by publishing books of noted authors, representing all genres. Its face and voice is **David Russell Tullock** (dtullock@parsonsporch.com).

Parson's Porch & Company *turns books into bread & milk* by sharing its profits with the poor.

www.parsonsporch.com

Cruise Of Miracles

Contents

Epilogue 7
Foreword 9
Chapter 1: Invitation 11
Chapter 2: The Itinerary 14
Chapter 3: Flight To San Francisco 18
Chapter 4: Boarding the Ship 28
Chapter 5: Leaving San Francisco 34
Chapter 6: At Sea 42
Chapter 7: Hawaii – Day 1 63
Chapter 8 – Hawaii - Day 2 82
Chapter 9: Four Days at Sea 97
Chapter 10: Seattle 115
Chapter 11: Alaska 139
Chapter 12: Unexpected Blessings 174
Chapter 13: Home? 180
Chapter 14: Thanksgiving 224
Chapter 15: Florida And Homeward Bound 251
Chapter 16: Last Leg 264
Chapter 17: Beyond Imagination 271
About the Author: 282

Epilogue

This novel is a fictional story based on both real and fictional events. Most all the characters in the story are real, but many of the names have been changed. The intent was to develop an autobiography of the dreams and outcomes we so earnestly wish to be true. It is basically a prayer from both the hope our lives were significant and that lives were changed along the way.

Upon entering retirement, one soon discovers that reflections can consume our thoughts in the desperate hope we walked this short life making a difference. A lesson learned in writing this novel was the reality that behind many of the fictional events were memories that, upon expansion, allowed the author to complete what he hoped marked the significance of his life. Most significantly, it reminded him of how God has intervened in his life and that his whole life has been one of miracles.

Primary characters in the story are Dorothy and Jim, the sister and brother-in-law of Shirley, the author's wife. It was in reality one of the greatest relational disappointments. Two sisters became so separated in their beliefs that it completely destroyed any sense of oneness between two who once loved each other deeply. The novel also brings out the destructive force of a false religion like Jehovah's Witnesses. It is anti-Biblical and destroyed the unity across families not to mention the intrusion into our family by attempting to steal the love and loyalty of our family from us. None of it in real life ended well. Both families are still suffering the effect of broken marriages, immorality and spiritual destruction with our children. The deepest pain is that many in these families will never see Heaven predicated on the indoctrination and acceptance of a faith that is so contrary to God and His Son. They deny the basis for which Jesus died and Who He is as Messiah. They hold no value to who Jesus claimed to be when He said, "I am the way, the truth and the life and no one comes to the Father except by me" (John 14:6).

While the stories also reflect the many who crossed the paths of Cal and Shirley Meyer for almost 75 years of their lives, it ends with the victory of the rapture. The surprise ending, the greatest miracle of this story, is the hoped-for salvation of Dorothy and Jim, as dreamed.

The author appreciates your walk with him as he took this Cruise of Miracles.

Calvin F. Meyer
September 17, 1943 – February 21, 2022

Foreword

Have you ever asked, "If I had my life to live over, what would I change?" I've often pondered that. I think of the many sad moments in my life, the many temptations, the many failures, the many people who disappointed me and whom I've disappointed, the many times I've failed to live up to expectations, the consequences of my actions and how they impacted my family. And yes, I've thought "if only I could relive that." But then it struck me that if I changed that, then the blessings I gained from it would not have happened, some job opportunities lost, the impending future of my life perhaps altered etc. For change in one situation would have altered yet another situation, the "Domino Effect."

Consequential to that have been the potential impacts my life may have had that I never realized. I don't know the ways God may have used me to help another person or situation make a dynamic change for which I never saw or felt tangibly. I lived my life as imperfect as it may have been and in it, I've seen both triumph and defeat. Yet would I have changed any of it? That I truly can't answer. But I still find some joy and comfort in contemplating it.

This then formed the basis for this book. I've pictured my life as a journey on a cruise, a Cruise of Miracles. When one looks carefully at true life situations, he/she cannot escape how much God blessed them in both the successes and failures. Those are the miracles we've often failed to see in our life's journey. The intent of this book is predicated on many real-life experiences but fictionalized a bit as to outcomes, outcomes that are plausible but were not tangibly experienced. However, one cannot but believe God would have been capable of each of these miracles. One day one of our greatest miracles will be to live in the eternal glory He promised us and when we get there it is anticipated we will see and experience that beyond our wildest imagination.

This book is dedicated to a God who loves each of us so dearly that He made promises to us and gave us a New Covenant through His

Son, Jesus. Join me in this journey and see miracles I dreamed, some of which I hope to see as true from the view of Heaven.

Calvin F. Meyer
Author

September 13, 2022: A note from Shirley Meadows-Meyer

A week or so after Calvin passed away, February 21, 2022, our son Chris found this completed book in Cal's computer and printed a copy for me to edit, hoping to get it published as soon as I could afford to do so. I read it cover-to-cover and deemed it "very good." I noted some errors and decided to leave them intact until I could read it a second time, marking them in red ink.

At this time, we have passed our 57th Wedding Anniversary and Cal would have been 79 on Saturday, September 17. My prayer is that you will enjoy his final book as much as I did!

Chapter 1: Invitation

Our typical retirement Saturday morning is to get up and review our emails and then have a late breakfast. In retirement it's okay to sleep past 8:00 am, sit in your pajamas and read the online news leisurely and peruse your emails. Then along about 9:00 am or 9:30 Shirley gets up and fixes breakfast. One thing we've done in retirement is structure our lives around a lot of routine. For example:

- Monday = Volunteer at Appalachian Outreach and Wash Clothes Day
- Tuesday = Study and prepare the Sunday School Lesson Day
- Wednesday = Grocery Shop and Gas Car Day
- Thursday = House Cleaning Day
- Friday = Clean Cars Day
- Saturday = Date Night/Movie Day
- Sunday = Church and Relax Day

With this also comes a very set routine of breakfast. Saturday is my omelets day. Throughout the week my breakfast menu varies from eggs and toast to eggs and grits and on Thursday its pancakes. But Saturday it's omelets. Well, this Saturday I had made plans for us to do a little shopping as I needed a new sprinkler for the backyard and I wanted to buy Plan of Salvation bookmarks for my Sunday School Class before going to the movies. However, I started the day by first watering the yard, given I had just had them aerated.

After breakfast I returned to the office and was previewing the news as I was listening to Christmas music via my Pandora, which I normally start in October, the doorbell rang. We weren't expecting anyone this morning. I went to the door. It was the Fed Ex man.

"Mr. Meyer. I have a Special Delivery for you. Please sign here."

Wow, I couldn't imagine what it could be. We were expecting new masks for Shirley's ASV Sleep Machine, but they typically ship that through regular mail. I took the package to the office.

Shirley was at her computer. "What do you have there?" she asked.

"I don't know. It's special delivery."

I opened it and found a letter and what looked like two tickets. I began reading the letter to Shirley:

DOVE CRUISE LINES
JERUSALEM
MH MKADDESH

Dear Mr. and Mrs. Meyer:

You've just been selected the award of a cruise via a new cruise line on which you will take a four-week cruise to sites you've visited before. We call this cruise the "Cruise of Miracles." Your ship is called the **"MH MKaddesh."** The ship line is a new line out of Israel called the Dove lines. If you have any questions, please call us a 555-537-8711.

Enclosed are your tickets. The trip will start on Saturday, October 29. I realize this is Homecoming at Carson-Newman and it is a special homecoming for Mrs. Meyer, given this is her 50th reunion, but this trip will be as special. Your trip will originate out of San Francisco, California. I am also attaching two airlines' tickets to San Francisco. You will be flying out of Knoxville via a new discount line called the MAT airlines. Please see tickets and itinerary below. You may read about us from your personal computers only at www.dovecruises.heav.

On Saturday morning please plan to arrive at the Knoxville airport no later than 8:00 am and proceed to the ticket window marked **"MAT Airlines."** Someone will be there to greet you and escort you directly to Gate 3. You will not need to clear security as we will have secured that for you. Your plane will depart sharply at 9:00 am and will arrive at San Francisco

International Airport at 10:00 am (PST). A set of hosts will be there to greet you and guide you to the buses that will take you to the ship. The ship will depart at 4:00 pm.

Sincerely

A. Gabe
Director
Dove Cruises

Chapter 2: The Itinerary

Hardly able to contain my excitement I eagerly read the letter to Shirley. Both of us were full of questions. Our minds were exploding with "Hows?"

"How are we going to be gone for four weeks with such short notice?"
"How are we going to get ready in time?"
"How are we going to plan for Gracie (our cat)?"
"How are we going to pay our bills while gone that long?"

It was mind boggling. Shirley seemed overwhelmed almost to the point of saying "We can't do this!" My first response was to get online and check out the legitimacy of this. I've never heard of Dove Cruise Lines nor MAT Airlines. This has to be a scam!

I decided to call the number and ask for Mr. Gabe himself. Without any difficulty I got right through to him.

"Hello, Mr. Gabe, this is Dr. Cal Meyer. I received your letter today inviting us to the four-week cruise and…"

Before I said another word, Mr. Gabe spoke in an ever so clear, authoritative but understanding voice, "but you're not sure this is real."

"Yes, you understand. I've never heard of you before and with so many scams these days and such short notice, this is pretty hard to believe."

"Cal, I understand. But it is real, and we ask you by faith to trust us. This will be a divinely inspiring trip for you and Mrs. Meyer. You've always lived by faith, and we ask you to do so now."

"But Mr. Gabe, my faith has been in Christ and not some ship or trip."

"Precisely. Cal, it is the faith you and Mrs. Meyer have had in Christ that is the reason for this invitation."

"I don't understand."

"Cal, do you remember the night you and Mrs. Meyer were on the Royal Caribbean Ship Majesty of the Seas and at the opening Welcome Program you and Mrs. Meyer were recognized for being married fifty years"?

"Well, yes, but how did you know that?"

"What happened next?"

"The Activities Director came off the stage and asked Shirley (my wife) what the secret was to our fifty years of marriage?"

"And what was her response?"

"She said we had centered our marriage on the Lord Jesus Christ."

"Cal, do know how beautiful choirs of angels sounded that night when they heard that?"

"Well, I've never thought of it that way. But what does that have to do with this trip. And how do you know all that?"

"Well, things are told around the ships. But the thing is this, you and Mrs. Meyer have been two lives full of miracles both in causing them and witnessing them. Thus, we want to award you for that with a Cruise of Miracles."

"Oh, man, how can I say no to that?"

"Did I answer your questions?"

"Well, in a way you did, and I do have some peace about this after talking with you. We'll be there Saturday morning."

Shirley chimed in after I hung up and asked, "Well, what did he say?"

"You won't believe it."

I proceeded to convey the conversation as closely as I could. "Hon, I feel we have to make this trip. I feel it in my soul. But I'll check out the site they gave us as well."

I went online to check out the Dove Cruise Lines. I never heard of ".Heav." Normally its ".org" or ".com." Sure, enough it popped up:

> *Welcome Calvin Meyer. We were expecting your visit. Dove Cruise Lines has been in operation for infinite years but with our efforts to provide comfortable ships, ones our patrons will find comfortable, we aren't publicized until patrons are invited to share a cruise with us. Thus, when we say it is "new" it is new to those patrons. We are headquartered in Jerusalem, but our beginning started in the little town of Bethlehem. We have eight ships traveling the seas for us at this time. Two of the most notable are the MH Jirah and the MH Shalom. Each trip is personalized for the patrons invited on that particular cruise. WE WELCOME YOU ABOARD.*
>
> *Please feel free to select your ship and peruse the ship's layout. Each ship is equipped with several main dining halls, a prayer chapel, a huge auditorium for joyful worship and plenty of areas for music, reading, games and fellowship.*
>
> *Although an itinerary has been mailed to you, please go to the site of your ship's sailing date and see your detailed day by day itinerary.*

Well, I found another site marked MH MKeddesh and clicked it. It had the typical detail information you find on most sites for the assigned or chosen ship:

MH MKaddesh
Sailing Date: October 29, 2016, San Francisco, California

DATE	DESTINATION
Saturday, October 29,	Depart 4:00 pm
Sunday, October 30	At Sea
Monday, October 31	At Sea
Tuesday, November 1	At Sea
Wednesday/Thursday, November 2,3	Honolulu 8:00 am – Thursday 11:00 pm
Friday, November 4	At Sea
Saturday, November 5	At Sea
Sunday, November 6	At Sea
Monday, November 7	At Sea
Tuesday-Wednesday, November 8,9	Seattle 8:00 am – Wednesday, 11:00 pm
Thursday, November 10	At Sea
Friday, November 11	Juneau 8:00 am – 8:00 pm
Saturday, November 12	Skagway 8:00 am – 8:00 pm
Sunday, November 13	At Sea
Monday, November 14	Ketchikan 8:00 am-5:00 pm
Tuesday, November 15	At Sea
Wednesday, November 16	At Sea
Thursday, November 17	At Sea
Friday, November 18	At Sea
Saturday, November 19	Panama Canal
Sunday, November 20	At Sea
Monday, November 21	At Sea
Tuesday, November 22	At Sea
Wednesday, November 23	Bahamas 8:00 am – 8:00 pm
Thursday, November 24	At Sea
Friday, November 25	Port Canaveral 8:00 am- Friday 11:00pm
Saturday, November 26	At Sea
Sunday, November 27	New York City 8:00 am

Chapter 3: Flight To San Francisco

As I read the itinerary and showed it to Shirley, we both had severe apprehension. Being on ship for four weeks, most of which would be at sea, we just didn't know if we wanted to do that. It's not like taking a train trip where you could see land or a car trip where we could make stops and see the sights a while. What in the world would we do for four weeks on a ship?

Then the thought of packing for four weeks was just too much.

"Cal, why don't you call Mr. Gabe back and tell him we really don't want to go." Shirley said, rather mournfully.

"Oh, I don't know hon. I think this is our initial reaction, but we might regret it this time next week."

She continued, "This means we've got just a little over a week to get our clothes ready, make plans for Gracie and get the house closed up, not to mention cleaned up, with someone to look after it. I just feel panicky all over."

"I know." I understood. There was a side of me that agreed and yet another side that urged me to go ahead and leap out in faith. "You know Ellen (our college friend in town) said she'd be glad to take care of Gracie if we needed her. I know it will be for four weeks, but let's give it a try. Then I looked after Jackson's house across the street when they went to their northern cabin for a month. I'm sure he'd do the same for us. It will all work out." Shirley sighed and we began our planning in our own way.

Over the next week, Shirley and I selected clothes we could easily pack and wash on board. Shirley called Ellen and she did agree to take Gracie and Jackson agreed to look after the house. I contacted all the utilities and we set up early payment so I could leave town without worrying on them. Putting the rest of our mail on hold would be no problem. We set the house heat on 68 degrees, left the living room light on and put a timer on a porch lantern. It seemed to me we had everything set. It meant Christmas shopping and setting up Christmas would simply have to wait until we returned but I normally didn't deal with Christmas until after Thanksgiving anyway. And, besides that, we could do plenty of Christmas shopping on the trip. I emailed all the kids and informed them of what was happening. Renee was excited for us. Chris only wished us well and Larry was eager to hear from us when we got back.

Well Saturday, October 29 finally arrived. We had planned to be attending Homecoming at Carson-Newman this day. It was after all Shirley's 50th reunion. We were regretful we were missing it as we had heard some of our classmates whom we hadn't seen in 50 years would be there. But my 50th reunion was last year and so many of our friends were in my class, so this was going to be a bit anticlimactic anyway.

To get to the airport in time, we needed to leave by 6:30 am. The airport is an hour away and I need to account for any emergencies. We got up around 5:00 am, got ready, Shirley put some coffee on and warmed up a cinnamon roll. Then about 6:00 am unexpectedly the doorbell rang.

I called to Shirley, who was in the kitchen, "I wonder who that could be?"

"Hello, Dr. Meyer."

"Yes."

"I'm Carlos Rodriguez, your driver."

"My driver?"

"Didn't they tell you?"

"Tell me what?"

"Tell you they were providing you and Mrs. Meyer a limousine to the airport."

Surprised, "No, no they didn't. Give us a minute. We were just about to have a cup of coffee."

"You go ahead, and I'll put your luggage in the car."

Quickly Shirley and I drank our coffee, ate our cinnamon roll, checked all the doors and headed to the limousine.

"I wonder why they didn't tell us." I quietly spoke to Shirley.

Carlos looked familiar but I have no reason why. He took us west on I-40 to McGhee Tyson Airport. Once there, he opened the door for both of us and unloaded our luggage. I went to give him a tip, but he would have none of it.

Soon a Red Cap came and picked up our luggage on a cart and took it to the MAT Ticket Booth. I didn't tell him where to go; he just sort of knew. I wanted to speak to Carlos and express my appreciation, but he was gone and out-of-sight as soon as I turned around.

"Hello, Dr. and Mrs. Meyer we were expecting you. Your luggage will be taken straight to the plane and then right to the ship. The next you see; it will be in your cabin."

"Oh, wow! That's first class."

"Please follow your stewardess to Gate 3, the Charter Gate."

I noticed that other passengers were going straight or to the left, apparently Charter flights were to the left. I wondered how many would be on our flight. We arrived at Gate 3. It was a small waiting area with several typical seats you see in any airport. Out of the windows was a small but new looking plane with "MKaddesh Air Transport" written above the door. It was a silver plane with a long blue stripe down its side. Rather plain looking. Then two thoughts struck me. First, MKeddesh, that's the name of our ship. Thus the "MAT" Airlines. How unique. Second, the last time I flew on an MAT airline was when I went with my dad (an Army Chaplain) back to Hawaii following a summer visit to Washington State to attend a summer youth camp at Mt. Baker. He and mom worked it out for me to fly via Pan Am to join our former church youth group. This would have been my first summer living in Hawaii. At the end of the youth camp, Dad arranged a flight on MAT to come and pick me up. MAT then meant "Military Air Transport." What a coincidence I'm going to Hawaii on an MAT airlines. Rather unusual. I wonder……..

I looked around and there seemed to be about 45 or so passengers. It wasn't a large plane. Somewhat like one of Delta Bombardiers CRJ regional jets. This seems more like a commuter flight than a long distance one, but I have flown long flights on commuter planes before. After all they are flying me out of Knoxville not Atlanta or some large city.

Around 8:30 am, the public address came on, "Ladies and Gentlemen. We are now beginning our boarding of MKaddesh Air Transport. The stewardess will assign you seats as you board."

Oh good, that gives Shirley the chance at a window seat. We got in line. We were about half way back. No one was in a rush. We walked out the door and onto the Jetway. As we got to the plane, I said to the stewardess, "We're Dr. and Mrs. Meyer."

"Yes, Dr. Meyer, Welcome aboard. You and Ms. Meyer please take Seats 30A and B."

We headed back to our seat and found them on the right side. 30A was the window and 30B the aisle. These were nice broad seats, four across. Seats 30C and D were across the aisle from us. We got in and for the first time in a long time I didn't have to ask for an extender. I have lost 30 pounds the last six months. We buckled up. Already feeling the excitement of take-off. It reminded me of Shirley's first flight back in 1999.

I had just finished authoring a math book for the Association of Christian Schools International. To celebrate they flew all the authors out to Colorado Springs for a book dedication and celebration. It was a book series from Grade 1 – 6. I wrote the fifth-grade book. At the time I worked at Liberty University in Lynchburg, Virginia. Shirley had never flown before and had made the comment she would never get on anything she couldn't drag her feet. Well, the morning came for us to fly. She was scared. She even tried to convince my daughter, who had taken us to the airport, to take her place. Wouldn't you know it, the plane between Lynchburg and Washington D.C., where we were to connect to our flight to Colorado, was a small 18-seater. My first thought, oh my, why this for Shirley's first flight? Well, we got in the air and sure enough my greatest fear hit, we flew into a rain storm. The plane began to swerve this way and that way. We were told to keep our seat belts on. I was scared. I looked at Shirley and she was glued to the window. I didn't know if she was in shock or what. Well, we finally landed in D.C. and got off the plane. Shirley didn't say a word. I was expecting a rush of tears or a scream or at the very least a very determined, "We're going home, now. Rent a car!" I said, "Are you okay?" She smiled and looked back at me, and her response almost knocked me to the tarmac, "That was fun!" Needless to say, she's enjoyed flying ever since.

As our seatmates in seats 30C and D got settled, Shirley was her usual self. "Hi, we're the Meyers."

"Nice meeting you, we're the Barkers."

Shirley continued; we're heading to San Francisco for a cruise to Hawaii but it's going other places."

"Well, so are we."

We should have imagined. We're on the plane named the MKaddesh going to a ship called the MH MKaddesh.

It then hit Shirley. This whole plane is full of people going to the same ship. With that realization Shirley added, "I guess then you've already been on a cruise to Hawaii."

Mrs. Barker responded. "Well, I haven't but my husband did years ago."

I know Shirley's curiosity wanted to continue the conversation but then the stewardess closed the doors and got on the public address.

"Ladies and Gentlemen, we've just closed the doors. The pilot informs us we are ready for take-off. Please turn off your cell phones and buckle your seat belts…." We all knew the speech by heart.

With that we felt the plane being pushed from the gate, the engines all being revved up. It is at this point my attention is looking out the window, as is Shirley. I'm always a bit uneasy until we lift off and we're in the air. With us away from the gate, we heard the engines revved higher and the plane began to move forward toward the runway. As we finally reached our take off runway, all of a sudden that thrust of power pushed us back a bit in our seats as the plane began its run down the runway for take-off. It is usually at this point I ask a little prayer for God's Guardian Angels to be under our wings and in the cockpit. Then that tilt upward as we could see the airport and city below get smaller. Finally, the sound of the landing gear having been raised in place as we headed toward our cruising altitude. Shirley and I both just stayed glued to the window.

Reaching 28,000 feet the pilot came on. "Good morning, ladies and Gentlemen. This is your Pilot S. Paul. I want to welcome you aboard. As your cruise is very special, we want you to have an enjoyable flight as well. Our flight time is four hours. We will arrive in San Francisco at 10:00 am Pacific Standard Time. We have completely clear skies in front of us and will arrive on time. Sit back and enjoy your flight."

After the pilot finished, the stewardess came on. "Ladies and Gentlemen, we are about to serve a Continental Breakfast of coffee, tea, various pastries and jams." Oh, good. I swallowed my small cinnamon roll at home in such a hurry I didn't really taste it and I only got to drink about half of my coffee as I was so conscious of Carlos waiting on us.

Well, as I eagerly waited for coffee Shirley again started the conversation with the Barkers. It was difficult given we were talking across the aisle. We found out they were from the Knoxville area. He had been in the Navy and was assigned to Pearl Harbor back in the late 50s and early 60s. I would guess them to be about 10 years older than us. How interesting. I wanted to pursue this.

"I lived in Hawaii in the late 50's and early 60's. My dad was an Army Chaplain assigned to Schofield Barracks. I graduated from high school at Leilehua High in Wahiawa."

Mr. Barker came in and said, "I was a young teenager at the time. I just got into the Navy, and they assigned me to an Army Transport Ship as my first assignment from which I would detach and go to my assignment at Pearl Harbor."

"Oh, we originally went to Hawaii on an Army Transport Ship named the Hugh J. Gaffey."

"That was my ship." Mr. Barker replied.

We were both dumbfounded. What a coincidence!

The noise of the jets and cabin were just too loud to have a personal discussion this revelation had opened.

I suggested. "Once we get settled on the ship. We need to find each other and compare notes about days together in Hawaii."

Agreeably, Mr. Barker responded "Indeed, let's do that."

I tried my best to figure out Mr. Barker's past. I wondered if he was on the Gaffey December 1957 when my family was being transferred to Hawaii. If so, we more than likely ran across each other, but that meant he was probably about 23 while I was in my early teens. There appears to be a slight chance we've had some historic encounters that we can share.

Shirley continued to be glued to the window, as she always is on an airplane. I can never tell if she is in a trance or if she is in shock. I moved over to look with her. By now we had been in the air at least two hours, meaning half way there. I couldn't see anything but beautiful clouds.
The wonder of this trip struck my mind. "Cruise of Miracles," I wondered how it came to be called that! We've certainly seen miracles in our lives through the years. About the time I was thinking this, we hit some turbulence, the seatbelt light came on and the stewardess got on the PA System asking us to remain seated with our seatbelts on. My mind began to wonder.

"Is it okay now?" These were the words back in 1980 when as the principal of a large high school in South Carolina I was invited to tour a Navy facility. We had a Navy Junior ROTC unit in our school. It was the year the Air Controllers went on strike. The Navy had intended to send a jet to fly us to the facility in Florida, but with the strike they couldn't get the plane they scheduled to us. At first, they were going to simply put the group of 30 educators on a bus for the trip, which would have meant an overnight ride. In unison we all let the Navy know that wasn't going to happen. Finally, they found an old DC 3 cargo plane that was heading in our direction and was already in the air. They arranged to divert it to us. Within the hour it landed, and we were all a bit mortified. As it pulled up to the small terminal for charters, not the main terminal, the doors opened and out came this rope ladder. Female principals and educators in high heels along with those of us in suits and briefcases, threw our briefcases and the females their shoes to the airmen on the plane and up the rope ladder we went. Once in the plane, there were no regular seats, there were swing fabric style seats, all facing the rear of the plane. After all, this was a cargo plane. We were all very apprehensive but soon the doors closed, the propellers started, and we began to move, it was too late to back out now.

Once in the air, our ears began to hurt unbearably. There was no air pressurization on this plane. One of the ladies needed to use the bathroom. The airman directed her to the back of the plane but first he opened the door to reveal they had a board bracing the floor and ceiling.

About midway in flight one of pilots came to the back of the plane. He opened what looked like an electrical panel and hollered to the front, "Is it okay now?" Needless to say, our stomachs, nerves and ears were doing all kinds of "didoes." Finally, what seemed an eternity in the air, the airman announced we were about to land. I kid you not, it seemed that within five minutes of that announcement we were on the ground. We took a steep slope downward and we landed. That seemed like a plane ride from you know where! We all felt that it was a small miracle we made it to Florida. Our only dread was we had to get back home the same way we came.

My mind back in place, the turbulence stopped, and I was ever so grateful for this nice jet taking us to California. It was overall a great ride and it seemed but a short while when the stewardess asked us to put up our trays, fasten our seatbelts as we're in the landing pattern for San Francisco.

I looked down as we came over the mountains, we felt the landing gear go down. Slowly we began to descend. Shirley grabbed my hand. Soon the cars and streets below became larger. The roofs of buildings were just below us. Then finally we saw the runway beneath us and quickly we felt the small bump and the push in our seats as we felt the reverse thrust, thus slowing us down. We soon began our taxi to the terminal. Instead of it being the end of our journey, we felt the excitement of knowing it was just the beginning. I looked at my watch and it was 1:00 pm. I remembered; we were now Pacific Standard Time. I turned my watch to that time, and it was 10:00 am, right on time.

As the plane neared our gate, I was amazed at all I saw surrounding the terminal at which we were to park. There were the seven other planes, a few regional sized, others huge, with the MKaddesh words and symbols. Apparently this was indeed a more prominent airline than

I had thought. We finally came to a stop. The stewardess said, "Welcome to San Francisco. As you depart hostesses will be awaiting you to direct you to your buses. Again, a reminder, your luggage will be transferred directly to the ship and into your cabins. Have a blessed journey and we felt it a joy to serve you on MKaddesh Air." With that, the doors opened, and we slowly began to leave the plane.

As we left the plane and walked up the Jetway into the terminal, sure enough there were several hostesses awaiting us, all dressed in beautifully attired light blue skirts and white tops inviting us to follow them. We walked past several gates, all of them empty. We seemed to be the only plane landing at this time. We came to an escalator and down to a large waiting room, where there were hundreds of other passengers who obviously had landed earlier. Lines of buses were outside, all were painted white on top, light blue on the lower and trimmed in gold with the words MKeddesh. The thought struck me. This being Dove Cruise Lines, why have they gotten so specific as to name their airplanes after the ship and their buses after the ship? There were plenty of buses and plenty of lines. The hostesses directed us to the buses we were to enter. We noticed that as the buses came to pick us up, they first stopped to pick up luggage at another door then proceeded to line up for passengers.

It wasn't a long wait before a bus parked where our line was to board. Uniquely we found the Barkers behind us about to get on the same bus. We were so glad to see them again.

"Once we get on the ship, let's do get together," I mentioned to Mr. Barker.

"Yes, we'll do that."

We got onto the bus, and it began to roll on past the terminal. I was so excited, as was Shirley. We headed out of the airport beyond downtown traveling toward the pier area. I knew we were getting close to the piers when we saw the bay and old Alcatraz. The last time I left San Francisco by ship was back in 1957 via the Hugh J. Gaffey, an Army Transport Ship. We left from what was then a military pier.

From the ship you could see the Golden Gate Bridge just in front of the bow. We'd have to go under it.

With several turns, this was all so strange to me. I do remember our short visit to San Francisco back in 1957, just before we boarded the ship. It was Christmas time. The hills of San Francisco were so gorgeous, and everything seemed so innocent. I loved it. But then a final turn and I felt like I was experiencing a de-ja-vu. We entered the pier area, and it all became so familiar. The pier was different, but the location looked so familiar. There stood the Golden Gate Bridge ahead of this humongous ship with the letters in gold "MH MKaddesh." The ship was absolutely gorgeous. All white trimmed in gold down its sides with light blue smoke stacks, trimmed in red. It had to be at least 17 to 18 decks. The bus pulled up to a large terminal with signs directing to the entrance. We got off the bus ready as ever to begin this journey indeed.

Chapter 4: Boarding the Ship

Entering the terminal building we faced a rather tall escalator taking us up to the second level finding stations listed numerically. We all had to get into a roped area that walked us around until we stood before the stations. It was obvious many had landed before us as the line was rather full. We headed to the stations and waited for one to be opened. Finally, a sweet lady dressed in the same beautiful outfit as the one awaiting us at the airport motioned us to come to her desk.

"Welcome, Dr. and Mrs. Meyer. We've been eager for you to come. I'll be giving you your room assignment and then you'll be free to board."

I was stunned. How did she know our names? I had to ask.

"How did you know our names?"

"Oh, we know everyone's name and we have your pictures before us."

Oh, well, that explains it.

She then continued. "Your room is number 4344. You will be on the fourth deck. Here is a ship's chart to guide you." Have a wonderful trip. You're free to board but they are still putting your luggage in your rooms, so we suggest you go to the buffet on Deck 1 for lunch until you're notified about your room."

I began to walk off and then remembered, "What about my key?"

"Oh, you won't need one. The door will open and lock by touch."

This is strange, I've never seen that. Wait a minute, she also said she knew us by our pictures. Just how did she get pictures of us? And why didn't we have to show her our passports?

The thought also struck me. Deck 4? In other ships that's the lower part of the ship. And Deck 1 is the bottom of the ship. I looked on the chart and this ship is totally reversed. Deck 1 is the top of the ship, and our deck is fourth from the top. Oh, wow! This thing is beginning to feel a bit strange.

As we moved from the pier building toward the ship, we were overwhelmed by the size of this large, beautiful ship. We entered through the side of the ship through two large doors. There to greet us were several ship officers dressed in white uniforms. They spoke kindly and directed us to the left, toward the elevators that would take us to Deck 1 and the buffet. It was magnificent. The ship was accentuated with mahogany walls and trimmed in gold throughout. The drapery was a variety of blues depending on the other décor. It would take a whole book just to describe the ornateness and beauty of this ship. As we walked the halls, we noticed playing softly a variety of Christian hymns, most were orchestral or piano. One almost got the sense we had entered heaven. Shirley and I found our way to the elevator, which overlooked the main core, center of the ship. It was a glass elevator that allowed you to view the height and depth of the ship as you went up or down. Based on where we entered, I would guess we were about mid-ship down, meaning deck 7 or 8. Thus, we wanted to go up to the top. We were so taken by not only the size but the beauty of the ship so that when we got to the top, we weren't that ready to get off. Turning to the right there were the doors to the buffet.

We opened the two doors and found the restaurant full. We noticed, as we had other cruises, everyone welcomed whoever to sit with them. We looked around and soon saw the Barkers. They had beaten us to the restaurant. We saw they had two extra seats at their table and asked if we could join them. Looking at our watches, it was about 11:45 am, Pacific Time. It has taken us about an hour and 45 minutes to get from the airport to the terminal and then to check in and get to the restaurant.

They hadn't been there long and had just gotten their food. Shirley put her purse down and I put my coat on the seat and we went to get our food. Oh my! What a feast! They had all kinds of stations with a variety of foods, American, Chinese, Mexican, cold cuts, hot meats, vegetables, desserts of every kind and I could go on. They say that on any cruise patrons can expect to add at least 10 pounds in a week. Well, I just spent six months losing 30 pounds, I knew I had to put myself under control. I had been faithful to my low carb diet, and this would surely blow it. I needed to be good. I got myself some cold cuts, a salad, unsweetened tea and some fruit. I was proud of myself. Shirley guarded what she got as well. I noticed she stayed with some soup and salad. With that we headed back to the table to join the Barkers.

Arriving back to the table, after a short prayer, we began our conversation with the Barkers. We found out they lived in the Halls area of Knoxville. Halls is an older neighborhood on the eastside of Knoxville.

"Have you ever met Jan and Lanny Walter? They were some of our dearest friends in college and we kept up with them for years but lost touch back in the 70s. They moved to Halls as it was developing." I asked.

Jan and Lanny were there for us when Shirley fell and broke her elbow in pieces due to a skating accident when in college. We went to football games together and after we were married, and they were married we continued our friendship but something happened to Lanny along the way. He lost his way and the last we heard the family split. We lost touch and have wondered what happened to them.

Mrs. Barker responded, "I know a Jan Walter. We moved there about 25 years ago before some of the areas began to decline. She moved in about four houses down from us. I think she moved back to Knoxville from the Atlanta area. She's about your age, I would guess."

Excitedly, Shirley joined in, "I think that's her. I think that's Jan."

Mrs. Barker continued. "We've seen some of who we think are her daughters visit but she appears to be a widow. She said she and her husband had bought a new home in Halls when the area was just developing back in the 70s, her mom and dad were from Knoxville, but she and her husband had moved to South Carolina."

"That's her," Shirley yelled. "Cal, when we get back, we've got to go visit her. Oh, this is some miracle to find her again."

I was truly eager to find out about our Hugh J. Gaffey connection. So, I turned to Mr. Barker.

"Do you remember if you were on the Hugh J. Gaffey during Christmas 1957?"

"Well, let me think." Pausing, "Yes, I believe that was the year. I can't remember if it was 57 or 58. But I do believe it was 57. I had to report to my base about a week before Christmas that year. I thought is so strange to be in transit during Christmas time."

"Then that means we were on the same ship to Hawaii. What were your duties on the ship?"

"Oh, they had me do several things. I served in the canteen, help set up the ship's chapel for services etc."

"You've got to be kidding me. That means I probably bought candy from you, and you probably met my dad as he held services on the ship while we were in transit."

"Really, then that means you're Chaplain Meyer's son."

Surprised beyond words, "Yes, how did you know?"

"I remember your dad well. He was a humble man. But the reason I remember him is that he and my dad were good friends in Columbia, South Carolina."

"Columbia, we have that connection as well!"

"Yes, I grew up in Columbia."

"What church did you go to?"

"My family took me to a church called Rosewood Baptist Church in the Rosewood section of town. That's where Chaplain Meyer and my dad came to know each other."

"I know that area well. We did indeed go to that church. Who was your dad?"

"My dad's name was Joe."

"Joe Barker? That sounds so familiar."

"You might remember him from the tattoo he had on his right arm. He too was in the Navy and lived a younger life not in tune with his later spiritual walk with the Lord. But he taught a class of young boys."

"That's it. Your dad was my Sunday school teacher. He had a tremendous influence on me. We shared a cabin with your family at Ridgecrest Baptist Assembly where I gave myself to the call of service to the Lord."

"Well, I was there too. By the way I'm Bill and my wife is Mary."

"Bill, I'm Cal. I can hardly believe this. This is nothing short of a miracle. We've been on this ship for less than an hour and already we've experienced two miracles. Bill, you were a young man then, not far from going into the Navy, is that right? I do remember, vaguely, you are joining us for dinner. I don't remember you that much as clearly you would have been involved in conferences with young people your age.'

"Yes, I'm sure I wouldn't have been able to handle the Navy had it not been for Ridgecrest that summer. After meeting your dad, I decided I wanted to become a Chaplain's Assistant and that's what I pursued once I got to Pearl Harbor. However, that's not the end of the story. After leaving the Navy I went to college and then on to seminary. I've spent my life pastoring."

My heart melted and tears began to flow involuntarily as I began to feel my own dad's presence in this conversation. Shirley saw my tears and whispered, "What's wrong?"

"I'll tell you later." I was feeling the void of years lost with my dad by losing him at such an early age of 57.

In this beautiful moment we found connections to our dear friend Joe, my Sunday school teacher, who had such an impact on my life and witnessed the impact of my dad on Bill's life. How can this cruise get any sweeter than this?

Chapter 5: Leaving San Francisco

We had had a delightful conversation with the Barkers and noted the time had slipped away. It was nearing 1:00 pm and I was eager to see the ship. I was also eager to go to see our cabin and unpack our suitcases. I went for a cup of coffee as did Mr. Barker and we talked for a few more moments of our children, our lives and found we had so many things in common such as living not far from them in Dandridge and my being a bivocational pastor. Shirley and Mary hit it off well and it seemed these would be good friend the rest of the trip. It wasn't long before we all decided to excuse ourselves and take a tour of the front of the ship.

As we left the restaurant, I was amazed at how so very similar this felt to being on the Gaffey back in 1957. We went toward the bow and there was the Golden Gate Bridge in the not so far distance. It was clear we'd be going under it. As San Francisco can be, it was a bit windy and cool, but I wanted to stand along the railing and view the bay.

"Ladies and Gentlemen, Welcome Aboard. We'd like to announce your luggage has now been placed in your cabins. Feel free to go to your cabins." I looked at my watch and it was right at 2:00 pm. We were scheduled to leave port about 4:00 pm.

I was eager to see our room. We moved back toward the elevators, as did the crowd that gathered in the buffet for lunch. By the way the restaurant was known as **"The Heaven's Abundance."** I hadn't noticed that until I looked on my ship's chart when attempting to find the location of our room. There were at least five elevators, each holding about ten. The lobby surrounding the elevators was full. We finally got onto one and didn't need to punch the floor as each button was already lit. We got to level 4, turned left and then to the hallway with a sign pointing us to the group of cabin numbers that included ours. We reached cabin 4344. On the door was "S. Cal and Shirley Meyer." I wonder why the "S." but I noticed all the doors around us had the name of the people and it started with "S." Opening the door, we were just purely overjoyed. The room had two beds to our right and a double sliding door leading to a small balcony overlooking the ocean. We had never had an ocean view before. I wonder how we were deserving of that! Our suitcases were placed on our beds on suitcase mats to protect the bedspreads. Our bathroom was to our left as we walked in and our closet space in front of that with a desk and small built-in dresser with drawers next to it. It was going to be a very comfortable room. By the way, I realized 4344 represented the years Shirley and I were born, mine being first.

We began our unpacking, putting everything into the closet and under the dresser. I wanted to get everything done before the required Safety Drill. On the night table between our two beds, I noted the daily ship's newsletter, it was entitled, **"THE MH MKADDESH SAINT."** I thought that rather odd, what a strange name for a ship's daily newsletter. It was dated **Day 1, October 29.**

I looked over the itinerary for the day and it listed boarding from 11:00 am until 3:30 pm with departure at 4:00 pm. I looked for the required Safety Drill but didn't find one. How did they get away without having that? However, I noted that at 8:00 pm there was a "Welcome Aboard Ceremony" scheduled for the main auditorium at the back of the ship. On the ship's map this auditorium was massive, it basically took up six to seven levels of the ship. It was called **"Heaven's Gate."** This meant we had plenty of time to unpack, see the ship, have dinner and go to the Welcome Aboard Ceremony.

After unpacking, I noticed a small card on the dresser. It said, "Your Cabin Steward: Carlos. Please feel to call for service 003." Carlos? I began to wonder. Wasn't it a Carlos who picked us up and took us to the airport? By the time we unpacked and got everything set up with our CPAP machines, it was nearing 3:30 pm.

"Shirley, let's go up on deck, I want see us leave port."

We both grabbed a small coat and headed to top deck. I wanted to see us pull away from the pier. As we arrived, they were still taking on last minute provisions, but I didn't see anyone boarding from the pier building. Apparently, all passengers were on board. However, I noticed something I hadn't seen with any other cruise, a small band had begun to gather on the pier. The last time I saw that was when on the Gaffey, the military transport ship. It wasn't' long before the gangway was pulled back to the pier, the ropes were loosened from the dock and brought back on ship. I looked again at my watch, and it was 4:00 pm. The ship blew several loud blows to let everyone know we were moving. This huge ship began to move away from the pier and all of a sudden, the band began to play "Anchors Away." How reminiscent of yesterday and how appropriate, but upon finishing that it then went into the tune of "Amazing Grace." Cold chills overtook me. It was awesomely beautiful. I couldn't help it, but tears came flowing. Here I am a 73-year-old, and I had the insatiable desire to find my mom and dad. The last time I was in this very moment I was standing on the deck with them as the Hugh J. Gaffey left what seemed this port for Hawaii.

As we pulled on into the bay the band became fainter, and our attention was now on our moving through the bay toward the Golden Gate Bridge. I motioned toward the front, beckoning for Shirley to move with me so we could see it. The breeze and wind were getting stronger and cooler. We were moving slowly but clearly getting into the center of the channel. The big orange monstrosity was getting closer. I stayed glued to the rail and watched as we came closer and closer and then we were underneath it, just like 59 years earlier. The memories of that very moment had not escaped me. Ahead of us was open sea and three full days of nothing but sea.

The wind was much too cold to stay outside, so we went inside, finding a coffee vendor. I just wanted to sit by a huge window with a nice cup of coffee and enjoy the beauty of the ocean and remaining land as we departed from it. After about an hour I felt the need to get a handle on this huge ship. It was time to explore. Using the map, we found at least three other main dining rooms. All were open seating. Not all were buffet. Only **The Heaven's Abundance** was a buffet. But on the sixth deck were restaurants name **Jacob's Well** and **the 5000**. On level seven was another restaurant called **The First Miracle**. There were no gambling areas as typical on most cruises, but there were numerous other areas to get food, like a pizza place, a hamburger place, an ice cream palace, and even a place to get funnel cakes. All of these surrounded the upper deck on the outside near the polls. There were a lot of pastry shops with coffee and hot chocolate near the stores toward the center of the ship. As for entertainment area, beside the main auditorium, there were several other main stage areas on different deck levels. There was the **Pearly Gate Theatre,** the **Heavenly View Theatre,** a theatre simply called **Joyful Joyful.**

At first my thought was this was truly thematic in all the names, but then it struck me, this ship is clearly a Christian ship and its whole atmosphere is a spiritual one. The whole ship is focused to get us to think about the spiritual. It's not a "Party Ship" per se but at the same time, I don't get the idea it's all about being so holy we aren't going to enjoy ourselves. Now I'm beginning to feel a bit awkward. After all wasn't I the one who just a few years back worked to get about twelve people to take a Charles Stanley cruise with us to Alaska. Dr. Stanley, pastor of First Baptist Church of Atlanta, made sure the atmosphere was one where we experienced the Lord. We went Holland America, but they closed down the gambling arenas, we had Christian entertainers and had a wonderful time. This is not a Charles Stanley nor any other Christian sponsored organized tour as far as I know. I don't recall responding to any such advertising about one. So how did they get my name and who is paying for this trip?

We made our way to the stores, and they had just opened. They had all kinds of shirts, hats, typical items you'd see in almost any small ship store, from clothes, to candies, to toys, to watches, etc. They had specialty stores as well, jewelry stores, a perfumery, an art store, etc. But I didn't notice any prices. We looked, but our past habit was never to buy the first part of the trip. It meant keeping something packed in a crowded room the entire trip. We usually waited toward the end of the trip.

Well, by now it was nearing 6:00 pm. Shirley and I decided to go back to our room and freshen up for dinner. We wanted to get good seats at the Welcome Aboard Celebration. As we approached our room, there was Carlos. It was Carlos, the very same Carlos who drove us to the airport. I was rather shocked. He had on a white coat. He had gone in to straighten our beds and put up the luggage mats. I noticed his name plate said "Panama."

"Carlos, I'm surprised. How did you get from Knoxville to San Francisco with us or ahead of us? And how is it you are our steward?"

"Oh, I've been assigned to you. I was flown to Knoxville for the purpose of being there for you. They had a separate plane to fly us back."

"That's quite an expense, isn't it?"

"In His Kingdom, it's a small amount."

I wasn't sure what that meant, but I went on. "I notice you're from Panama, where in Panama?"

"I'm from a small town in the mountains. It's called Vulcan."

"Carlos, this is quite a coincidence. I was on a mission trip to Vulcan two years ago."

"Yes, I know." I turned for a moment to share my surprise with Shirley, but when I turned back around, Carlos was gone.

This had to be pursued.

We decided to go back to **The Heaven's Abundance** for dinner. I really didn't want to change clothes for a more formal dinner. These were the clothes I had been in all day, so a buffet was fine with us. I had only had a few cold cuts for lunch, so I was a bit hungry. They again had all kinds of food I simply can't describe. I got some lamb with gravy, small white potatoes, Italian green beans, a roll and butter, with unsweetened tea, and we headed for a table. We didn't see the Barkers. But as is the custom on most of these ships, you share a table. We found a table for four, but only Shirley and I took it.

Shortly a couple came to join us. I looked out over the horizon and all you could see was open sea. It was still daylight, but the sun was clearly beginning to set. Soon a couple came to join us.

"May we join you?"

"Certainly."

Our new friends sat down. "Hi, we're the Meyers from Tennessee."

"I'm Mike and this is my wife JoAnn Kirkville from Florida."

Shirley looked at me and me at her. Could it be?

"Where in Florida are you from?" Shirley asked.

"We're from a little town in the center of the state called Auburndale."

Shirley giggled. "You wouldn't have known a Tommy Kirkville, would you have?"

"Yes, he was my dad," Mike responded.

"I can't believe this," Shirley continued.

"Your Dad and I went to school together. We were very close."

"Are you Shirley?" Shirley wasn't sure how to answer.

"Yes, how did you know?"

"My mom died several years ahead of my dad, and he loved her so very much. But in his last years he began to reminisce a lot about high school. He brought your name up. He indicated you were his first love but that you had met a guy in college."

"Yes, this is my husband Cal, we've been married 51 years now."

Mike continued "Dad met mom after high school and from what I hear, they fell deeply in love at college as well."

"Wasn't your dad going to go into the ministry?"

"Well, he was but in college he decided to pursue a business degree then go to seminary. However, after college he got a job offer in insurance and it became his life's career. But he was very active in his church."

The dinner went on from there with Mike, JoAnn, Shirley and me talking about families, Florida and how our lives took different directions. What seemed liked five minutes was almost two hours.

I interrupted Shirley and the keen conversation that was taking place, "Hey, it's almost 8:00 pm, we'd better head to the auditorium. Listen, it is so good meet you! I hope we'll get to see you some more. This has been a small miracle to run across each other."

With that we got up and made our way toward **Heaven's Gate.** The place was packed. We had spent a bit too much time talking. I would guess there had to be almost two thousand people in this auditorium.

The drapery was red. Everyone was talking. Quiet worship music was playing in the background. All were anticipating the first evening program. Soon the lights went down, and a spotlight went to the left side of the stage from whence came a man dressed in a white suit.

Coming to the center of the stage he took the microphone and started speaking.

"Ladies and Gentlemen. Welcome aboard. My name is A. Gabe. Tonight is the beginning of a very special trip, a Cruise of Miracles. As we make this trip, that will become more and more evident to you. You've probably noticed all the names of the ship are thematic. That's in keeping with what we are as a ship line and in keeping with our purpose. This is more than just a cruise. In many ways this cruise will reveal to you sights, sounds, experiences and unbelievable phenomena you've never anticipated. It is truly a Cruise of Miracles. The success of this journey will in part be dependent on you seeking answers to the many questions you are about to have from the extraordinary experiences coming your way. You have Cabin Stewards specifically assigned you. Don't hesitate to ask them. Don't forget to read your daily **MH MKADDESH SAINT.** To get you started, the name of the ship the MH MKaddesh meaning Most High MKaddesh. It comes from the Jewish term "Jehovah God of Sanctification." That should get you started in unraveling some of the other mysteries about your trip. In the meantime, enjoy your evening as we have a program full of music and joy."

All of a sudden, the curtains opened up and there was the full orchestra backed by a full choir that serenaded us for two hours with some of the most heavenly music you could imagine. I truly felt like we had experienced Heaven.

Chapter 6: At Sea

Following a wonderful evening of glorious music, Shirley and I finally retired to our room, both very tired and weary. We had a difficult time wrapping our minds around all we had already experienced just since leaving home, boarding ship and meeting the people we already experienced. It had been a very long day. While eager to see what else was to occur, we weren't sure we were ready for it. Once back to our room, we found Carlos had pulled our covers back, put a chocolate mint on our pillows and set our first day off in a sweet way.

With no urgency to feel we had any time constraints on us, we both went into a very sound sleep. However, around 6:00 am my body clock nudged me to get up. Keep in mind that back home it was already 9:00 am. My body hadn't made the time change yet. I rolled over and tried to go back to sleep but only tossed and turned. I finally gave in and about 6:30 am got up, bathed and got myself ready for the day, awaking Shirley about 7:30 am. While she prepared herself, I noticed the next edition of the ship's newsletter, **THE MH MKADDESH SAINT.** It was dated **Day 2, October 30.** I breezed over the agenda for the day, and it was full. At 10:00 am there was Morning Devotionals in the main auditorium. Throughout the day were various activities, from an Ice Sculpturing Demonstration to a Hawaiian Tour of the various islands, to piano playing in the center venue of the ship, to Pineapple Sculpturing, to making leis. Or you could just go to the ship's library and read, go to the game room and play table games, go to the center ships outside deck and lounge, go to any of the outside eating venues and eat. Almost every afternoon a Christian movie was also played such as "God Is Not Dead," "Courageous," even "The 10 Commandments," "The Robe," etc.

Shirley and I finished dressing and made our way to top deck to **The Heavenly Abundance** buffet. Indeed, the food offerings were so tempting. You just wanted to try everything! We got our food and made our way to a table. To our delight Carlos came and asked if he could get us some coffee. I was eager to see him.

"Carlos. I have to ask a question. How is it you are our personal steward and server as well?"

"Dr. Meyer, I am assigned to you and several others, but you have something very special in common."

My curiosity was clearly eager to hear what he meant.

"You all came to my home."

"I did what?"

"Do you remember my brother Carlos Junior?"

"No, I can't say that I do."

"Yes, you do!"

"You served my little brother his meal at the church in Vulcan, Panama, when you went as a missionary from your church in the states."

"Oh, little Carlos with the sweet smile on his face."

"Do you remember the little plastic cross you gave him?"

"Well, yes I do."

"When you came by our home that afternoon, after you told him and the other kids the story of Jesus, Carlos came home and tried to tell us the story you told. Dr. Meyer, my brother was hungry, and you helped feed him and you gave him something that helped him understand there was a Jesus."

I began to shed some tears.

Carlos continued. "I had to find out more. I went to that church the week after you all left, and over the next year or so, I gave my life to the Lord. But I wanted to do more. So I asked if there was some kind of ministry I could do. I have no education, but I have a willing heart. They referred me to Dove Cruise Lines. It turns out there have been many who have come to my village with the Word of Jesus. They, like you, have reached a point in their lives where they too were invited to take this cruise. My role was to be their steward, as I am with you."

"Carlos, I am blessed and, indeed, touched. This is another miracle I wasn't expecting. Thank you for sharing this and I'm so glad you are here for us."

"Thank you for being there for my little brother Juan Junior."

"How is Juan Junior?"

"Sadly, he's at Home with Jesus. Two years after you were in Vulcan, he got very sick. He had been so malnourished, as we all had. We all survived the sickness, but little Juan didn't make it. He's with Jesus. While making this cruise, I feel I'm closer to him as well."

What more could I say, other than grab Carlos and give him a hug and try to stop sobbing.

Finishing our breakfast and still feeling both blest and emotional over our time with Carlos, we headed to the auditorium for morning devotions. Upon arriving, there was a soft melody of music coming from an organ. At 10:00 am, the auditorium filled, a gentleman got up and led us in the singing of "To God be the Glory." What a rousing song of praise that early in the morning, particularly with a piano and organ duo leading us. Then our morning speaker. He was a tall man, looked so much like Adrian Rogers, former pastor of Bellevue Baptist Church, Memphis, Tennessee. His topic was "Are you Saintly?" His message proposed to us that we were all saints and became so upon accepting Christ as our savior. But he went on to share that we've lived fallen lives. None-the-less, our saintliness wasn't surrendered over that. He reminded us that the cross was once and forever. God saw us as forgiven from the moment Christ entered our lives. Throughout our lives God has proven his love for us by the miracle He's sent our way and in so doing, allowing us to be reminded we are saintly. So, he proposed, when you greet each other, it's okay to call each other "Saint." He said, as a reminder, "There's a daily hint for you each day you enter your room. Now I'll let you figure that out." I left the morning encouraged and curious. What a rousing start to a cruise!

Shirley and I had our daily newsletter with us and as so often on a cruise, we pondered what next. We just had breakfast; thus, it was way too early for lunch. This afternoon there was going to be a Gospel music program by several quartets in **Joyful Joyful Theater.** I clearly wanted to take in that. Tonight, there was going to be a live Christian musical stage show at the **Heaven's Gate,** the main auditorium.

I really wanted to walk the ship and see the people and try to figure out the hint the speaker gave us this morning. As we went to open deck, we were clearly in open waters. Being November, it was cool even though in southern waters between San Francisco and Honolulu. My mind went back to 1957. That trip too was in late fall, in fact December. However, the Gaffey had no amenities like the Kaddesh. It was after all an army transport ship. It was basic but at the time it was the largest ship I had ever seen and to a young boy it was as grand as the ship I was now enjoying. As I walked with Shirley, I remembered being there with Mom and Dad. My mind went to our going to top deck and seeing the sea spray behind us. I recall Dad having to leave and prepare for Chapel services, which he held with the other on-board chaplains. There wasn't much entertainment to be had on the Gaffey except a daily movie and a general game room with board games and a sitting area. But in those days, that was enough. Our day centered around the call to our dinner sitting. We had Sitting #2, and our table was in the center of the dining hall. Third day out we hit a storm and we were advised to stay inside. We bounced around a lot that day and night. No one seemed alarmed. If you dare go out on deck you pretty well took life into your own hands, as the winds were blowing pretty hard. Sailors were there to guard the way and pretty well keep you inside. I remember going to dinner that night. My baby brother, Dan, was only about three at the time. Mom had him sitting next to her in a high chair. Just as our meal was served a big wave hit us and the ship definitely rolled to an angle, with our food, Mom's chair and Dan's chair beginning to slide across the room. We couldn't save the food, but Mom reached, grabbed Dan's chair and they both went sliding. I grabbed onto the table as it seemed to be bolted to the floor, so I didn't go anywhere nor did my dad or my brother Tom. Several servicemen ran to save Mom and Dan. All were saved. The food on the floor cleaned up, new dishes brought, and dinner continued on as normal, if you could eat with a rolling ship.

As we travel these three days to Honolulu, each day seemed full of delightful entertainment, from singers to plays to movies we had already seen to just spending time reading and going to the game room and playing Yahtzee. On the second day out, we went to breakfast but decided to visit one of the other restaurants, **Jacob's Well.** At this restaurant our waiter placed us with an elderly couple, much older than ourselves. Their names were Mr. and Mrs. Carl Walters. In these restaurants you were served as they weren't buffets. As we sat down, I felt something rather unusual. They were sitting across from us, but we were facing this huge glass window, with the sun shining in very brightly. It seemed to have surrounded them with a golden halo.

"Hello! I'm Cal and this is Shirley, my wife." And even though we had been placed there by our waiter, out of courtesy I said, "May we join you?"

Mr. Walters responded, "Certainly, Cal." It was spoken as though there was such a familiarity in his voice. "I'm Carl and this is my wife, Sue."

How strange. This all sounded so familiar.

"Have you been on any cruises before?" I continued.

"Oh, only once, many, many years ago, when in the Army."

"Oh, were you in the Army?"

"Yes, I was an Army Chaplain."

My attention clearly peaked now. Then Sue picked up and began speaking to Shirley.

"Shirley, how are you enjoying the cruise?"

Shirley chimed in to the discussion. "Oh, it's fine. We've been on several, but this is more of Cal's thing rather than mine. I'm getting to the point my walking is an issue for me. But I love the scenery, the relaxation and the programs."

"I understand what you mean. I used to love traveling a lot until Carl got so ill. It cut our ability to travel almost completely out until this cruise. And we wouldn't have come on this cruise had it not been by special invitation."

I began my conversation with Carl again. "Where are you from?"

"We lived in South Carolina."

"Oh! Where?"

"Columbia."

Now I knew we were traveling down a path that was leading to some very common ground.

"You wouldn't have known the Meyers would you have, a Chaplain Meyer?"

"Yes, we knew them very well."

"How?"

At that point the waiter came to take our orders. I gave him mine and pointed to the Walters for him to get theirs', but they were gone.

"Do you know where the couple sitting across from us went?" I asked the waiter.

"What couple?"

"The Walters!"

"I'm sorry, but I haven't seated anybody but you and your wife at this table this morning."

Chills overtook me. Could it have been an illusion brought on by the sun through those windows? But what about the discussion Shirley had with Mrs. Walters? This was clearly unnerving.

I think our breakfast came and I think I ate it, but I couldn't swear by it as my mind was on the experience or illusion we had at that table. I'm not sure we'd eat at **Jacob's Well** again. We had either experienced another miracle, or our minds had become delusional.

We walked away from the table with several questions. They knew my mom and dad. They were an Army family. They were from South Carolina. They were an elderly couple much older than Shirley or me, but there was a sense of familiarity.

Oh well, we needed to head to our worship service in the main auditorium. Our speaker, who again sounds so like Adrian Rogers, is dynamic. I so want to hear what he has to say today. This morning they had a great quartet that blessed our souls. They reminded me of some of the great quartets we heard at the Southern Gospel Festival held at Dollywood. The message this morning was on "Realizing your Sainthood." The speaker challenged us to realize that although we aren't perfect, God puts opportunities and people in our lives to remind us of His love for us. He asks us to think of times in our lives when we knew it was God and only God that opened or closed a door for us. He asked us to remember those whom God sent to bless us. He shared several from his own life. The point was that God was using all of this to speak to us and in so doing accepting our sainthood as He accepted us as forgiven and gave us security in our salvation. He only does this for the sanctified. Wow! What a message!

After the message, Shirley and I returned to walking the decks. I had my mind on both the encounter with the Walters and the sermon. Could it be coincidence the Walters came into our lives this day and, in so doing, gave us a reality we needed for this day. My mind was drawn back to a day recently when Shirley and I were driving from the movie theater in Morristown to our home in Dandridge, Tennessee, when we witnessed a beautiful sunset of pink, blues and yellow. I said to Shirley. "You know, my mom and dad used to see this type of sunset when they went to school at Carson-Newman back in the '50's."

I went on to say, "I also recall the sunset we'd see from campus while we were students in the '60's. Of course, 11E was not a four-lane highway then, nor was it at the location we're now driving. It used to go through the center of the old downtown Jefferson City. But as I look at the sunset, I recall the dreams you and I had when dating. I recall the eagerness of getting married and our leaving campus to chase that sunset to our future. It held such promise. I held such hope. Now here we are, retired and my career is over. Our children are grown and have gone their ways. We often find loneliness and long to return to the days of our youth. Those fifty-three years have gone so fast. The dreams in large measure came true but I kept chasing that sunset. We made full circle. We left Carson-Newman to chase it and returned to face the same sunset of our lives."

Shirley sat quietly as she often does, reflectively. She lets me expound in the deepness of my contemplation. But I continued.

"You know, I so wish I could just one more time talk with my mom and dad and ask how they felt when they traveled these same roads. Here we are seeing the same sunsets, the same beautiful mountains they saw. They were only in their 30's when they were here as Dad was preparing to go into the Army Chaplaincy. I know they had dreams, and I would love to ask. Dad, what dreams or hopes were you imagining? Mom, what did you fear or look forward to at the time? What were your thoughts as you drove down 11E?"

It would take a miracle for that to happen, but just maybe.

But, at the same time, I knew Mom would have to share the pain their dreams endured. Dad had a wonderful career, getting to serve in Korea, Seattle and blessing me with my high school years in Hawaii. Dad also went on to serve in Europe in such countries as France, Holland, and Germany. Dad got to give twenty years of his life to the Army. He left Carson-Newman at the young age of 34 and by 54 he was retired. By 57 he was dead, as we lost him to a terminal disease. I'm sure none of this was in their dreams. Mom went on to live into her 80s but lived her remaining years mourning the loss of her beloved husband and then in her final years faced the devastation of strokes that literally stole her body and mind. Do I really want to have such a conversation with my mom?

Oh, well, I let it go for the time being as we enjoy the ride across the Pacific. I so loved the memories of our first trip to Hawaii. As my mind was getting settled, all of the sudden the captain addressed us on the Public Address System.

"Ladies and Gentlemen, we are only one day out from Honolulu, but I need to share there has been an earthquake off the coast of Mexico. They have sent a tsunami warning to all ships. I must ask that every one report to their cabins as we are expecting waves 30 to 50 feet high. We ask you to pray as it is heading to the Big Island of Hawaii, and it could be devastating. At this time, we feel our ship will be safe, but we will certainly feel it. At the speed the wave is traveling, we anticipate a direct hit within the hour. Following the major hit, there will be several others following. Your stewards will be in the hallways to guide you. Once in your cabins. Please put on your life jackets for safety's sake. We will give you a warning prior to the waves reaching us. Needless to say, all ship services are closed at this time. After the danger has passed an 'All Clear' signal will be given."

At first, I think we all felt a bit of panic. Everyone seemed to take it calmly but clearly you could see the concern on their faces. I wondered if we would be safer in our room versus the upper decks. I remember the movie "The Poseidon" and fear of our ship being capsized did momentarily rush through my mind. Upon entering our room, we went to our closet, secured our life jackets and put them on. Then we sat on the side of the bed and prayed. It was about 5:00 pm in the afternoon. The anticipation was about to overwhelm me.

I recalled the day we hit a squall on the Hugh J. Gaffey. The ship did rock and roll, and we were about a day out from Honolulu just like this trip. However, at that time, my brother and I were perhaps too naïve to recognize the danger. We were intent on trying to play Chinese Checkers in the large game room of the ship. The only problem was that we couldn't keep the marbles on the board. We even tried to go out on the deck, but the wind was blowing so hard we couldn't open the doors to get out on the deck. At the time, it was great fun and part of the great adventure of our first cruise.

However, this is a bit more than a great adventure. This has the prospect of being life threatening. Finally, about 5:45 pm the ships horn went off and within minutes we felt the pitch of the boat take a sharp movement upward, more so than any move I had ever experienced on any cruise before. Afterward, the Captain came on again.

"Ladies and Gentlemen, that was the initial wave. There is no damage to the ship. We do have several other waves coming our way. Please stay calm. Another twenty or so minutes passed, again another jolt of movement, then twenty minutes later another. Finally, after about an hour, things calmed down and the "All Clear" horn was sounded.

"Ladies and Gentlemen, it seems the waves have passed, and all is clear. And, I have some good news. According to our radar, the waves are going east of Hawaii and will miss them. Hopefully they will dissipate before hitting other islands to the north. I have instructed the crew to return to normal duty and all restaurants and services will be open within the next two hours. We can give praise to our Almighty God. We have, indeed, lived through a miracle."

I'm beginning to understand why this is a cruise of miracles!

You know as I look over my life, I've often felt there were earthquakes of emotional pain that shook my faith and the issues that followed often were waves of doubt that overwhelmed my spirit. The day I was fired by a church for reasons I did not understand at the time. My one and only venture into full-time church work ended sadly but at the same time victoriously. It took a miracle for me to later see that. As Minister of Education, I did not have a handle on exactly my role, nor did I grasp my own depths of spirituality at the time. I got caught up in the politics of playing church and at the same time confused by the emotions being expressed around me, including church leaders, as well with what was real in doctrinal understanding. I made some personal mistakes which led to some spiritual mistakes that led to some leadership mistakes. In the end, I was told to resign. The pain came in that I had nowhere to go, and my baby girl was only two months old. I was panicked. I was hurting. I had left the field of education to go to this church and now that the school year had begun, all the jobs were taken. What hurt the most, is that in my firing many of those I thought were friends abandoned me, except a few. One of my last nights at the church I was in such anguish that as I was driving home from the church, I lowered my car window and yelled at God, screaming, "God! Why?" I had just gone through an earthquake of pain and the waves of worry were overwhelming me.

The final night of service came on the Sunday night before Thanksgiving. I remember thinking that there wasn't going to be much for which to be thankful. On Monday morning, I did the only thing I knew to do, I called the county school office and ask if there was a need for a substitute teacher. Though the pay was very minimal, it at least would put some groceries on the table. Delightfully, they had a need at the local high school, in the physics class. I knew nothing about physics, but I really didn't have too. A substitute basically hands out worksheets left by the teacher and attempts to keep order. About 10:00 am, the Public Address System called my room telling me I had a phone call in the main office. Worried it was my wife and we had some emergency at home, the office sent a staff member to my class so I could answer the phone.

"Hello, is this Cal?"

"Yes, it is. Who is this?"

"Cal, this is Mr. Pelfrey, your former principal."

"Oh, Mr. Pelfrey, how good to hear from you. What can I do for you?"

"Cal, a little birdy told me you need a job."

"Yes, Sir, I certainly do."

"Well, do you remember Mrs. Maldenaldo?"

"No sir, I can't say that I do."

"Of course not. Well, she took over your class when you resigned and went to that church."

"She did?"

"Yes, and last Friday we learned her husband, a Captain out at the army base, got orders for Germany. She has resigned effective as of this week. Would you like your old classroom back?"

Tears in my eyes, and joy in my heart and hardly able to control myself. "Yes Sir, I sure would."

"Well why don't you come in after you finish today and complete all the paper work, then enjoy your Thanksgiving and we'll see you next Monday back in your class."

Talk about miracles. I could hardly wait to call Shirley. You know I can look on my life and see miracles throughout it. I certainly haven't felt I deserved it, nor have I felt like a saint, but it has to be something called Grace. That experience occurred some forty-four years ago but in the interim God put me back into the field of education where I had a wonderful forty-three-year career as a teacher, principal, professor and dean.

Now I wonder what the preacher meant when he said there was a daily hint to our being a saint as we enter our rooms. I'm certainly seeing a lot of hints about why this is a cruise of miracles but being a "saint?"

We awoke Tuesday morning and just decided to make it a leisurely day. We had been out to sea for three days and were scheduled to dock in Honolulu tomorrow morning. So much had happened Sunday and Monday! We enjoyed the leisure of the cruise on Tuesday morning, just taking in the devotions and the beautiful day at sea. Our devotion this morning was a morning of prayer and thanksgiving led by some beautiful music sung by two of our special soloists. We've already experienced so much I wondered what could behold us now. I wondered if there would even be a program at **Heaven's Gate** given, we had such a scare with the tsunami, as they had cancelled it the night before, deferring to smaller programs around the ship Monday evening such as singing, local artists etc. Then the Public Address system came on.

"Ladies and Gentlemen! May I have your attention please? Following dinner tonight, all are invited to the Heaven's Gate theatre for an evening of celebration. The program will begin sharply at 8:00 pm. Enjoy the rest of your afternoon."

Well, I guess that answered that! Shirley and I went back to our room. We felt we had been at sea for a month, so much had happened. But we hadn't even been to our first port. This was going to prove to be one very long, adventurous trip. We arrived at our cabin door, and I saw our name S. Calvin and Shirley Meyer. It hit me "S," "Saint!" That's the hint. This whole trip has been to remind us of our sainthood and there it was in front of us all along. I motioned to Shirley as I pointed to the "S" on the door. She got it about the same time I did. What a daily reminder! Now, if we could only live up to it in our daily living and witness. On this ship, no problem, but what about home?

After a day of contemplation, dinner time was approaching. We changed clothes into something a little more formal and headed to the **5000**. We hadn't eaten there before. Noting the story from the Bible of feeding the 5000, I figured this had to be the place of sea food specialties and I was right. I particularly wanted some shrimp or if possible, lobster tail. But maybe I was being a bit decadent and selfish. I'd settle for some good ole salmon or flounder. The dining room was full, and we had to wait to be seated. After about 20 minutes, a formally dressed waiter came and took us to table with four others, placed beautifully pressed napkins in our laps and menus before us. The room had a warm atmosphere with candles providing the light at each table and dimmed wall lights surrounding the room. You had the sense you were definitely in for some fine dining. Looking over the menu, I saw a various mixture of seafood I clearly wanted to try. I couldn't decide. Shirley, not being one for much fried seafood, likes salmon or grilled trout. She settled on the salmon, but I wanted shrimp and found they had a plate of fried, coconut shrimp, and a whole variety of differently styled cooked shrimp. I wanted to try them all, so that's what I ordered.

I looked across the table and saw others having the same dilemma in deciding. I didn't see any lobster tail. Normally, on other cruises, there is one night that lobster tail is on the menu. Only one night. But you better get there early as they run out pretty early. I haven't heard if this cruise will serve that on any night. I was looking forward to my shrimp. After we placed our orders, with soft, celestial, Christian music playing in the background, we began to introduce ourselves. One of things I always enjoyed about cruises was the different people you meet from all across the world. I started.
"Hi, I'm Cal Meyer and this is my wife, Shirley. We're from Dandridge, Tennessee, having just moved there recently."

I looked over and to my delight there was Carl and Sue Walters. They were the ones we saw earlier but no one seemed to confirm their presence. Was I delusional again?

"Hello, Carl and Sue. We saw you earlier. So glad to have dinner with you."

"Cal, it is a pleasure to be with you and Shirley again. I'm sure we'll see you throughout the trip."

I wanted to jump in and start asking questions, but then our other guests spoke up. Another couple I should have recognized but, with the dimness of the light, had not.

"Hi, Cal and Shirley. You know us. I'm Ross and you remember Cornelia." Oh, my goodness, the Nicholson's! These were the folks we had come to know when I was a teenager in Hawaii. He was stationed with my dad at Schofield Barracks. In fact, I babysat their daughter while I was in high school.

"Ross! I'm speechless. What are you doing here?"

"Enjoying the cruise just as you are!"

"No, you know what I mean." Ross died some 25 years ago and Cornelia about 10 years later. They were both in their 80's. Now, they both looked as they did in the 1950's when we first met them, in their late 30's or early 40's.

Ross looked over to Carl and gave him a wink.

"You know each other, don't you?"

"Cal, haven't you figured it out yet?" Carl asked quietly.

"Well, no! Except, I'm terribly confused."

Carl continued.

"Cal, you are remembering rather vividly your first cruise on the Gaffey, aren't you?"

"Yes, this whole trip is such a side by side living episode of that trip back in 1957."

"Well, it was the real beginning of your adult life. The life that would set in motion what you would become as a man. We had a part in that, and the Nicholson's did as well, but a little later in your journey."

Then, it slipped out. "Your mom and I have always followed your career be it here or where God gave us the view.'

My mom and dad. Carl, Sue? Before Mom died, she shared that before Dad left for Moody Bible Institute, where they met, he also left his German Lutheran heritage. He had his name changed to Charles William from Carl Walter and became Baptist.

"Dad! It's you?"

"Yes, it is!"

"But why the charade of Carl Walters?"

"I wanted to share it at the right time, and this was the right time. I hadn't lied to you; I simply used a former name."

By this time, Ross and Cornelia were smiling from ear to ear, thrilled they had witnessed our surprise. Shirley was so overwhelmed; she tearfully went and hugged Mom and Cornelia. I had long forgotten my shrimp.

Ross and Cornelia became a second mom and dad to us while my mom and dad were in Europe. We hit some rough times financially and career wise. It was the time I lost my job at the church I mentioned earlier. It was at that time I hit rock bottom financially. We had three kids and suddenly we found we had secret benefactors leaving us money and groceries at our doorsteps. It was sometime later when we found out it was the Nicholsons. We loved them and for years would visit them, as they grew older, in their Elizabethtown, Kentucky, home. I loved his leathernecks, sun dried green beans. Ross was much like my dad, a sweet, gentle spirit. They were so much alike. It was no wonder they became good friends while in Hawaii.

"Dad, Ross, I have so much I want to share."

Dad, responded, "I know, but we'll have more time later."

About that time our dinner arrived, I looked up and both the Nicholsons, Mom and Dad had left. I clearly didn't feel like eating. My basket was full of joy from having seen them. Clearly a miracle! I looked at my watch and time had passed quickly. It was going on 7:30 pm, with the Celebration Show starting in just 30 minutes. Shirley and I ate about half our meal and quickly left for the theater. As we left the restaurant, the waiter wished us a good evening and then said, "I trust you enjoyed the table by yourselves tonight. I guess everyone wanted to get to the show." Not again. He hadn't witnessed what we had just witnessed!

As I left the restaurant for the theatre, my mind went back to something my dad said when referring to our first cruise to Hawaii, "It was the beginning of your adult life." Now that I'm 73, I've often stood on top of the hill at the top of my driveway and pondered is this where I want to be in retirement. For years I longed to return to East Tennessee and now that I have retired there, I often asked if my life lived up to what I had hoped it would when I left Carson-Newman as an aspiring graduate with my future about to unfold before me.

When we were about to land in Hawaii I had no idea of the monumental joys, thrills and life changing events that were about to take over my life. I entered Leilehua High School as a scared freshman with no knowledge about life or what skills I had for it. It was there I began to change from preadolescence to adolescence and found out what it meant to be a leader, a friend and stand firm on your dreams while being challenged on your values. Growing into adulthood within a cosmopolitan environment was indeed a privilege that would help shape my drive and world view. I had the rare experience of being there when Hawaii became a state. I had the joy of having Waikiki as my backyard playground and the unique privilege of dating a Japanese girl without a sense of prejudice. I learned the art of politics by leading my high school to vote for Nixon in the Kennedy/Nixon election year, in a Mock Election Campaign as a Senior Project, although Hawaii has and always has been a solidly Democratic state. At the same time, I committed myself to the gospel ministry as my church, First Baptist Church Wahiawa, licensed me to preach. These are the gifts I was on the threshold of enjoying as we were about to enter Honolulu on that first cruise via the Gaffey, when I was but 14 years old. Is this to what Dad was referring?

When I left Leilehua, I had so many dreams. Did I live up to them? After four years at Carson-Newman I once made the comment to Shirley, "It is my dream that one day I will return and teach at Carson-Newman and earn $10,000 a year." That was back in 1965. Today, I return to the Carson-Newman campus and see so many young people, as I was, chasing their dream, with aspirations for their futures once they finish their degrees. I can't help but look back and remember those moments Shirley and I walked across the campus and talked about our hopes and what we wanted the future to be. I wonder if God had sat me down on one of those college benches and laid it all out to me if I would have been happy or sad and willing to accept it. Here's the conversation I might have imagined.

"Cal, you want to know your future? Well, there will be many, many excellent experiences for you and successes beyond your wildest expectations. But along the way, you will also face many disappointments and setbacks that also comes with life. Which do you want to hear first?

"Well God, let me hear about the successes first."

"Okay. Well, first, you and Shirley will get married and as you grow older you will fall deeper in love. You will become one in spirit and come to understand how I brought you together in one heart. You will exceed your 50th Wedding Anniversary and will be admired by many for your commitment to each other. Second, as you both have verbally shared with one another, you will have three children, but your first will be adopted. Your children will be a joy through their early years. Shirley won't graduate with you but will finish her degree 26 years later, when you become a college professor, as you hope to be. Third, you won't become a military chaplain as you initially thought but you will be a school teacher, a high school principal, will work briefly in a State Department of Education and then the last part of your career you will become a college professor teaching in both small colleges and also large universities. One day you will run a graduate program, will teach doctorate students and eventually become a dean. Oh, and along the way you will bi-vocationally pastor some eight churches. I do need to mention that you will also earn your master's degree and doctor's degrees. You will also write a Fifth Grade Math Textbook and several personal books. You will gain the reputation as a scholar. As for your earnings, I know you indicated you want to earn $10,000 at Carson-Newman. Well Carson-Newman will never hire you, but you will earn about $100,000 toward the end of your career and when you retire, you will have a home with no mortgage and a solid retirement income. How does that all sound?"

"God, that sounds terrific. But what about the setback?"

"Well, Cal, this can be tough. Are you sure you want to hear it? Regardless of the path we choose there is just no guarantee life will have its pitfalls. But it's those pitfalls that will strengthen you and get you ready for the next challenge."
"Okay, let me hear it."

"Well, first. You and Shirley will have a rocky start in your marriage. Both of you will have to overcome your own self-centered desires and misguided views about each other. There will be times you will think about why you got married and your tempers will get the best of both of you. Your greatest disagreements will come over your children. But you will get through this as you begin to realize what true love is. Second, as you start your career, you're going to hit some rocky financial times. You're going to be cleaning floors and toilets at a rest home, doing taxes, and delivering newspapers in the early am before heading off to school just to put food on the table. You will try to handle all of this while going to graduate school at the same time. Third, you will attempt to go into full-time church work and find that's not what I wanted you to do. You will be fired and it will break your heart only to find I will open a way back into education in a miraculous way. Although one of your proudest moments will be to become a high school principal, and in fact you will be named "Outstanding Administrator for the State," your superintendent will undermine you for reasons you'll never understand. However, it will be the challenge that will ultimately challenge you into college teaching. Once into college teaching you will find much success earning tenure and promotions but always finding political back biting. You will find one dean literally attempt to murder you professionally, another to discredit you and another tell you to do some unethical things. But you will survive with your happiest moments at Marshall University where you will work for 10 years and could stay permanently. Marshall will come about due some of the early pitfalls you will experience in other universities. As for your children, your daughter will rebel at a young age and she will break your heart but she will come back years later as a mature mother. Your birth son will never allow you to know your grandchild as his wife will totally isolate you from their family. Your dad will die at the young age of 57 and never get to be a part of your career. "

"God, this is just too much!"

"Well, Cal, that's why the future is never revealed but lived day by day. You will have what most would call a successful career. And, I imagine it far surpasses your greatest dreams but the hurts are probably far beyond what you can dare to think of. I'm sure you're thinking, how can I avoid the hurts? Well, you can't and after this conversation you will forget we even had it. Your future is what you make it. It's not that you face the pitfalls but how you face the pitfalls. You can either crumble under them or grow under them. I am predicting you will grow under them because I'm seeing a relationship with you that will only grow stronger, that's what sainthood is all about.

With those thoughts in mind, Shirley and I reached our seats in the auditorium awaiting the program to begin.

Soon the curtains opened and a great choir and orchestra sang the "Hallelujah Chorus." We sprang from our seats in a tremendous uproar of applause. I thought, where in the world does this program go from here? Soon, a music director came and led us in singing "Victory in Jesus." By this time my heart was in such a crescendo of praise I didn't know if I was going to be able to contain myself. We then shared in prayer and I found my hands springing into the air. I'm never one to raise my hands into the air but I did that night. Then a speaker came to the microphone, again, that Adrian Rogers style speaker. I could have sworn it was Adrian Rogers, but he's been dead for over a decade now. He said, "Ladies and Gentlemen, tonight I want to share a few words and what it looks like to be a saint." I had just had those thoughts and now this!

"We've already experienced on this cruise some near disasters such as a tsunami but we came through it. Our Captain was able to maneuver our ship over the waves to safety. In your lives, many of you have hit waves of near disaster, waves of hurt, waves of pain, waves of doubt, waves of despair. As Job, you cried out 'Why?' You see being a saint never means you avoid the storms of your life. Being a saint never means you won't question God's timing, or even His will for your life from time to time. Being a saint is always knowing the captain has the ship under control and is guiding you over those waves of distress. Being a saint is not living in a past that can never return, or wishing for the perfect future on this earth without pain or hurt, but it's accepting your sainthood on a daily basis and rejoicing in an Omnipotent God who paid the ultimate price for you to have and enjoy it. What does sainthood look like? Try these words; love, peace, tranquility, acceptance, calmness, eternal."

By the time he got to "eternal," I was out of my seat yelling "Yes!" Soon the choir and orchestra came back on and sang a concert of beautiful music including "At Calvary," "He Lives" and ultimately concluded with "Amazing Grace." By the time the program was over, I was ready to dock in Heaven, not Honolulu.

We returned to our cabins in such a joyful exuberant spirit. I almost felt docking in Hawaii would be anti-climactic. But I set my alarm clock for an early wake-up as I wanted to see Diamond Head as we rounded it and headed into port.

Chapter 7: Hawaii – Day 1

I got up early. I truly wanted to be on deck when Diamond Head came into sight. If I remember back to that December morning back in 1957 when we first docked in Honolulu, on the Gaffey, my first sight of Diamond Head came from the deck of the ship after we docked. That was my very first view of Hawaii. As a young 14-year-old, I was mesmerized. I knew very little about Hawaii only that it was an island and at the time, I didn't know the different names of the islands. I thought Hawaii was Hawaii and thus when I was told we were on the island of Oahu, I had some confusion. I never imagined mountains nor had heard about this steep ancient volcanic mountain, known as Diamond Head, which greeted you as it welcomed you to Hawaii.

On this cruise, it was 5:00 am, local time, I rushed to get my bath and wanted to be on deck by 6:00 am. We were scheduled to dock at 8:00. I wanted to have full view of Diamond Head as we came around the island. I awoke Shirley and encouraged her to get dressed and told her I'd meet her at the buffet on top deck between 7:30 and 8:00. As I approached the elevator, there were many who had the same idea. It was just getting light but darkness still prevailed. It wasn't quite 6:00 am. As I got to top deck you could see daylight to our stern just beginning to come over the horizon and, in the distance, to the west, some dark shadows that couldn't yet be identified by shape. I found a great place to view it on the top deck at the bow of the ship. As the minutes passed, the daylight behind us was brightening the sky and the shadows in front of were coming closer and becoming more obvious. Then by 6:45, there it was. The silhouette of Diamond Head stood there as though pointing to the sky and reminding us it was the gate to a paradise of God's beauty we would forever remember.

As we drew ever closer, we seemed to round the edge of Oahu in front of Diamond Head. There was Honolulu and Waikiki Beach glistening in the morning sun. It was nearing 7:30 am, time for me to meet Shirley. I wasn't ready to leave the deck. I went down to the buffet and she was waiting inside where we normally entered. I was too excited to eat and beckoned her to come on deck and see the sight. I rushed back to the bow and sure enough we were heading into the dock with the Aloha Tower just in front of us. My mind went back to 1957 again, with the military band there welcoming the Gaffey playing the tune "Aloha Oe." My heart was thumping as though I was 14 years old again, full of excitement entering an adventure unbeknownst. I had this sense of de-ja-vu and lost consciousness expecting to see my mom, dad and brother surrounding me as we were about to dock, forgetting this was 2016, not 1957.

As they threw the lines to the pier to secure the ship, Shirley and I headed on to breakfast. We ate quickly as I wanted to get to my room, get my coat and hit the pier. I hadn't made any shore tours plans, figuring we had time to go to a local travel agent near the pier and make some plans to take the Graylines to various events. Nor had I read my daily ship's newsletter. I had been to Hawaii several times and figured if anything I could just rent a car if all else failed. However, as I was thinking this, Carlos came by and asked:

"Dr. Meyer, did you get my note?"
"What note Carlos?"

"The note I left with your daily ship's newsletter last night."

"No, Carlos, I didn't. I didn't even pull the newsletter out of my cabin's box outside the door."

"Oh, do you think you can be ready then."

"Ready for what?'

"Dr. Meyer, I am driving you and your wife in your own private limousine for the day. I'll meet you at the pier where you leave the ship and escort you to the car at 9:00."

"Oh, my it's 8:30 right now." I motioned to Shirley, "We need to hurry."

We rushed to our cabin, brushed our teeth. Got our things and headed to the departure deck.

Sure enough there was Carlos. He walked us through the terminal, past the boarding rooms and onto the street side. There was a long white limousine awaiting us.

As we drove past the terminal, I noted something rather strange. The last time I visited Hawaii, which was only five years ago, in 2011. We came to celebrate my 50th year since graduating from high school at Leilehua. Unfortunately, we missed the official homecoming as they planned that for the fall and my job just wouldn't allow me to attend. So, Shirley and I made it a vacation in the summer. The highways were four to six lane thoroughfares. Honolulu and the cities had all meshed. The pineapple fields and sugar cane fields were very limited. But today Carlos is taking us on what I remember as the old King Kamehameha Highway. That was the only road to and from Honolulu when we lived on Schofield Barracks. Pineapple fields are plentiful, as are the sugar cane fields and it seems they are full of workers.

"Carlos, I thought the pineapple and sugar industry had long left Hawaii or had gone to the other islands."

"Not in this day."

"What do you mean 'in this day'?"

As we neared Pearl Harbor, I could see the harbor, but I didn't see any signs of the Arizona Memorial. In 1957, the only memorial was an old wooden platform over the sunken hull of the Arizona. There was really no memorial. And if I recall, not all the debris was completely cleaned from the harbor in '57. There was some rusting hull of an old landing craft LSD amphibious ship. As we neared Wahiawa, it was looking so much as it did in yesteryear. I note we have but two days in Hawaii. I just wonder about all that I'm about to experience. As we drove into the Wahiawa area, I began to recognize the Schofield Barracks area. Sure enough, Carlos takes a turn onto the base. He was waved right on through the gate as though he has special privilege. But it isn't what

I anticipated. What I see is an active row of battalion quads. We come down the main thoroughfare and pass the 35th Infantry Quad, then pass the 27th Infantry and sure enough we're upon the 21st Infantry Gimlets, the battalion in which my dad was assigned. Carlos soon takes a turn onto Rainbow Avenue. That's the street on which I lived. The old green quarters in which we were assigned were the original officers' quarters dating back to WWI. This is the Schofield Barracks I knew in 1957. Shirley looked over and saw my astonishment.

"What's wrong, Hon?" she asked.

"Something's wrong! This isn't 2016."

"What do you mean?"

"I mean, we've gone back in time. This is somewhere between 1957 and 1961 when I was a student."

"You must be imagining things!"

"No, I'm not. All the old battalions have long left Schofield Barracks. The 25th Infantry Group is no longer here. This was a staging point for Vietnam at that time."

"Carlos, what's going on?"

Carlos, wouldn't answer. He simply parked the car and opened the door for us. He pointed to the front door and encouraged us to go and knock on the door.

We went to the door and knocked. Soon the door opened. It was Mom. But it was Mom back in 1960.

"Welcome, Calvin and Shirley. I've been expecting you."

Okay, I'm speechless. I've already had an encounter with Mom and Dad via meeting the Walters on ship earlier. God is conveying so much through living again the memories of my parents. A miracle not many can relive in living memory.

"Mom, how? Why? I don't know what to say?"

"Cal, you and Shirley have been granted the Miracle of Time."

"The Miracle of Time. What does that mean?"

"Simply, you are able to go back in time and see it from the experience and wisdom of your years. Yes, you are who you are and I am who I am. I am younger than you, but God has given me the wisdom to see into your 73-year-old heart, even though at this time I am but 46 years old. To me, as with all mothers, you are still my baby boy."

Talk about strange. But you know, I don't think any of us ever think of our mom and dad as younger than we are.

Mom went on to say, "However, I only know of you what I experienced with you at that point in your life. You know my future. You must not convey it to me, even though I might be tempted to ask. I know Shirley is your wife as that was revealed to me when I was told of your coming and I understand we developed a loving relationship. But again, that conversation cannot be further detailed."

"Who told you all of this?"

"I had a visit by a representative of Dove Cruise Lines. At first, I didn't accept it, but then it was reinforced by a dream I had night before last."

"Does Dad know about this as well?"

"Yes, we were both told and we both had the same dream. Come on in and let's talk. Your dad will be home for dinner right before we go to church."

"Go to church?"

"Yes, after lunch, Carlos is taking you over to the high school and a tour of the island, then this evening we're all going to church together for dinner and prayer meeting. Brother Dan is leading us in Bible Study on the Psalms."

Now that is strange, as I just recently read that Pastor Kong, his full name was Pastor Dan Kong, died at the age 76 back in 2005. Pastor Kong left our church, Wahiawa Baptist, back in 1960, to go and pastor the larger church in Honolulu, Olivet Baptist Church. Pastor Kong was raised in Wahiawa and was converted as a 12-year boy there. He was of Chinese heritage. After college and seminary in the mainland, he returned to pastor his home church. I loved Pastor Kong. But embarrassingly, I have to admit that as a high school student I had a crush on his wife Eleanor. She was our youth group leader. In those days we could take Bible as a high school course and we sometimes met in the home of the pastor. Mrs. Kong was an attractive Caucasian lady and as a young teenage boy I just somehow misguidedly developed a crush on her. She was always a good friend to all of us teenagers. I would fain problems on which I needed counsel. She soon caught on, called in my mom and redirected me. The crush soon came to an embarrassing end.

Time was fleeting but soon Dad came in.

"Hello, Cal."

"Hi, Dad."

It all seems so normal.

"Hi, Shirley. It is so good meeting you again and I'm truly looking forward to getting to know you even more. What's for lunch, Sue."

"Oh, I fixed our favorite Saturday night meal."

I knew what that was! Every Saturday night Mom fixed chili dogs. Sure enough, we sat down to the table and Mom brought out buns, hot dogs, a pot of chili and tea.

This is where I learned to smother my hot dog in chili. I don't just take a spoon full and put it on my hotdog. I take and cover the bun, hot dog and all with chili, then ketchup, relish and mustard. I eat it with a fork. Mom never asked me what I was doing. She just learned that's the way I eat chili dogs. That's why a pot full of chili.

Dad led us in Grace and we ate. Mom asked about our trip. I really didn't know how much I could share.

"Oh, it's been exciting. Something I never imagined. It has reminded me a lot about our Gaffey trip."

"Oh, that was fun, wasn't it Chuck." Chuck is what Mom called Dad.

"I remember the evening that storm hit us and Dan and I went sliding across the dining room floor." We all began to smile.

I responded, "Yeah, we had a similar experience this trip but a little more threatening. We had a tsunami hit us but it went on past and no harm."

"Oh, my!" Mom looked rather alarmed.

"Oh, we're okay, it all went well." I reassured her.

"Cal, did you know we have orders for Fort Lewis? Your dad got to extend his stay for six months so you could graduate from Leilehua." She paused. "Of course, you knew.'"

By our coming in mid-1957, Dad was only supposed to stay in Hawaii for three years but that would have meant my having to leave in the middle of my senior year in high school. Dad asked for a six-month extension so I could graduate. You know as I look back upon that now, I realize how much priority Mom and Dad gave me. He in essence put his career on hold for me to graduate. I've never fully given them the credit they deserved for that.

I reached over and hugged Dad.

"What was that for?" Dad inquired.

"I just want to say thanks for sacrificing your time and career in thinking enough of me to allow me to graduate from Leilehua."

It's a miracle that I have this opportunity to now realize that and finally thank them.

"Cal, I wouldn't have had it any other way."

We soon heard a knock on the door. It was Carlos.

"It's time to go. I'll have them back at the church by 5:00 pm."

Carlos took us straight to Leilehua.

"Dr. Meyer, go on into the main office and explain you are an alumnus. Even though in today's time frame this is 1960, they won't know you are a student here. Your present age certainly will convince them. Just tell them you date back several years. They won't want to ask your age. Then ask if you have permission just to walk around the campus. By the way, you won't see yourself as you can't occupy two time frames. Given you are 73 years old and you are visiting 1960 when you were 17 years old, you are here but you aren't here. Just enjoy the moment."

Shirley and I went into the office.

"Hello, my name is Cal Meyer and this is my wife, Shirley. I am an alumnus of Leilehua and we're here from the mainland just for the day. I was wondering if we could have a Visitor's Pass and simply walk around the campus. We won't attempt to enter any classes; we just want to view the grounds."

The lady behind the desk said, "Let me speak to Mr. Kwan our principal." I remember Mr. Kwan. He is Mr. Manuel Kwan. He was my principal. He came to the desk and I repeated my request. He said,

"Oh, sure, we're going to be making class changes before long, just be sure you aren't in the pathways, you could get run over. Would you like a student to guide you?"

"Sure, if you don't mind. I wouldn't mind at all." I figure if a student were with us Mr. Kwan would feel a bit more comfortable with our visiting places on campus I'd want to see.

Soon a sweet Japanese girl came out. "Hello, I'm Rosemary Herano." Rosemary! I couldn't believe it. I once dated her. I took her to a football game across the island one Friday night. It was on a school pep bus. We played Kailua that night in Kailua. I so wanted to respond to her but I knew I couldn't. Rosemary was one of the major campus leaders and class officers. I never figured how I got a date with her. However, she was also a fine Christian girl and went to my church. I figure that had something to do with it. We only had that one date as Rosemary's circle of friends eventually grew larger than the church group and I never felt comfortable in asking her out again. Basically, I sat with her on the bus to and from the game as well as at the game and that was the extent of the date. Besides that, I was going back to the mainland upon graduation so dating local girls generally wasn't all that accepted. The locals generally dated among themselves. That's another reason I felt privileged to have had that one date with Rosemary. But here she was working in the principal's office, about to escort us around campus.

We left the main office and started walking down the main hall. Leilehua is laid out with outside walkways connecting the rooms.

"Are Mrs. Anderson and Mr. Tiara still teaching here?" I asked.

Rosemary looked puzzled that I asked the question. "Yes, they're here. Mrs. Anderson's room is down this first hall to the left and Mr. Tiara's room is two hallways behind us. Would you like to drop by them?"

"Yes, if you don't mind."

We took a left and headed toward Mrs. Anderson's room. There she was just as I remember her. An elderly looking women with a sweet continence. Rosemary shared, "She taking several classes to see Macbeth in the spring."

I remembered that trip. That was a great trip. It was an evening field trip to a playhouse near Diamond Head. I never liked Macbeth and I think that's the only Shakespearian Play I ever understood. But the trip spoke more about Mrs. Anderson and what she would do to help us learn and love what she taught us.

Rosemary then guided us back to Mr. Tiara's room. Ah, my very favorite teacher. A teacher of Japanese heritage but did he ever love America! He taught American History and instilled in his students a love for this country, as well. Everyone loved Mr. Tiara. He, too, was a wonderful Christian man. His smile and continence also showed it.

I couldn't help but notice that all the ROTC cadets were in full uniform today. It was Wednesday and every Wednesday was parade day. In my day, Junior ROTC was tied to the Army base. Our commandant was on active duty, assigned by the Army. We had honorary female officers who accompanied the various companies on Parade Day and about noon every week there was full parade of all the school's companies. We had missed the parade. I so regretted that! I was on the Drill Team, but I didn't stay my senior year and thus never became an officer. I really did regret that.

As we took a turn back toward the office, I looked up and there was my best friend, Ken Burke. I wanted to yell out, "Hi, Ken." But I couldn't. This was 17-year-old Ken and I was 73-year-old Cal. He wouldn't understand and I'm sure it would have scared him. He looked just as I remembered him! Ken and I were best friends. He had a car, I didn't', but we did a lot of pal things together, just like good friends do. We often went to a Post Exchange movie followed by a visit to the Post Exchange Canteen for a sub and chocolate shake. We truly lived the life as depicted in the Ron Howard show "Happy Days," a show made in the '70's about high school life in the '50's. Today's generation would never understand that, but Cal and Ken were two characters who lived it and we did understand it. The movies, the canteen hangout, the '57 Ford, the football games, etc. Yep! All were "Happy Days." On Graduation Night, my folks did what I, at the time thought was unforgiveable, but it wasn't their fault. The General had a command reception my dad had to attend. So, following graduation, Ken's family had me join them for dinner. It was okay, as I didn't realize it at the time, but it was going to be the last time I'd be able to be with Ken. Within days of graduation the moving truck picked up our things from our post quarters and we moved down to Waikiki for a few days before out flight back to the mainland.

I don't think I'll ever forget that summer following graduation. We landed in San Francisco, with our car awaiting us. Mom and Dad's things were headed toward Fort Lewis, Washington. That summer was going to be my last few months to be with my family as I was heading off to college that fall. Mom and Dad planned a trip across country from California to Tennessee via Texas and back toward Washington State via the Badlands of South Dakota. Our car tags had our Hawaiian plates. At every gas station Dad took delight in telling people we had just come from Hawaii. Our trip felt like it was extended by weeks because Dad took all that extra time at every gas station to tell them about Hawaii. We stopped in Texas to see my grandfather, Pa Pa, and his wife Rose, as well as my uncles and aunts. We didn't know it at the time but soon my Uncle Hal would suffer a life changing heart attack that would alter his energy laden lifestyle.

Then on to Tennessee as I was so eager to see my potential dorm, my life for the next four years. I was excited but at the same time extremely nervous. With Mom and Dad still there and all summer being with them, I wasn't yet facing any separation anxiety. That was coming. As I walked that small Baptist campus on a hot July afternoon, I felt a sense of pride I was going to college, but very unsure I had the ability to make it. Dad cleared the way financially for me to enter. I didn't know how they were paying for it, all I knew was that my college was being provided by them, something that, to this day, I am so very grateful. When I look at all the debt young people are facing when they leave college today, I realize that even at the prices of the ,60s it had to be a major sacrifice for my parents. We left Tennessee and headed up to South Dakota to see the Badlands and Mt. Rushmore. That was the first time I had seen it. It was awesome! Following that, we headed on across Wyoming, Montana, and into Washington State as Mom and Dad relocated and settled into their new quarters on Fort Lewis. I spent my last few weeks of the summer preparing to get on the train and go to my new life at Carson-Newman College in Tennessee. It was, indeed, a summer of which I still have so many fond memories.

Well, so much for remembering the past, I'm living it. Rosemary continued the tour. She took us to the football field. Oh! I do recall those Friday night games. Of all the mascots, we were the "Mules." This was taken from the fact we were considered so closely related to Schofield Barracks, the Army Base, such that when the school was built back in the '20's, they took on the identity with the base and became the Mules just as are the cadets of West Point. At one time that was an honor. But today, how many schools do you know are called "The Mules." None-the-less, we yelled "Go Mules" with pride and must assume the students do the same today. Leilehua's colors are Green and Gold. I still love those colors even though when I became principal our biggest football rival, Spring Valley, had the same colors. As we circled on around the facility we came upon the cafeteria. What memories! In my day, students could volunteer to work in the cafeteria. I really don't know how we were chosen or how we got out of our classwork, but we did love working in the cafeteria. The cafeteria was a unique design. It was enclosed but the bricks were open-air, meaning every other brick one was missing leaving an open space to the outside, thus birds and outside critters had access to the cafeteria. I do recall loving those tuna salads and homemade rolls. We finally made our way back to the office. The afternoon had gone so quickly. I really wanted to talk but I knew I couldn't. I was living in one dimension and Rosemary, this day, was in another.

Carlos was waiting for us and, with his smile, opened the door as though beckoning us to enter. I didn't want to leave but time was fleeting.

I asked Carlos, "Can I stay just a few more minutes?"

"Dr. Meyer, school is about to be dismissed."

"Okay, I understand."

About that time a line of big green Army busses drove up and turned down the side of the school. I so remember that! All the kids who lived on Schofield Barracks were brought to school and taken home on those busses. I rode one of those busses. I remember it well.

We got into the car and Carlos turned right out of the school, not left back to Schofield Barracks.

"Carlos, where are we going?"

"Oh, I thought you'd like to see the first house you lived in when you moved to Wahiawa, before your dad got quarters on base. Remember Karsten Drive?"

Boy! Do I remember that! It was a mile up the hill from the school and I had to walk it to and from school. No bus, just walking. Thank goodness Dad got quarters by summer and we only lived there one semester. But I do recall having a paper route with the Honolulu Advertiser. I won some trips and dinners which featured hula dancers and the like. However, once on base, my paper route was a thing of the past. I did not miss that walk. Karsten Drive was a small house, and I don't remember much about it, only that we were all so thrilled when post quarters came through.

As we drove on back through town there stood the old Wahiawa Bus Station. We could catch a bus to Honolulu. In my day, there were no major four laners, only King Kamehameha Highway. The only thing you saw most of the way between Wahiawa and Honolulu were pineapple fields and sugar cane fields. I do recall taking the bus to Honolulu on Saturdays. I don't know why. The streets were full of military and to be honest I felt it a little unsafe. The atmosphere was well, I guess you might say, a bit on the adult side. I felt out of place. Back in the '60's, a fellow by the name of Hugh Heffner had just made his mark with a new magazine called Playboy and regretfully, the age of innocence had changed. Rather naïve I realized that even going into a drug store was not a safe place to browse. I got back on the bus and went back home. That's a memory I'd rather forget.

By now it was going on supper time, given we had church to attend. I recall we had to be at the church by 5:00 pm. I gathered we were having dinner at church. We arrived back at our post housing.

"Cal, I'll let you and Shirley ride with your folks, and I'll be back to pick you up after church."

"Okay, that's fine with us."

Shirley and I went inside. Talk about surreal. There I am at 73, Shirley at 72 and my mom is but 43 or 44 years old and my dad only 39 or 40. It would be interesting how this would be explained at church.

"Hi, Mom," I said as I entered the house. Did that ever seem strange! I felt like a teenager again.

"Cal, we don't want the church crowd to become overwhelmed at this Miracle of Time that is happening. Why don't you just call me 'Sue' as I'll introduce you as acquaintances from South Carolina? They'll never make the connection you're Calvin, the Calvin they knew as a teenager."

Feeling a bit embarrassed, I said sure. I had no idea how I would call my mom 'Sue' as that was simply never in my vocabulary growing up. But these were indeed unusual circumstances.

About that time Dad came in the door, in uniform. I almost melted in tears. Oh, if only I could truly go back in time and be that teenager truly again. But then again, I wouldn't have Shirley.

"Are we ready?" Dad asked Mom.

"Yes, I think we are, let's head to the car," came Mom's response.

We all headed to the coral pink 1957 Pontiac I remember well.

We drove on back through Wahiawa to the side parking lot of the church. Upon arriving we headed to Fellowship Hall.

"What is the wonderful aroma I smell?" I asked.

Mom shared, "Oh, they're doing a special dinner tonight of Korean Chicken." I could hardly believe it. That was the one meal I remember so well from one of our youth nights. A church member prepared that dish and it was the first time I had ever eaten it. It was like heaven to the lips. If prepared right, it has a tang unlike any other Oriental food. It's served in a light brown sauce that is out of this world.

As was the custom, we entered and immediately we were recognized as guests. There was Sue Seito, one of Mom's great Women's Missionary Union friends. There was Pastor Kong and his wife Eleanor, the one I had such a crush on in high school. Then there was Mr. Tiara my history teacher, not to mention some of my classmates. My heart was leaping in joy. I was exhilarated I could hardly keep my emotions inside. I wanted to yell, but I dare not. They were seeing me as some 73-year-old man, not the young 15- or 16-year-old when they knew me. What a joy to be in their presence!

One by one they came and introduced themselves. I found it hard to refrain from saying their names before they did. As they came, I simply said, "I'm Cal Meyer and this is my wife Shirley, we're acquaintances from South Carolina." I wondered if any of them would make a connection. However, back in my high school days most at church called me "Calvin." The shortened "Cal" didn't really become common until college. In fact, Shirley and I became such a thing that when people saw us together, they simply called us "Shirlcal" rather than have to say "Hi, Shirley. Hi, Calvin."

Soon Pastor Kong indicated it was time for prayer. I so appreciated his prayer. It seemed so appropriate.

"Father, we come to you this evening for this time of fellowship and praise. We thank you for bringing these our friends, Cal and Shirley Meyer, from across the waves and across time to be with us tonight. We thank you for this food and for the reminder of how you love us across generations and across cultures. Lord, may we be reminded this night that you are Lord indeed and that the miracle of life is life itself. Amen!"

How prophetic. Did Pastor Kong truly grasp the miracle in which he was living? It had to be the Holy Spirit nudging Him and putting these words in his mouth.

We all went to the serving tables. Ladies of the church served our plates. I do recall the beauty of the mixture of Polynesian ladies in our church. We all sat at our table enjoying every morsel of Korean Chicken. Nothing on the ship matched this. Time passed quickly and it was soon time to go to the auditorium for services.

Mom and Dad led the way and as per their normal, Mom guided us to the front.

After a couple of hymns, Pastor Kong called on Dad to pray. I always loved it when I heard, "Chaplain Meyer, would you lead us in prayer." Wherever we were stationed it was our practice to be dedicated to the chapel in the morning but to our local church in the evening and on Wednesday nights. That was true in Seattle, and it was true in Hawaii. Dad was respected by the pastors of the churches to which we belonged. It was as though they felt honored, he had dedicated himself to the military and yet felt obliged to serve in their church. I always remembered Dad for his humble spirit and I'm very confident that's what impressed his fellow ministers. Following Dad's prayer, Pastor Kong asked for prayer requests and following a session of many requests we broke into small groups of three and four where we were seated and prayed. I was at home in hearing about the Sakagawas, the Otas, the Nunotanis, the Ignacios and so on. It has been well over 55 years since I had heard those names as common to the culture in which I lived. In some ways I felt I was back in high school. It was truly surreal. I wanted to join in and start thanking God for allowing me to be with my mom and dad again, but I had to catch myself. Instead, my prayer expressed thankfulness for the church, how it had reached young people and influenced lives and for Pastor Kong and the blessing he has been as a pastor and the blessing I know he would continue to be. Little did those around me know he would be moving on to a larger church in Honolulu in just over a year and leading in the development of the State's major Baptist Academy.

After the prayer, Pastor Kong, got up and said, "Tonight I felt led to speak on the topic 'Sanctification and Growing Through It.'" Oh, wow, I knew that had to be the Holy Spirit. He went on to speak about how he was raised as a small Chinese boy in Wahiawa and growing up in a Chinese culture. But how at a very young age he was led to a saving knowledge of Jesus Christ. He went on to share that while he didn't realize it at the time, he was sanctified at the moment of his salvation. "**Sanctification** isn't included in the "we have been saved" part of **salvation**, but it is **synonymous** with the "we are being saved [1https://www.9marks.org/article/what-role-does-sanctification-play-salvation/]-" But it's a matter of the Lord taking one's life and through the power of the Holy Spirit guiding it through the pitfalls of temptations, trials and stages of life. Though we sin in life, the cross was all about forgiving that sin once we let Christ in." He reminded us of Isaiah 1:18 "Though your sins be as scarlet they shall be as white as snow." "The blood of Jesus took our black hearts, our black sins, our black thoughts, our black deeds and put them through the machine of time, with the detergent of His cleansing blood and we came out white as snow, purified, justified, sanctified before God." But he went on to say, "It's a daily walk with Him. As long as we're on this earth, no matter the age, be we high schooler, young adult, parent adult, middle career adult or retiring adult, our lives are continuously living the struggles and battles of this life. Yet we have the assurance we are sanctified through life regardless of what it throws against us. He then added, one day you will get to life's twilight, you'll ask 'Lord, my life has passed so quickly, and I wonder are you okay with me? Is it well with my soul?' And He will respond 'It is Well! It is well! Well done, thou good and faithful servant. I saved you, I sanctified you, because I loved you and you accepted my grace.' That's sanctification through time."

Oh, Wow! What a sermon! I surely needed that. Shirley looked over at me with her pretty blue eyes and smiled. Shortly after the message the service was over. We got up to leave and as I did, Pastor Kong grabbed my shoulder and said, with a twinkle in his eye, "Cal, it was good having you with us tonight." With that I felt he knew. He knew I was the Calvin that was the teen aged Calvin some 55 years ago. That message was placed on his heart by the Holy Spirit and with it the insight to know we weren't completely whom we were introduced to be. He knew, I believe, a Miracle of Time was taking place and that in itself was yet another miracle.

As we left the church, we noticed to the side, Carlos was in the parking lot awaiting us. I thought we'd be going back to Mom and Dad's home, but I guess not. I was saddened to realize we'd be leaving them.

Mom grabbed me and said, "I love you, Calvin, we'll see you again soon." Then she went to Shirley, hugged her and gave her a kiss.

I went to Dad, "Dad, I love you. Always have, know that."

With that we got in the car and Carlos drove us on back to the ship through the island of the late '50's. But my thoughts were too much on the events of the evening to think about the sights on the way back.

We arrived back to the ship between 9:30 pm and 10:00 pm. I was pretty tired and full of thought. I was so glad we had a second day on the island. I wondered what would amaze us tomorrow. As we boarded the ship, I thanked Carlos for his patience and kindness. As he turned to leave, he said, "I won't be escorting you tomorrow, you will have another special day of many surprises. Your instructions will be awaiting you in your room."

My, oh my! How could anything be more fantastic than this? Shirley and stopped by the upper deck at **The Heaven's Abundance** for a late-night cup of coffee. I wanted a piece of chocolate pie and Shirley just wanted some water and some fruit.

About 10:30 pm we headed on toward our room; there in our door box was an envelope marked "S. Meyer – Agenda for Day Two – Hawaii."

Chapter 8 – Hawaii - Day 2

Well, we could hardly wait to open the envelope to see our agenda. I wondered why it was addressed to S Meyer, why only to Shirley. Then I remembered, our door plaque said S Meyer and that was for the both of us. It meant Saints Meyer, meaning the both of us. Well, we couldn't go to sleep wondering. Opening, the agenda it read:

Welcome Cal and Shirley to the Big Island of Hawaii:

You have been chosen to travel by air to the Big Island for a one-day tour via our subsidiary airlines Blue Skies Airlines. You are to meet your airport shuttle at the port dock at 6:00 am. Your Shuttle will be #6116. Look for the sign on the window. You will be taken to Honolulu Airport where your flight, #1123, will be awaiting you, along with your co-passengers. Your Itinerary is as follows:

7:30 am	Depart Honolulu
8:30 am	Arrive Hilo
8:45 am	Continental Breakfast in Airport Guest Lounge
9:15 am	Depart for City Tour
10:30 am	Arrive Volcano Park
12:00 Noon	Thurston Lava Tube
12:30 pm	Buffet Lunch
1:30 pm	Visit Orchid Gardens
3:00 pm	Visit Rainbow Falls
4:00 pm	Visit Macadamia Nut Farm
5:00 pm	Island Luau
8:00 pm	Depart for Hilo Airport
9:00 pm	Depart Hilo
10:00 pm	Arrive Honolulu
10:30 pm	Arrive Back at Ship

We trust you will have a beautiful day. Please take this itinerary with you as it also serves as your tickets to board the plane.

**Sincerely,
Your Hosts of the MH MKaddesh**

Oh, my, we clearly had a full day, and it was already going on 11:00 pm. We had pretty well gotten to bed. I set the alarm for 4:00 am, noting we had to get up early to get ready and off the ship and to the Port Deck by 6:00 am. I'm not sure how we'd make the day on just four to five hours sleep. Oh, well, we will have several days at sea to catch up on our sleep.

With five hours sleep, I rushed through the typical morning shower, brushing of teeth and assorted amenities and rushed Shirley up. If we wanted any breakfast, I knew we had to be at the diner no later than 5:30 am. Waiting until 8:45 am, as on the agenda, wasn't going to work for me. However, along about 5:15 there was a knock on the door. Barely dressed, with Shirley still in the bathroom, I opened the door and there stood Carlos.

"Dr. Meyer, knowing you and Mrs. Meyer would be in a hurry I brought you some pastries and fruit along with a small pot of coffee."

"Carlos, which is most gracious! I didn't know how we'd get any breakfast before heading to Port Deck. Thank you ever so much."

Shirley, yelled, "Who was that?"

"Carlos. He brought us some breakfast!"

"He did what?" Shirley yelled back in amazement.

"I said, he brought us some breakfast."

I went ahead and helped myself to the cinnamon buns, some coffee and some fresh pineapple, not before giving thanks for what had already been an amazing trip.

Soon I heard the hair dryer and Shirley was finishing in the bathroom.

"I finished my breakfast; you might want to eat fast. We need to head to Port Deck in about 15 minutes." It was nearing 5:40 am.

Both of us were rather sleepy and not sure we were going to make this day. Shirley had her blessing and helped herself to the pastries and fruits, as well as coffee. I remembered to pick up the itinerary/ticket and we headed to Port Deck. Upon arrival there were crew members guiding us to the exit of the ship and toward the airport shuttles.

Noting there were numerous shuttles I looked for #6116. Finding it, Shirley and I boarded it with about 30 others. Numbers always meant something on this trip. Why #6116? What did we all have in common? All I could think of was that 1961 was when I left Hawaii, and this is 2016. So, I guess all 30 of us have much in common with the years 1961 – 2016. It was a comfortable bus and within minutes after all the shuttles were loaded, we all headed to the Airport. The Honolulu Airport is on the edge of town and in departing you can see the city lights in the background as you leave it behind on the Highway #1, which is one of the major freeways on Oahu.

As the busses pulled into the terminal, they took us to the doorway marked Blue Skies Airlines. I had never heard of Blue Skies before. When I went to high school in Hawaii the big inter island airlines was Aloha Airlines. But after a major accident in which the roof blew off one of its aging planes as it traveled between islands in the '80's, it wasn't long before it went out of business.

Once into the terminal of Blue Skies, it was full of passengers from our ship. Apparently, the shipping company had booked a fleet of planes for all these inter island excursions. There was a gate to each island, all departing at different times. I looked at the lighted board and there we were, "Flight #1123, Hilo, Departing 7:30 am." Again, what did

#1123 mean? Well, this is November and we will have been in Hawaii the 2nd and 3rd. This trip is indeed adventuresome just in figuring out the meaning of the numbers. It was going on 6:30 am, so we had a little time. Soon the public address system came on.

"Ladies and Gentlemen. Let me welcome our guests from the MH MKaddesh. Each of you have tickets to visit various islands today. Your tickets are the same as the itineraries you received in your guest rooms last evening. Please check your tickets for the time of your departure. We will board you approximately 30 minutes before departure. In the meantime, for your convenience we have a table of fruit, pastries and beverages for your comfort island side of the room. Please help yourselves and welcome aboard Blue Skies Airlines." Now I wish I had waited, rather than eat that first cinnamon roll in the room.

I had forgotten that on one side of the airport was the Island of Oahu, but the airport was boarded by the Pacific Ocean on the other side. It was still dark outside so in coming in all we could see were the city lights, not the ocean. Having about 25 or so minutes before boarding, I went for another cup of coffee.

As I got my coffee my mind wandered back to the '60's in those last high school years. My mom had the thrill of being named the first State Women's Missionary Union leader for the State Baptist Convention. Hawaii became a state in 1959. When we moved there in 1957, it was still a territory of the United States. One of her official duties was to travel to the other islands and visit the various WMUs of the churches. I so envied her as during my entire time in high school I only saw Oahu. I somehow wish mom could be here to enjoy this day with us.

"Ladies and Gentlemen, we are now boarding Flight #1123, Gate #1, please have your tickets ready." Shirley and I headed to the gate and presented our itinerary/ticket to the stewardess, a beautiful Hawaiian girl, wearing a flower in her hair and a gorgeous dress trimmed in light orange and pastel red.

As I presented my ticket she said, "Welcome, Dr. and Mrs. Meyer and the guest you are bringing with you."

I went on through, then it hit me, "Guest with me! What guest?" I looked around and saw no one except the other passengers who boarded the same plane. I guess she must have meant them.
We boarded the plane and, as always, I let Shirley have the window seat. I noted the plane was full, but this was about a 50 to 60 passenger sized plane. I wondered how many of us had the same itinerary. Like clockwork, one of the stewardesses shut the door, the engines revved up and I felt us, being pushed from the gate. I looked at my watch and it was 7:30 am. The sun was coming up over the horizon. I felt a chill of excitement as we taxied down the runway. We soon made the turn for take-off and with the compression back in the seat, the plane was rushing down the runway and we were soon lifting into the air.

To our right was the Pacific and to our left was Honolulu. We were on the left side of the plane and we had a beautiful view of Honolulu and of Diamond Head as we looked down into it while flying over it. As it turns the old extinct volcano is a park along with businesses in the heart of it. Of course, we were over the water in just a matter of seconds. We had about an hour's flight to Hilo, but along the way we'd pass the other islands of the chain. Actually, the flight time wasn't all that long, but gate to gate was.

The sky was beautiful. I just felt so at peace and eager to see the Big Island. After yesterday, I didn't see how anything could be more wonderful! Time passed quickly.

"Ladies and Gentlemen, we are in our landing pattern to Hilo. Please put your seatbelts on, we should be landing in about 15 minutes."

My, goodness, it felt like we just boarded! Soon, we felt the plane descending and indeed the mountains rose high to our left. It is amazing that Hawaii has two major mountains, Mauna Kea and Mauna Loa both rising about 13,700 and 13,800 feet about sea level. You can have winter and summer on the same day in Hawaii. From the air, as you land, you get a perspective of just how huge they really are. It was awesome! The airport, as in Oahu, is next to the ocean. We soon saw the runway and with the wheels touching down, we had landed on Hilo. Our exciting day was about to begin.

I was ready for another cinnamon roll. I never get tired of cinnamon rolls! We deboarded the plane and were guided to the airport guest lounge and to my delight there were trays of fruit, yes, wonderful fresh pineapple, a large tray of Cinnabon cinnamon rolls with fresh coffee, a mix of cheeses, other tropical fruits and other pastries. We only had about 30 minutes before boarding our shuttle. I wondered if it would be a large sized tour bus or small shuttle style bus. The tour bus is clearly more comfortable but not as open to visiting with others. I also wondered with whom we might get to share the trip. I noted there were several Blue Skies planes when we landed and the airport guest lounge will pretty well packed. But I didn't see anyone on the plane or in the lounge that I recognized.

Soon the public address system came on.

"Ladies and Gentlemen, we are ready to board our shuttles. The shuttles are numbered as they were in Oahu. However, there will be two shuttles with the same number. Feel free to board either.'

Given we boarded Shuttle #6116 in Oahu I had to assume we would board the same here in Hilo. However, there were only 30 people who were boarding that shuttle and now we have two with the same number, meaning we have smaller shuttles taking 15 people each. I think that's great we'll get to know people. We were told to go to the exits and drivers dressed in light blue would be by their shuttles with the shuttle number in the windows. There were a line of shuttles and we walked past several until we got to #6116. I always like being near the front of the line when going somewhere, although I feel a bit selfish in doing so. Sure enough we got on the first shuttle with the number #6116.

Others followed and it wasn't long before our shuttle was full. I made an observation. All of the others were approximately our age. Most looked like they also graduated from high school around 1961. A coincidence? With it approaching 9:15 am all the shuttles along the line seemed to be full and our driver entered the bus.

"Good morning, ladies and gentlemen. My name is Alex Nakamura. I have the privilege of being your host and driver today. We'll be departing soon. As your printed itinerary so notes, we have a rather full day ahead of us. I will do my best to make it comfortable and keep you informed about the events and sights along the way. We will try to stay on schedule unless something unexpectedly occurs, or you may have special requests I can honor. Sit back and enjoy. We will depart momentarily."

I looked at Shirley and we both felt excited. We had an exciting day ahead of us. What did he mean something unexpectedly occur or special requests. The other shuttles began to pull out in front of us and we soon followed. As we did, I felt a tap on my shoulder. I looked behind and heard.

"Hi I'm Elaine Turner and this is my husband, Tom."

I turned a much as I could and said, "Hi, I'm Cal Meyer and this is my wife, Shirley. Where are you all from?"

"Oh, we're from Seattle, Washington."

"Seattle! I lived there right at 62 years ago as a middle school student, my dad was in the Army stationed at Fort Larsen. It is no longer an Army post."

Elaine, came back with "How coincidental! I once lived in Hawaii as a high school student and met my husband Tom when he was stationed at Schofield Barracks. I was a senior in high school just finishing up and he was a young private, freshly stationed here. My dad was a colonel on post when I met Tom. We got married there and once he left Hawaii he was stationed at Fort Lewis where he finished his Army duties. He went to work at Boeing and made his career there. We retired in Seattle."

"My, oh, my, what a lot we have in common! I bet you went to Leilehua."

"Well, yes, I did. How did you know?"

"Because I went there as well. Elaine, what was your maiden name?"

"I was Elaine Robins."

"I can't believe it. Elaine, I remember you! I can go to my yearbook and point to your picture. We were both active in Student Government and I remember catching a ride from school one day with a classmate after I had a late meeting at school. You were in that same meeting. I had to go to work at the Post Exchange Gas Station and you simply wanted a ride home. We shared a ride."

"I'm not sure I remember that."

"Well, it's been a long time."

I didn't want to convey that Elaine hung around a different class of kids than I did. She was considered a part of the beautiful set. My dad was a company grade officer, meaning Captain and below. Her dad was a Colonel, a field grade officer, meaning Major and above. In the Army the old saying goes, "Rank has its privileges." Well, that applies to the families as well. We were separated by housing communities and as in off base communities you have upper class, middle class and lower class. Company grade meant middle class, field grade meant upper class. So, when we got to school, having been picked up by those green Army busses in our respective communities, we came in on busses that tended to bring us in by communities. Not only that, many of the field grade officer's kids had their own cars. Elaine fell within the ranks of the "elite," the "upper crust," the "upper rank" kids. However, she was always friendly with me, I just knew I'd never fit into her circle of friends. It surprised me she fell in love with a Private at the base.

Well, we seem to move on toward Hilo and the driver began to share the history of the town. First we drove by the shoreline where he told the story of the Hilo Tidal Wave of 1969. It seems Hilo is susceptible to tidal waves. They had one in 1946, 1960 and 1969. And the scare we had on the ship was that such a wave was possibly heading to Hilo, but it went further north. I can't imagine the fear of living through a tsunami. We passed landmarks showing the height of the water in the 1969 wave and he described in detail the devastation that hit the City of Hilo.

As we drove past Hilo, we headed toward our next stop, Volcano Park and then to the Lava Tube. All of a sudden, we felt a shaking and weren't sure if it was the bus or something else. Mr. Nakamura appeared a bit alarmed and almost immediately he was on his cell phone. His conversation appeared somewhat concerning, but yet not that alarming. He soon got on the bus speaker.

"Ladies and Gentlemen, I just need to announce that the shaking you felt was a small earthquake but nothing alarming. We have been assured it was small and we can continue our trip. We've had them before and if something unexpectedly occurs, we will return you to the airport."

I felt reassured. I could hear Elaine and her husband, as well as the rest of the group sigh in relief. Although I think we all pondered if we needed to continue the tour. Oh, well, we trusted Mr. Nakamura and the company wouldn't put us in harm's way.

We arrived at the caldron on the top of Volcano Park. As we went inside the museum, a ranger beckoned us to meet with him first before we went out on the observation deck. As we gathered together, he began to inform us about Kilauea's activity since 1983. It seems it has been active ever since, although for the most part the lava has been pouring into the ocean and can only be seen at that point. However, some vents are opening up in the crater where sulfur dioxide is emitted and some volcanic ash has erupted. Of course, in the museum there are photographs and spectacular moving pictures of the lava eruptions over the years. We took some time to look over all the various pictures of the volcano and then proceeded out to the observation deck.

As we walked across the various paths allowed around the observation area, we noticed what appeared to be an increased amount of sulfur dioxide smoke. We also saw a vent spew some volcanic ash and I wasn't certain, but I was sure that when the smoke cleared, I saw a clearly red flow in the vent hole. Was I the only one who saw it? We all began to smell the sulfur and it became stronger, so much so we needed to retreat to inside the museum. I approached the ranger.

"Sir, is there an active flow of lava in the crater?"
"Yes, but it's hundreds of feet below the surface."

"I think I saw some red flow coming out of the vent."

The ranger didn't wait and ran out to the edge of the observation deck. By this time the smoke had cleared and the activity appeared to die down a bit. The ranger came back.

"I didn't see anything but we're going to check on it further."

I know it wasn't my imagination. I asked Shirley if she had seen it and she hadn't. It was 11:45 am and we needed to move on to the Lava Tube. Mr. Nakamura beckoned us to our bus. We boarded as the lava tube was only about a 15-minute drive from the crater. The old lava tube was discovered back in 1913 and has been taken over by a fern forest. Of course, it was carved out of hot lava flowing from Kilauea. But it has been extinct for years. It is now a beautiful, cool, 1/3 mile walk through lava stalactites.

The afternoon was cool, the clouds above were beautiful and the air filled with sulfur. I felt a bit unnerved.
"Ladies and Gentlemen, I'm about to pull into the parking lot of the Lava Tube. You'll have twenty minutes to walk to it, go inside and return. You won't have time to walk the entire length of it but where the stalactites begin is just a five minute walk from the entrance. If we take a few extra minutes that's okay as we have a full hour for lunch and that shouldn't take long. Enjoy yourselves. I'll meet you back at the bus no later than 12:25 pm."

As he finished talking, we pulled into our parking spot along with other busses. We all headed to the entrance. As we walked, we felt the cool air coming from the tube. The path was surrounded by lush ferns. We walked inside and proceeded about 20 or 30 feet. We saw some of the stalactites and they were amazing. Suddenly we felt a shake. I grabbed Shirley's hand. Elaine and her husband were just behind us. It stopped but then another shake and this time it was a jolt. The lights to the tube flickered and then all of a sudden we heard a loud "KOWAM!" We looked around, the lights were out. It was total darkness. We looked toward the entrance and saw nothing. Then we began to smell the stench of sulfur getting stronger. Shirley pulled out a pen light from her purse. The air looked smoky. We couldn't tell if it was smoke or dust. Heat began to fill the room. At first there was silence and then everyone began to talk in sounds that clearly indicated we were all very scared.

"Cal are you there?" I heard from behind me. It was Elaine and her husband.

"Yes, Elaine, we're here, Shirley's pen light is on."

Others pulled out pen lights and phone lights. Others in our group began to yell, "Help!"

It was obvious no one heard us. The four of us began to feel the wall and walk back the way we came. The longer we were in the tube, the warmer it was getting and the smell, stronger.
It was obvious the shaking was an earthquake the magnitude of which we weren't sure but clearly it caused damage to the tube and blocked the entrance. I felt confident those outside were working to get us out, the question was how long and what were we facing on the inside.

We moved ever so close to what we thought was the entry point but we couldn't tell.

"Lava, lava," came a faint but ever so panicky sound in the distance.

Some yelled, "Did you hear 'Lava!'?

By now there was screaming and everyone rushing to the entry. I grabbed Shirley's hand, who grabbed Elaine's hand, who grabbed her husband's hand. I felt panicky. We were either going to die by Sulphur poisoning, heat from lava or being crushed by the crowd coming toward us.

"Lord, please open the entry" I cried out. I then heard a silence and what I thought was my mom saying "Cal look up!"

The silence ended abruptly and again the screams. I wondered if I was the only one experiencing the silence.

"Shirley, did you say something."

"No, I didn't say a thing."

At that very moment, another quake. I looked up toward the ceiling of the tube. All of a sudden daylight entered and another quake. This time the major boulder and rocks that had blocked our entry had fallen. There were plenty of police and emergency workers helping us to climb over the rocks. Everyone was dashing to the entry. Thank, goodness! We hadn't gone that deep into the tube when all of this had begun to occur. Smoke from the tube came pouring out around us.

"Ladies and Gentlemen, we have ambulances and paramedics for any who need them. If you are okay, we urge you to return to your shuttles."

I looked to where Mr. Nakamura had parked our shuttle. He was there waving for us. I also looked in the distance toward the crater of Kilauea and you could see a lava explosion towering from it. I guess the lava I saw in the vent was for real after all.

Everyone was running from the lava tube as the police forced everyone to leave and urged all to board their shuttle or get in their cars as quickly as possible. Fortunately for us, we got there just as it began to happen so that none off our shuttle had time to go deeply into the tube. Mr. Nakamura kept waving his hand for all of us to board the shuttle. It took about 25 minutes but while shaken we all were safely back on. We were eager to hear the news.

Mr. Nakamura got on the speaker.

"Ladies and Gentlemen, we just had an earthquake on the Island of Hawaii which has caused Kilauea to erupt more actively. The end of the lava tube is again active and we fear a few people who entered earlier may not have escaped. The shipping company has directed me to take you back to the airport where your plane is ready to fly you back to Oahu. All activities for the day have, of course, been cancelled. We need to get you back to the ship safely."

We were shaken but glad to be safe. Not getting to go to a Luau was the least of my concerns now. As we drove up to the airport, we noticed all the shuttle busses pulling in and people being rushed to their gates. We were quickly rushed to our plane, not even time to go to the rest room. As soon as everyone was accounted for, the doors were shut and we were on the taxi way ready for take-off. We were grateful no one from the ship was missing on our plane. But we were all saddened that some may not have made it out of the tube. We so hope they knew the Lord! We looked in front and behind us and it seemed planes were in line to take off, nothing was staying behind.

As we got into the air, we could see the red hew of lava flowing from the crater of Mt. Kilauea. While it was spectacular, we couldn't but help feel concern over any lives that may have been lost in the Lava Tube, or surrounding area. We sat back in our seats feeling exhausted and yet somewhat in shock over what we had just experienced. The flight to Oahu seemed so short as our thoughts of just getting back to the safety of our ship occupied our minds. As we were about to land, the pilot came over the public address system.

"Ladies and Gentlemen, due to the situation of this day, all passengers have been called back immediately to the ship. All tours for the islands have been cancelled. As soon as we land, the busses that brought you to the airport will be available to take you immediately to the ship. Please make your way directly from the plane to the busses. Flight personnel and ship personnel will be at the airport to guide you. Please let me assure you that as far as we know no ship passengers were injured on the island of Hawaii today. We are certainly glad you are safe. I think each of us needs to give thanks to our Almighty God for the miracle that allowed all of you to escape a very dangerous situation today."

I said quietly, "Amen!"

Then behind me I heard a few quiet say, "Thank you, Lord."

We soon landed and were ushered off the plane quickly.

As we entered the airport, we noticed all the gates for Blues Skies were full of exiting passengers, all being directed to the exits and awaiting busses. We found our shuttle, #6116, and boarded it. The driver had a list of passengers and waited until all had arrived. Given most of us were on the same flight, the bus was loaded quickly and we left the terminal heading out past Honolulu. Though we had experienced a nightmarish day, everything seemed rather normal on Oahu. We wondered if maybe we might get back to the ship and simply stay on board until scheduled to depart the next day. With all the activity, it was nearing 5:00 pm. We had missed lunch and I was starving. I imagine most of the passengers were similarly so.

As we arrived at the pier, the ship's crew was there waiting us and the line to re-board was a bit backed up. It seems the entire ship had been called back. Originally, we weren't scheduled to return until 10:30 pm. I asked of one the crew members.

"Sir, why the long line?"

"We've called back all tours and all passengers are to be back on board by 6:00 pm. The ship is leaving at 7:00 pm."

I was a bit confused. According to schedule we weren't scheduled to leave Hawaii until later that night and then be at sea the next few days. I wonder why we're leaving three hours early.

We passed through security and went to our room. I was famished. Shirley and I headed up to the buffet at "The Heavens Abundance." When we got there, we found it packed. Apparently everyone on board had arrived back at the ship and all are faced with the same situation we found ourselves. One of the attendees came down the line.

"Ladies and Gentlemen, the other restaurants are open for your benefit. Please feel free to go to any of them."

We thought about it but I really didn't want to be waited on. I just wanted a quick meal, although it looked like all the tables were full and it was going to take some time.
Just then the Captain came over the public address system.

"Ladies and Gentlemen. May I have your attention? As you are well aware, we have suspended the events of this day and are departing the waters of Hawaii within the hour. This is purely precautionary. The Island of Hawaii suffered a major earthquake today which caused a new eruption of Mt. Kilauea. As far as we know the earthquake was centered within the volcano itself. However, with concerns other earthquakes may follow and some surrounding the island, there are other considerations and thus the Civil Defense for the State of Hawaii has declared a State of Emergency, for the time being. They are fairly certain no other island will be impacted but we feel it necessary to act with great precaution and thus we are leaving the Hawaiian waters. Please do not be alarmed. You are completely safe on-board. We regret many of you did not complete your tours, but we know you understand. All the restaurants are open. All ship services are open as well and available to you. Please try to relax and be at rest as we head out to sea this evening. In the meantime, I've asked our ship's Chaplain to lead us in a prayer."

The Chaplain came over the speaker. "Almighty God, we come before You, humbled. Humbled by your awesome power and by Your tender mercy. While our hearts are stirred by the events of this day, we thank You that all our passengers have returned safely. Now as we head out to sea, we pray for your guiding mercies that no danger will come to us and that our passage will be safe. We pray for those people on the Island of Hawaii who have been impacted by the eruption this morning of Kilauea and prayerful for the families of those who may have been killed or injured. While we see the power of such an event, we see the awesome power of your creation, as well. May we live in humble obedience to you, Father, while remembering you are a God of Love and Hope as shown us on the Cross of Calvary. Lord, help us to be at peace, knowing You are the real Captain of this ship. In Jesus Name, Amen."

Chapter 9: Four Days at Sea

Following the Chaplain's prayer, we all found our way to the top deck. I'm not sure any of us wanted to go to bed just yet. We were too excited by the day's events. The lights of Honolulu were lost in the distance as we headed out to sea and around the island. We headed out past Diamond Head and then northeast with a setting toward Seattle. I knew we wouldn't see much of the volcanoes again as we were a distance from the Big Island to see any further eruption from the ship.

Not every passenger was on the Big Island when Kilauea erupted, but they wanted to know what had happened. It was a good time to meet folks, share our experience and find comfort. Soon Elaine and her husband found their way to us. I could tell she was still a bit shaken. We had been in the Lava Tube together.

"Cal, how are you feeling about this morning?" She asked.

"Still a bit unnerved, but clearly relieved however, I never had a sense we wouldn't get out of there."

"Wel, l I did, particularly when the screams began at the other end and the smell became so suffocating."

"We were fortunate. What surprised me is that the heat didn't get any worse than it did, if indeed some had seen lava as they yelled. I'm not sure that wasn't a figment of someone's imagination. I'm quite sure had there been lava the heat would have been so intense we wouldn't have survived. However, I'm positive had we stayed there much longer, we wouldn't have made it."

"Cal, I noticed you praying, as were all, but you seem to be very specific in your prayer and about God's opening the entrance. I also noticed you looked up just as the opening cleared as though you saw something rather unusual."

"Oh, you noticed that. Well, I asked the Holy Spirit to provide the way and at the time I felt His presence doing just that. Also, for some strange reason I also thought I heard my Mom say 'Look up' and when I did, I thought I saw an army of angels pushing those stones away from the entrance. I'm convinced the Spirit of God was in there with us."

I looked over and saw tears in Elaine's eyes.

"Cal, I'm not crying over today only, but it has awakened a sad time in Tom's and my life. Soon after we were married, I was expecting. We anticipated a beautiful angelic girl. We were going to name her 'Lehana.' We had read where it was a name for one full of allure and spirit. That's what we wanted our little girl to be. At the time, Tom and I didn't know the Lord and I wanted a spirited little girl in our lives. Well, one day when Tom was at work, about my eighth month, I was trying to reach a box of rice I had put in the upper level of our pantry, and I couldn't reach it. I grabbed the kitchen step ladder and climbed it but as I was coming down, I missed a step and lost my footing and fell. I took a really hard fall onto the kitchen floor. I knew something had happened. All of a sudden, the little vibrations I had been feeling had stopped. My stomach ached. I called Tom and he rushed home and then we rushed on to the hospital. The diagnosis was grim, the baby was still alive, but its vital signs were not good. I went home and cried pleading with God for a miracle. But it didn't happen, within a week it came prematurely and was stillborn. My little Lehana wasn't going to be. I was devastated. I wanted to die. Where was God? To make things worse, a month or so later my doctor informed me that I would probably never be able to have another child. Not only did God ignore my plea about Lehana, but He now took my hope of ever having a child from me. How cruel a God!"

"Elaine, I am so sorry."

"Oh, Cal, don't be. You see I spent the good part of the next year in total rebellion against God, life and, often times, against Tom. It's a wonder Tom stuck with me. I was miserable. I began to wonder if I wanted to live. Then one Sunday morning in reading the newspaper, I saw this gorgeous little blue-eyed girl's picture. She was about three years old and above her picture was the caption, 'This Little Girl is Full of Spirit and Needs a Home.' I yelled, 'Tom, its Lehana.' Tom was so used to my ups and downs, he had learned to ignore me. I grabbed the paper and ran to him and threw the paper in his face. 'Tom, this is our little girl, it's Lehana.'"

I began to giggle a bit as this seems so familiar. It reminded me of the day Shirley found our little boy, Larry, similarly in the newspaper.

"Why are you giggling?" Elaine sounded a bit offended.

"Oh, I'm sorry, but I have to share, we have an adopted son, Larry, whom we also found in the newspaper. It seems God had led us both down the same road. I'm just giggling with happiness because I know your joy. Please continue and tell me how it all came to be."

"Well, we called the adoption agency and they told us we were among many who had inquired and at first, I was a little discouraged but at the same time I felt this had to be our little girl. I really didn't feel close to God, as I felt He had let me down, but at the same time, I had no answers. There was a nudge in my heart that Tom and I needed to go to church. We went ahead and requested an application form for consideration of an interview. In the meantime, Tom and I decided it was time to visit a church. We had heard of an active Baptist church down the street from us. Sunday we got up and made our way to the services. It was a bit unnerving as we felt a bit strange, although everyone made us welcome. That Sunday, of all Sundays, the pastor spoke on the topic 'Why Bad Things Happen to Good People.' He told of the story of Joseph, how he was sold into slavery but yet God saved him, then how he was put into prison by being falsely accused by Potiphar's wife, then God miraculously put him into the seat of power in Egypt and he saved an entire nation. It struck me. Did God have a purpose for me? I know I must be boring you."

"No! No, you're not! Shirley and I are there with you Elaine. Please go on."

"Well, we went home that night and I prayed like I had never prayed before. I asked the Lord to help me find purpose again and to forgive me for blaming Him. Tom and I both went back to the church and met with the pastor. He talked with us about how much God really does love us. Within weeks we found ourselves walking down that aisle giving our lives to the Lord, asking for Baptism and getting involved in Sunday School and the church. We were developing a home for what we hoped would be one for our little girl as well. We did get an invitation to interview for adopting but we were one of many. Well, one Sunday morning I asked our Sunday School class to pray with us over the matter. Our teacher asked the class to devote our prayer time solely for this and while in prayer I felt a tap on my shoulder. I looked up and no one was there, but above me I felt I could see angels all around the room giving me comfort. I knew it had to be the sense of the Holy Spirit that His power was upon us. We interviewed and that next week we got the call that we had been chosen and we could come in to make final arrangements. The little girl's name was Mary, we were allowed to give her a middle name if we so chose and I decided to make it Lehana. The next week our home was full of the joy of our little Mary Lehana Robins."

"Oh Elaine, I couldn't be happier for you."

"Well, we called her Mary, as we never wanted to forget how God used Mary to bear the Savior in her womb and how our Mary was used by God to bring us to that Savior. This morning, we experienced a miracle but I had already experienced a dynamic one. Today, our little Mary Lehana is a missionary serving the native Indian people of Brazil, she is indeed full of spirit sharing God's Spirit."

About this time, Tom looked at his watch. "Hon, it's going on 1:00 am. We've got to let these folks get to bed."

Indeed, the time had passed quickly. But I wouldn't have wanted to miss the miracle story Elaine has just shared. We all said our goodnights and headed on to our cabins.

The next morning brought a bright sunshine. I felt like it was indeed a wonderful day, a new start. I had remembered Elaine from high school but never knew her spiritually. But, oh how God used her to bless me with her miracle story! You just never imagine how your classmates turn directions spiritually. How they bless people. I look back over so many of my high school classmates and wonder what ever happened to them. I know that, at my age, seeing them again or crossing their paths is all but an impossibility. Whatever happened to Stacy who was on my high school Red Cross Committee and volunteered to work with me in teaching the preschooler Sunday School class at the post Sunday School? What about Rose Marie, the Hawaiian girl who was in our church group at First Baptist Wahiawa? She was always the opinionated one, but she was faithful to all the youth meetings and Training Union meetings on Sunday nights. What happened to Alex, the son of one of Dad's fellow chaplains who got caught in the major cut back, but rather than leave the Army took a cut in rank and came back as an enlisted man? Something they allowed back in the '50's and '60's, even though he was a chaplain? I could go on and as I take out my school yearbooks from time to time, I often wonder "Where are they now?" That would be some miracle to get to see them again. Oh, well, now I'm daydreaming.

Strange, but in terms of sequence, this trip is a bit reverse of reality. We went to Hawaii after leaving Seattle, my junior high years. Now we're leaving Hawaii and going to Seattle. Ah, Seattle, the happy years of my middle teens. For so many those years hold poor memories, but for me they were some of the best. We had a happy home life as Dad loved his assignment at Fort Larsen. We had a great church at Calvary Baptist, in Renton, Washington, and you can't beat the beauty of the Cascades, Mt. Rainier, Lake Washington and Puget Sound. For Dad it meant a lot of salmon fishing. And for the family, loads of sightseeing and doing things we've never done before such as clam digging, going up Mt. Rainier in the midst of mounds of snow 15 feet high, taking the ferry to Victoria, Canada, going up to Vancouver, B.C., and my catching my first trout on Spirit Lake at the base of Mt. St. Helens (before it exploded). Given this is a cruise of miracles, I do wonder what miracles we'll be experiencing on this leg of the journey!

As we got further away from Hawaii, Hawaii began to feel like a distant experience. My mind looked forward to the next adventure. We had at least four days at sea ahead of us.

As we made our way toward Seattle, I not only began to think of the happiness of my middle teens but of the innocence of my early years. Maybe it was just my being blinded by my own sweet memories, but it does seem the late '50's and early '60's were much more innocent. Yet, I have to remember the transition between our leaving Seattle and moving to Hawaii was a short period of time when the Korean Conflict had ended and the Vietnam Conflict was just about to begin. But, it was in that same period of time I remember churches were still having evening services. It was a time that Southern Baptists had as their theme, "A Million More in '54." We had the opportunity to take Bible courses for credit in our public schools. It was still a period of time when there was intense pride in our country. Smoking was the major issue for suspension at our high school, not drugs. Having a baby out-of-wedlock was still a social taboo. Abortion was against the law; thus, unborn babies were still safe. Television was very much censored and our children's programs were accentuated with appropriate models, such as Roy Rogers, Sky King, Gene Autry, Howdy Doody, etc. Then Playboy, Roe vs Wade, LSD, R-rated movies, cable television, drugs, Blue Laws suspended, prayer taken out of schools, Gideons thrown out of schools and the march was on. Innocence soon was lost. I watched all of that happen. I was a teacher seeing that and found myself teaching Values Clarification courses that basically taught no absolutes. I saw myself teaching children they were all important without a framework of teaching them of about God who made them in His own image. From 1960' on, I've slowly seen the seed of moral decay eat away at the very foundation of our educational system, the church and our nation. And now I'm at sea and I wonder what kind of country it will be when we dock for the last time. Will there be any miracles along the way that will change the course of our nation?

After breakfast, I had read in our ship's newspaper that there would be a worship service in the main auditorium, **Heaven's Gate**. My goodness! With all that had happened in Hawaii and our stay there, I was ready for a worship service! Shirley and I made our way to the auditorium and found our favorite seat, which tended to be on the upper left level. We could see the whole stage from there and the acoustics were always good. A music director came out with an orchestra of violins, trumpets, drums, etc., a full symphony. We were led in some truly praise and hymn music including "In Christ Alone," "Blessed Redeemer," "His Name is Wonderful," concluding with "Amazing Grace My Chains Are Gone." With hands raised our hearts were overpowered with outreached joy; then our speaker, the same man who so reminded me of Adrian Rogers.

"Ladies and Gentlemen, I want to speak to you today on the topic, 'Saints Surrendered to Leave It All Behind.'"

He started by asking what we left behind to go on this cruise and wondered how we would feel if we knew we could never return to any of it? Man! That began my thought process. I thought about my home, our cat, Gracie, our children, our church and my roles in the church. Was any of it necessary for my true happiness, I wondered was any of it permanent? In time, whether ready or not, I would leave it all behind. I thought about my mom as active as she was when that life-taking stroke ultimately stole first the quality of her life and then her life. I thought of my dad and how he retired and four years later, at the young age of 57, he left this world. Both left a lot behind. In terms of stuff, my brother and I found so much of mom's things were not things we needed or wanted and thus much was sold in an estate sale. So, the answer to the preacher's question was I guess I could leave my stuff behind but what about this world? As for the church, years have taught me that no one is indispensable. Oh, a few will make comment about one's contributions but after the funeral, you are soon forgotten, someone takes your place and life moves on, just as it did when I retired from my career. As for the world we leave behind, I so fear what it has become and what is left for my grandchildren Chelsea, Genee' and Kaelen.

The preacher went on to say, "I suspect many of you who were near the volcano on the Big Island of Hawaii, particularly if you were in the Lava Tube, you began to ponder what would happen if life were to end. You prayed. You hoped. You began to have flashbacks. But did any of you trust? Did any of you simply feel a sense of surrender?"

Surrendered? How could anyone feel surrendered in the midst of feeling near death, when the smell of death was surrounding you? My thoughts were going haywire, but I was beginning to feel a sense of needing to get closer to that stage. What was his point? I scooted to the edge of my seat.

"My point is this. As Saints, we need to be so in tune with Jesus that nothing else matters, realizing nothing on this earth can take eternity from us, nothing can steal truth from us, nothing can deny our salvation, and the gates of Hell are sealed to us. There was an old saying on television, a secular saying, 'What goes on in Las Vegas, stays in Las Vegas." That was a message from Hell. But the truth of it is, in time, "what goes on in Earth, will stay in Earth, until Jesus comes to reign and makes a new Earth.' As saints, we are not shackled to this world nor ever will be. So, when trials come, when death threatens, when our culture literally commits moral suicide, remember what Jesus said on the cross, 'Father unto your hands I commit my spirit.' Thus, as Saints, be surrendered to leave it all behind."

Oh, what a powerful message. I needed to hear that this morning. We closed by singing a favorite of mine, one Dr. Falwell used to close all the services with at Thomas Road Baptist, "My Jesus I Love Thee." Putting that to symphony, we left that auditorium feeling we were half way to heaven not Seattle.

Leaving the service, Shirley and I clearly weren't ready for lunch, although it was going on 11:30 am. So, we decided to go to top deck and just look out over the ocean and the skies. We sought out a deck chair. It seemed another couple did as well. We wanted out of the wind, but at the same time in the open air. So we procured a couple of deck blankets. Shirley, always the extrovert, wasn't shy about initiating the conversation.

"Hello, may we sit by you? I'm Shirley and this is my husband Cal."

"Indeed, we'd love to have company, I'm Stacy and this is my husband, Bill."

"We're the Meyers, but only if you see us both at the same time," Shirley continued.

"We're really Meyer, but so many want to add the 'S' on."

"Well, we're the Grangers from Oklahoma, originally."

"We've traveled around so much, we really don't have an 'originally,' but my family was from Florida and Cal's settled in South Carolina, although we live in Tennessee right now."

"Oh, where in Tennessee?"

"In a little town called Dandridge, near Pigeon Forge, Gatlinburg, the Smokies."

"Yes, we know it. We've done vacationing there. It's beautiful there."

"We don't know much about Oklahoma."

"Well, we're from there originally but we've been on the mission field most of our lives."

"Oh, really! Where?"

"We've just come home from Central America having served in Costa Rica and Panama."

"How amazing and coincidental. Cal did a mission trip to Vulcan, Panama, a few years back."

"Oh, we know it well. It's a beautiful up there."
"Yes! Cal was impressed with the work and loved the people. Carlos our steward is from there.'

"Well, that's unique! He's our steward as well."

"What led you to the mission field?"

"You know I'm not all that sure, but I got my first taste of service back when I was in high school. I was asked to be a Sunday School teacher with pre-school children on the Army Post my dad was stationed. I didn't give much thought to it at that time but it became a seed. God used to ignite a hunger of service within me."

I was awe struck. It can't be, I thought.
"Stacy, did you go to high school in Hawaii?"

"Yes, I did."

"Leilehua?"

"Yes!" She was apparently as surprised as I was.

"How did you know?"

"Stacy, I don't know if you remember me or not. But I'm Cal Meyer. My dad was the Post Sunday School Chaplain and you and I taught in the class of pre-school children."

"Oh, Cal, I do remember you! You were the one who invited me to teach with you. I didn't take it seriously at first, as you were probably well aware, but we were just kids in high school. I didn't take a lot of things seriously then. I didn't know what I wanted to do when I got out of school. Where I wanted to go to college? What I'd major in while in college? I was rather flighty in school."

At this point, I was rather amused as that's exactly how I remembered Stacy. I never took her as the serious type. In fact, she rather annoyed me and I regretted inviting her. She was late to class and was just somewhat cavalier about it.

"But you know Cal, God takes hold of a life. I don't recall our seeing each other much at school. You had your circle of friends and I, mine. My interest wasn't the church. My mom and dad weren't that involved. Oh, we went to chapel on several occasions but we really weren't all that involved in a church off base. But I finally had to decide what I was going to do upon leaving Leilehua. Upon graduation my dad received orders for Fort Sill, Oklahoma. I didn't have a clue about college. Once we got settled on base in Oklahoma, I took a job at a bank in downtown Lawton. I didn't know anyone but I developed friends with a colleague at the bank. Her name was Sue. She was a true believer and began talking about her church, Calvary Baptist. I listened at first, with little interest. But the longer I stayed at home, just working in the bank, the lonelier I got, feeling I had no purpose. Finally one day I told her I'd meet her for church. Cal, I went and heard a sermon on God's calling the ordinary and using them to do bold things. I thought back to my teaching those little kids in that Sunday School and remembered God's using me to teach little kids even when I wasn't all that close to Him. I asked why? It struck me, God was talking to me then, for now. It just so happened that on the back table of the church were materials from Oklahoma Baptist University. I grabbed a brochure and my heart told me to call them. Then I told myself I had no reason to go there. What would I major in? My mind wouldn't let go. So within the week I called and made an appointment to speak to the Admissions Office. They sent me materials and, in the process, invited me to an On-Campus Day for new prospects. By this time Fall semester had well begun, so my entry would be 2nd Semester at best. But then I thought, how am I going to afford this? Sue and I became closer and I continued to attend Calvary Baptist with her, joining with the young adults and eventually going forward and joining the church, after acknowledging I was letting Jesus in my life. I also was baptized."

"Stacy, my heart is so thrilled about this. I want to hear it all."

By this time Shirley was listening in on the conversation, as well as was Bill. Finally, Bill spoke up.

"Go ahead Hon and share how we met."

Stacy continued, "Well, I talked with my parents. They weren't all that religious but they weren't at all opposed to my feelings either. Dad came around and shared that they had been prepared to help me through college once I had decided where and what I wanted to do. They were happy for me but curious what I would major in at Oklahoma Baptist. As you might have guessed, I put my application in and was accepted for entry for 2nd Semester. I had some funds saved from my banking job and they had a dorm room open for me. But I had no idea on a major. Knowing the first two years are general liberal arts courses, I simply got into those, feeling I had time to decide. I considered teaching, and social work. But none really captured my heart. Once on campus I got into the life of a student, enjoying life in the dorm, going to the school cafeteria for my meals, studying in the library and attending a few athletic events. I was taking Biology 101 and we had to dissect a fetal pig. I hated it. I had no idea what the difference was between the kidney and the spleen. All I knew, it smelled. But I was assigned to a lab partner, a cute boy named Bill. Bill kind of grabbed my heart. At dinner, he had a way of finding his way to my table. Then when we had a major test over the parts of that fetal pig, he joined me in a study review over a pizza at the dorm. We began to date going to a few basketball games, etc. It wasn't long before I realized Bill and I were more than just lab partners. During the summer I returned home and worked the summer again at the bank. Bill was from Kentucky. His dad was a professor of missions at Southern Baptist Theological Seminary. All summer long, we exchanged letters. Absence did, indeed, make our hearts grow fonder. I could hardly wait to get back to school to see Bill."

Bill joined in. "What she didn't know, is that she stole my heart the day we met in class. I knew she was going to be my bride one day. But I knew my calling and I wanted to be sure God was calling her and gave her the time to realize it."

Stacy, blushed, "Well, yes, after that summer, I knew it had to be Bill. But neither of us talked much about our future. Bill and I went to the local church near campus and just rather took our faith for granted. I knew Bill was interested in some field of science but wasn't sure what. We were both freshmen. He hadn't indicated if it would be research, medicine, teaching or what.
August came, and I could hardly wait to see Bill's parents arrive with him. In those days, we just didn't have cars. I was still a freshman and Bill would be a sophomore. Bill and I continued to date and I wondered if and when it would ever lead to a proposal. Finally, the night before Homecoming, Bill said, 'I've got to talk with you.' He took me to our favorite park bench on campus. His folks had arrived that afternoon to enjoy the weekend with us. Then he laid it all out for me."

"Stacy, I love you. I've known it from the day I met you in class last spring. But I have to share my calling. I'm preparing myself to go to the mission field as a medical doctor. I am majoring in pre-med with the intent of going to med school and seminary. I have long years of school ahead of me and to ask anyone to be a part of that is asking a lot of sacrifice. But I want you to be my partner in this ministry and I ask you to join me in this ministry. If you feel you can, will you be my wife?" At that time, he pulled out a box with a beautiful engagement ring which his parents had brought with them. Bill had bought it that summer but wanted it prepared and brought at Homecoming.

I didn't know what to say. I just knew I loved him and that whatever he wanted to do I wanted to be there with him. I didn't understand the calling at the time, but I didn't need to. God would reveal that. However, it opened the door to my major. I knew it immediately, nursing. I looked into his eyes, hugged him and gave him the sweetest kiss I could and said, "Yes! Yes!"

Bill just took me and said "I love you so much."

By this time, I grabbed Shirley's hand and both of us had trouble containing our tears. It seemed so reminiscent of our courtship.

By this time Bill and Stacy both had tears in their eyes. Bill chimed in.

"We finished college at OBU and I immediately entered med school at the University of Oklahoma. With residency and all, I was there another four years. Then on to seminary in Louisville, at the Southern Baptist Theological Seminary, where my dad taught. I was in the Bachelor of Divinity program."

I asked, "What years were you there?"

"Let me think. I think it was 1974-1979."

I responded delightfully. "Well, we just missed you then. We were in Louisville from 1970-1973. I was a school teacher and then Minister of Education at a church out in the Valley Station area. Stacy what did you do while Bill was in school?"

"While he was in med school, I took a job in nursing that helped get us through financially, although we had to take out some loans. While in seminary I worked part-time nursing and Bill had a part-time job in a local hospital. I entered the Master of Religious Education program."

"My! Oh, my! That was a lot of years in school and a lot of money." I had a hard time wrapping my head around that much time. But then I realized I did the same thing as I was in school until 1979 earning my two master degrees and doctorate.

Stacy came back reassured, "Yes, but God blessed us. With my folks and Bill's folks helping with our OBU schooling, we basically left with no debt there. The biggest debt was Bill's M.D. We had to get loans on that and it took years to pay that off, but with the Lord's provision and help from Bill's parent's church and the Southern Baptist Foreign Mission Board, we did in time get it paid off. As for seminary, with the Cooperative Program basically paying much of the tuition, our part-time jobs paid for our seminary housing and it was enough to get us through."

"I take it then you became Southern Baptist Cooperative Program Foreign Missionaries (meaning the Southern Baptist Convention provides salaries for missionaries, they don't have to depend on securing their own funding from the churches)?"

Bill spoke up. "Yes, we did. We weren't at first sure where we wanted to serve but we knew that we wanted to go somewhere in either South or Central America. Then, in the fall of 1979 a young man from Panama came to our church and spoke of the many opportunities there, particularly in the Highlands. He spoke of the responsiveness of the people, of the poverty, of the openness to the Gospel and of the need for medical missionaries. He also spoke of its being critical in timing as the country was going through political changes with President Carter turning the Panama Canal over to Panama and how the country could be in for changes for good or bad. It was a time for needed Christian influences. That got our attention and we applied for Central America, particularly Panama."

I realized we had been in conversation for a while. Bill went on to talk about their years in Panama, telling how things got difficult under Noriega and the threat to American Missionaries, particularly during the American invasion in late December 1989. But he shared how churches were planted and how people became receptive to the Word. Eventually, Bill and Stacy transferred to Costa Rica and finished their service there. I would have loved to have had more time with them, but I realized we had spent several hours with them as it was and that perhaps they had other things they wanted to do.

"Bill and Stacy, this has been a real joy and blessing. Stacy you can't imagine how humbled I feel in knowing I was the one inviting you to teach that class with me back when we were in high school. Who would have ever known how God would use that. I feel I've witnessed a miracle in once again getting to see you and hear your story. I feel your whole life has been a miracle. I trust we'll come across each other on this cruise again. I'd love to hear some of the stories from the mission field."

Shirley and I rose from our deck chairs and headed back to the restaurant. I felt like some ice cream and perhaps some coffee. I just wanted some time to reflect on what God allowed me to experience.

Oh! Wow! Stacy, that reluctant rather uncommitted pre-school Sunday School teacher, becoming a nurse and missionary to Central America! God is so good!

You know I'm learning that life is full of situations where God uses you in some of the most insignificant ways, insignificant to us, but not to God. He is constantly changing lives. We never know when or how. I know that on a ship we'll more than likely see Stacy and Bill again, but I'll never see or think of her as I once did. I'll always see her as a giant of Christian service and faith. This trip can't get any better than this!

We're spending four days at sea before arriving in Seattle. But I discovered on previous trips, those days become somewhat seamless. You lose sight and sense of what day is what. The days on a ship are often so routine, a routine of rest, dining, entertainment, etc. On this ship, the entertainment is all so inspiring as we have daily morning worship services and evening top notch musicals and Christian oriented entertainment. You'll not find many pianists, quartets, soloists or speakers that can be as uplifting as we've found on this ship. But blend that with the personal experiences of personal miracles and I just don't know how much more I can be filled. Life off this ship is going to be a big let-down. I feel we almost need to go on to Heaven for that not to happen.

Well, Friday and Saturday went by quickly, all we had was Sunday and Monday before docking in Seattle on Tuesday. We were to be in Seattle for a day and a half. That would be exciting. I was looking forward to Sunday, knowing it would be a special day of worship. That evening our newsletter, the **MH MKADDESH SAINT**, was in our door box. I was delighted by the proposed events including:

- 6:30 am – Sunrise Service – Deck 1 (Top Deck)
- 11:00 am – Morning Worship Service – Heaven's Gate
- 5:00 pm – Vesper Services – Deck 1 (Top Deck)
- 9:00 pm – Musical, Gaither Revisited – Heaven's Gate

I wasn't sure why a Sunrise service, as this was fall, nowhere near Easter. But I can't imagine a more beautiful morning being out to sea and seeing the sunrise come over the ocean. It meant getting up early, but what else did we have to do?

Noting services began at 6:30 am that meant getting up around 5:30 am. I figured, we could probably bathe Saturday night and simply get up in time to shave, take our pills, etc. in order to be on deck by 6:30 am. Even at that hour it would be dark but the purpose was to see the sunrise. Morning came quickly. I'm not sure we were ready for it, but who is that early in the morning? We made our way to Top Deck and as we got closer heard a beautiful rendition of "To God Be the Glory," led by an ensemble of young singers, supported by a keyboard, guitar and a small horn line. Slowly the deck began to fill with passengers and all joined in the singing. Song after song began to bring us in one harmonious praise of the Lord. By the time we got to "Victory in Jesus" the sun was rising in the East. The beauty of the morning could only be matched with the moment all of us joined our hearts in loud, joyous, uplifting, glorious worship to our loving Savior. The entire day was one of continuous worship as we heard such outstanding messages on the "Glory That Is in Sainthood." One cannot look at the prophesies of the Old Testament without seeing the Messiah throughout. One cannot see the Messiah of the Old Testament without seeing the Christ of the New Testament. One cannot see the Christ of the New Testament without realizing He gave His all so that ALL could be saved by His grace through faith or as John wrote, "Whosoever will." And as one of my favorite pastors, Dr. Dean Haun, First Baptist of Morristown, Tennessee, stated it, he died for "All" and the plural of "All." The plural of "All" is "All Y'all!"

After a day that seemed like a walk in Heaven, we gathered in Heaven's Gate, and to our delight there was Bill Gaither and Gloria Gaither, as well as singers that have traveled with them for years and new ones. The concert started at 9:00 pm and went on for two hours, but I believe it could have gone on all night. They sang their favorites and new ones, as well. I'll never forget the concert "Alleluia." I loved that musical. My first taste of Bill Gaither was back in the 1970's when "Because He Lives" became so popular. At first it was sung as choir specials then it became a part of most hymnals. I mean that song could raise me to glory when a choir raised the roof with it. By Midnight, I was exhausted but uplifted. I didn't know how it could get any better than that! Talk about a revival!

Monday morning we needed to sleep in and that we did. We'd be in port Tuesday morning. As we neared Seattle, the seas got a little rough. The Captain encouraged us to stay inside as they closed off Deck 7, the outside deck. The winds were a bit heavy. If I understood correctly, we were facing wind gusts up to 75 mph. We were rockin'. You couldn't walk a straight line anywhere. I know elevators only go up or down, but I could have sworn on that day the elevators were also going left and right. Strangely, we didn't get sea sick and I didn't note others doing so either. It didn't seem to affect the dining schedule or the normal activities. We just had to hang on to the rails a bit tighter. Getting closer to port, you could definitely feel the air getting colder. Yep! We were nearing Seattle!

Chapter 10: Seattle

Well, Tuesday is upon us and I awoke early to see us approach port. Seattle with Mt. Rainier in the background is always such a picturesque view. We have two full days in port. There is so much I want to see, but what can you do in two days? There is, of course, Calvary Baptist in Renton where I had two wonderful years of spiritual growth in my youth and met a young girl that, at the time, I thought would someday be my wife. It was but a teenage heart throb but it opened my heart to the true love of my life who I would meet in college. There is Bellevue Junior High where my social studies teacher made such an impact on my life and presented me a Bible upon my leaving. There is the Space Needle and the memories of the 1963 World's Fair. There is the area that was once Fort Larsen, the military base where my dad was stationed upon his return from Korea. There is Mercer Island, where we lived while in the Seattle area and where I delivered the Seattle Times. I also recall beautiful Lake Washington which surrounded it. I want to see it all, but where do I begin?

Shirley and I got ready and headed for the upper level for breakfast. While dining, we noted again only one table available and it had one other couple.

"May we join you," Shirley asked.

"We're the Meyers from Tennessee."

"Well, hello, we're the Groves from Renton, Washington."

"Renton?" I inquired.

Mr. Grove responded. "Oh, that's been years ago. It was originally our home and we're coming back just as a part of this trip. We haven't lived here for at least 40 years. We now live in Texas, but Renton has always been considered home. I thought I'd share that since we're back here now."

"I understand. I lived here in my youth some 60 years ago. I was just a Junior High School student then. My dad was stationed at, what was then, Fort Larsen."

"Yes, we were aware of Fort Larsen. It was a beautiful place and still is. It has been turned over to the city as a park and other development."

"Renton?" I asked quizzically.

"We went to church in Renton. Calvary Baptist Church."

"Yes, we know Calvary, our daughter attended there. But that was years ago. Her mom and I weren't much involved in church then. We didn't find the Lord vital to our lives until years later."

This whole conversation began taking a unique twist. It struck me. "Grove" that was the last name of Riva, the girl who stole my heart as a 14-year-old. This couldn't be! For this to be her parents, they would be at the very least in their '90's by now and this couple doesn't look much older than us. It would take a miracle for us be sitting with them.

I passed it by as just a coincidence and we continued our conversation.

I inquired further. "What did you do for a living?"

"Oh, I was in business for myself at first, but eventually I went to work for Boeing."

"What kind of business did you do?"

"I was into minerals, so to speak. I collected rocks and polished them."

Now, I know this is too coincidental. Riva's dad designed a rock polisher and that was his business when I met her. I used to wear those western Bolo ties with polished rocks she gave me. This conversation is beginning to take a very eerie turn!

"What made you give it up?"

"I couldn't make a living doing it. Soon everybody had their own polisher and Bolo ties weren't all that popular. So, I had to find a real job."

"What led you to Texas?"

"Our daughter. She married a preacher. After his schooling they eventually found their way there and that's where our grandchildren were born. We wanted to be near them."

Mr. Grove then began inquiring about me.

"What about you?"

"Oh, I became a teacher, college professor and bi-vocational pastor. I thought I would one day be an Army Chaplain like my dad but God had other plans. I met my wife Shirley at college and we've been married for 52 years, have three children, one of which is adopted, all grown now."

He continued. "Chaplain Meyer? That sounds so familiar, but I'm not sure why."

I then had to ask. "What was your daughter's name?"
"Riva."

I was momentarily stunned. "Riva? Did she attend Renton High School in 1957? Was she on the dance team and was she the one who attended Calvary Baptist Church?"

"Well, yes, she was. How did you know?"

"Mr. Grove, I'm Cal Meyer. I met your daughter as a 14-year-old. I took her to the Valentine's Banquet at Calvary Baptist as my date. My very first date. My mother, Sue Meyer, led her to the Lord. As a 14-year-old, she stole my heart and I truly thought at the time I would marry her one day. We attended several youth retreats at Mt. Baker and went on skating outings with the church. However, I only got to know your daughter for one year as my dad was transferred to Hawaii."

"Yes, I vaguely remember. Didn't your dad come one summer to pick you up from that retreat?"

"Yes, after moving to Hawaii, I wanted to go back the next summer for the Youth Retreat at Mt. Baker. Pastor Johnson offered to pick me up at the airport and take the youth to the retreat. That was the last time I got to see Riva. My dad flew from Hawaii via Military Transport to take me back home that summer. You and your sweet wife had us over for dinner the night before we left."

"That has been so long ago. You know Riva did, indeed, marry a preacher."

"Yes, I heard that, but once in high school, I lost touch with her. Upon leaving Hawaii my dad was stationed back in Fort Lewis, down in the Tacoma area. Mom tried to find Riva again. She had it in her mind we were meant for each other. However, as Riva found her true love, I found mine as well. I never knew what happened to Riva, though I have wondered."

"Riva had a wonderful life but sadly our sweet daughter passed on to be with the Lord about 10 years ago. She left us three wonderful grandchildren, two daughters and a son. Our grandson is a preacher himself now, serving in the Renton area where it all started. Our granddaughters married and both of them are faithful to the Lord. One is a nurse and the other a high school music teacher."

My eyes watering, I realized so much common ground between us. "I am so sorry. I would have loved to have seen Riva at least one more time in our lifetime. Several years back we made a trip back to the Seattle area on vacation and spent a Sunday at Calvary Baptist. I wanted to see if the church had changed. And, of course, it had. But I also wanted to check out if anyone knew of Riva and what had happened to you all and her. The church had changed and none of the members knew anything about Riva or you all. We left a little disheartened. I'm so glad we've had the opportunity to see you again."

Mr. Grove continued, "No, once we left Renton, we never returned. We had nothing here to keep us here. And, as you know, we weren't faithful in any church in this area. We didn't find the Lord until later in our lives. Riva and her family were instrumental in bringing us to the Lord."

"Well, that explains it. But what brings you here now?" I asked.
"Let's just say, a miracle. We're just passing through. You'll have a couple of days here. If you want, Riva is buried at the Memorial Gardens in Renton. Maybe you could visit her grave. She moved back here when her son began his ministry here. Her husband died shortly before she moved here. He died suddenly with a heart attack. Riva left us having fought a good fight with cancer. Her son has two children and she wanted to be near her grandchildren. You see, he's the new pastor at Calvary Baptist."

My heart jumped into my throat. Riva's son now pastor at Calvary, the very church in which my mom led Riva to the Lord, the very church I had my very first date and that date was with Riva. I could never imagine in my wildest dreams the miracle of all this.

"Well, we must go," as Mr. and Mrs. Grove got up to leave.

"Thank you! Thank you so much for joining us." With that, we saw them blend into the crowd that morning, never to see them again.

"Shirley, it just hit me. Riva would have been 75 years old if she were still alive, one year older than me. That means the Groves would have been in their late 80's to early 90's, at least. That couple didn't look that much older than us. Are we sure of what just happened?" Miracle? Wonder? What just happened?"

Having the unexpected just hit us over the head, we weren't quite sure what we needed to do next. We really hadn't planned our time in the Seattle area, although we had considered stopping by Calvary Baptist. I guess we need to do that now. We went back to our room to find Carlos. I realized now we needed to rent a car. As we made our way to the cabin, just as unexpected as everything else, Carlos came down the hallway.

"Hi, Dr. and Mrs. Meyer. I was hoping to see you this morning. A car will be waiting for you dockside to take you wherever you'd like to go."

"How did you know?

Carlos, just grinned and went on his way. I should have realized by now this is, indeed, a Cruise of Miracles. We only had today and tomorrow. I knew we needed to make them count.

By now it was nearing 10:00 am and, if we were going to get anything done, we needed to be on the road. Shirley indicated she needed to brush her teeth. I learned a long time ago, it was no simple brushing of teeth. She usually had to do a makeover, finish those last minute getting ready chores. What I normally would consider a five-minute delay, Shirley could always find a way of turning it into 20 minutes. I love her anyway!

Sure enough along about 10:45 we were heading down the stairs to the ship's Level 6 exit. Once off the ship, a gentleman in a black suit with a sign "Dr. Meyer" waved to us. We approached him.
"We have your car waiting just out the exit door; follow me." We did and to our delight there was a white limousine awaiting us. I've never ridden in a white limousine.

"Are you ready to visit Calvary Baptist?" the driver asked.

My mouth halfway open. "Well, yes, how did you know?"

He just smiled and off we went. We headed across town, going east, toward the floating bridge which crosses Lake Washington. I used to ride my bike there regularly, given we lived in the Shorewood Apartments just a mile or so from it, back in the '50's. Once on the other side of Mercer Island we were on the interstate heading south toward Renton. When we lived in the area 60 years ago, there was no interstate, only a four-lane highway, which we traveled on to church

Sunday and Wednesday nights. With it going on noon, we finally arrived at the church. It was Tuesday, but to our delight there was the pastor and a group of older adults gathering. They were putting their things on the church bus.
I felt like we were intruding. But we got out and I went to the pastor.

"Hello, I'm Cal Meyer. I know you don't know me and I'm sure you weren't expecting me. But I knew your mother and I just found out this morning who you are and that you are pastor here."

"Oh, Dr. Meyer, we were expecting you. The ship called to tell us you were coming. We're going up to Mt. Baker for an overnight Senior Citizen Retreat. We'd like you to join us. We've made reservations for you."

"You, what? We don't have our clothes nor are we prepared for an overnight stay." At that time, the driver of our car came over with a suitcase.

"Here's all you'll need, for the both of you." Again, flabbergasted, we took the suitcase, found a seat, put the suitcase in the rack above us and off we went. Both Shirley and I were without words, but then again, we've been like that since this morning.

I knew this was going to be a quick trip and one that would use up our entire time. It was at least a three-hour trip to the retreat grounds. Everyone was so friendly. We didn't even know the pastor's name, only that it was Riva's son. After everyone boarded, the pastor got on board and welcomed us.

"Hi, everyone. I'm so glad you've decided to come. Let me introduce you to two special guests. We have with us today Dr. Cal and Shirley Meyer. Dr. Meyer is someone my mother knew years ago when they were both teenagers in this church. Dr. Meyer and Shirley are on a cruise via the ship MH MKaddish. It is in port only today and tomorrow but we've fortunate enough to have them join us. What Dr. Meyer doesn't know, is that I'm asking him to lead us in the morning devotions tomorrow?"

Oh, my! I wasn't expecting that! I was taken back and my mind became to buzz on what I might talk about.

The pastor continued, "Before we leave, let's ask the Lord's blessings on our trip." With the closing of the prayer, the pastor came back and sat in the seat in front of us.

"I hope you're okay with leading a devotion. I understand you pastored several churches and I knew you'd have something to share. By the way, I'm Roy. My mom has mentioned you and told us how she was saved, that it was your mother who led her to the Lord. She also told us about that Valentine's Banquet."

Somewhat embarrassed, I responded, "She did! How did you know I was a pastor?"

"Oh, we found that out when we heard you were coming to visit us today. A fellow from the ship, Carlos, told us all about you and we already knew the connection with my mom."

I should have known. Miracles, whether great or small seem to never cease. As we traveled on the bus, Pastor Roy told me all about his mom and their home life, his dad and his last years with his mom, Riva. I was touched and wished somehow Shirley and I had had the privilege of knowing them. Riva apparently was such a godly mother and obviously so, her son is a pastor, noting also his dad was a pastor as well. I felt so blest to know my family, particularly my mom, had a part in Riva's finding the Lord. I already knew about Riva's parents; we met them on board. But, asked about them anyway. Roy confirmed most all they had told us and then the shocker.

"Riva and I loved her mom and dad. It was such a loss to us when they died about 10 years ago."

Shirley and I looked at each other rather mortified. This couldn't be, we just had breakfast with them. How do I tell Roy we had breakfast with them without his thinking we had lost our minds or were delusional? I know we weren't speaking to spirits. They were as real as we are and as alive as everyone else. Shirley and I looked at each other again in silence. I put my finger over my mouth as a signal for us to just keep silent. We can't explain it. It was real but to mention it would be something we knew he would never understand. It was a miracle and we'll leave it at that.

My mind began to focus on the devotional I was to give. This was a group of Senior Citizens; most were about my age or five to ten years younger. What could I say that would be of interest, would be motivating, and would glorify God? Then I thought about sharing a little bit of the story of Riva, how she was saved, the Valentine's Banquet and then go into my own testimony.

Having a rest/lunch stop along the way we finally arrived at the campgrounds around 4:30 pm. Upon leaving the bus, I found to my amazement, the retreat had replaced wooden cabins with a modern hotel. Pastor Roy led us to the foyer where we were all checked in and given a schedule of events. First on the schedule was dinner at the hotel dining room. I was rather disappointed as I remembered youthful days when we stood outside in the brisk morning cold, waiting in line to enter the old barracks cafeteria building that was then the dining hall. There was just something rustic about it, that I felt was rather romantic and energizing. Shirley and I checked into our room, a nice typical hotel room but the view was gorgeous as it looked out toward the peeks of the mountains. They were snow-capped. The air was brisk. Dinner was scheduled for 6:00 pm, with evening vespers in the chapel at 7:30 pm and an outside marshmallow roast around the hotel fire pit scheduled at 9:00 pm. I kept thinking, when am I going to have time to prepare my devotional?

Dinner was great as we were served delightful salmon and/or roast beef, red potatoes, Italian green beans, a salad bar with every mix you could ever desire and a great selection of deserts. It was a wonderful time of fellowship as we got to know the wonderful people from Calvary Baptist. It reminded me so much of the great love we had when we were members back in the '50's. While many were near our age, none of them were at Calvary when we were members. I met retired Boeing employees, retired military, retired teachers, just so many with whom we could relate. The 90-minute dinner hour was over quickly.

"Okay, folks, we need to head to the chapel for our evening Vesper Service," Pastor Roy reminded us.

I followed the group out of the dining hall and to my utter delight the chapel was just as it was back in the '50's, a rustic A-Frame building with gorgeous stain-glassed windows. My mind raced back and I recall the youth singing, the great young preachers and the utter spiritual excitement we felt in those earlier days.

As we entered the building, one of the group was a pianist and she was playing "At Calvary." It wasn't long before we were singing it. Then the pastor led us into other hymns of our day, such as "Tell Me the Story of Jesus," and "Blessed Assurance." Noting Fanny Crosby's hymns were probably the most prominent songs in our youth, it was a joy to sing them again. These hymns have been replaced by others and so many new choruses. Pastor Roy then asked if there were prayer requests. Many had friends and loved ones to lift up in prayer. He made a list of all the requests as they were named. He then suggested we each take one and lift them up as we prayed. Then, uniquely, he had someone play over the audio system Tennessee Ernie Ford's "There Will Be Peace in the Valley" as we prayed. It brought me to tears as it was so strong in my memory that on those cold mornings at the youth retreat, we'd be awakened by the public address system with gospel music of the day, one of which was Tennessee Ernie Ford. We each prayed individually and then the pastor called on three others to lead us in prayer, one was to pray that during this retreat we seek to get to know Christ, another was to pray that we would seek to Glorify Christ and yet another that we would find ways to make Him known. The pastor then led us in prayer.

Following our prayer time, we sang another chorus we grew up loving, "His Name Is Wonderful." Of course, the pastor had the words printed to all the music we sang. He then divided us into groups of four. The pastor gave each group a two-foot length of twine. He asked each member of the group to think of their lives.

"As you look on your life right now, you will see yourself on a part of a storyline of your entire life. Each of you have a moment in time where you are seeking God's leadership to lead you in doing something. It may be to pray for someone specifically, to ask someone to come to church with you, to reach out to a long lost relative, to heal wounds with a family member, to say 'I'm sorry' to someone, to be honest with God when you know you haven't been, to respond to a gift He has called on you to use, etc. I want you to think of this moment in your storyline and then tie a knot on the twine to represent it. After you've done that, I want you to share it with your group. Then as a group lift up each other in a bond love to seek God's leadership to follow through on this storyline."

This was a fantastic exercise. It got personal. I had to think about where we were. I gave great thought to this and realized my knot represented that as I face the closing years of my life I wanted to still be significant for Christ in the way I served Him and not be retired. I needed to be open to both the small acts of kindness or acts of service, as well as the greater call of service that may challenge my ability. I want to teach again, but I may need to simply find happiness in bagging groceries. I need to realize God is glorified in both.

After the four in our group tied a knot, we each shared our storyline. At the end of the group exercise, the pastor asked if any in the entire group wanted to share their particular storyline. At this point many did, but the pastor had to draw it to a close and he made a transition to his devotional.

"You know, the point of this exercise was to draw our attention that for each of us to find our way through our storyline of life, we have to have a close relationship with the Lord. Tonight I want to take a few moments and ask that we consider this topic, "How do we get to really know Christ?"

With a prayer, the pastor turned to Philippians 3:10 and read "That I may know him and the power of His resurrection, and the fellowship of His sufferings, being conformed to His death."

The pastor indicated he wanted to share the thoughts of a great preacher from First Baptist Church, Morristown. We know Jesus by knowing the power of His resurrection. It is only that power that our sins are ultimately forgiven, it was that resurrection that defeated sin. We know Jesus by sharing in the fellowship of His suffering. We totally acknowledge Him when we face the crisis that life throws at us. And finally, we die to self by being conformed to His death. <u>In each point the pastor emphasized that in order for us to experience the power of His resurrection, the fellowship of His suffering and conformed to His death, we have to Yield, then we have to be Filled, filled with His Word, filled with His Spirit and filled with Prayer and finally Spilled out daily for the Lord. [1 – Dean Haun – 1/14/18].</u> It was a great message and spoke to our hearts. It blended well with the exercise we each had just completed.

Pastor Roy then led in an altar call asking if anyone wanted to come to the altar and allow the Holy Spirit to lead them in spilling it out on the altar in prayer, as we sang, "Just as I am." It was a deeply soul-searching encounter. The whole evening was like a retreat of old. After the service, we were invited to the fire pit behind the hotel, but it was much more than marshmallows, they had the fixings for S'mores. I hadn't had a S'more in years. Gathering around the fire, we were given metal prongs on which to roast our marshmallows and then to the side were Hershey chocolate bars and Graham crackers to complete the S'mores. Hot chocolate was also available. The air was chilled enough to sit around the fire enjoying our S'mores and hot chocolate. Couples sat next to each other and began to converse about days of old and memories of youth trips. One of the fellows came out with his guitar and began to play tunes. We sang along anything from "My Jesus I Love Thee," to "Beulah Land." Talk about heavenly!

Noting it was nearing 11:00 pm and I had a devotional to prepare, I nudged Shirley as a hint we needed to head on back to the room.

Others were beginning to do the same and a lovely evening came to an end.

Our schedule for the day was breakfast at 8:00 am, Prayer Meeting and second cup of coffee hour 9:00 am, Song Service and Bible Study (which I was leading) at 10:00 am, Personal Time to pack and load the bus at 11:00 am, lunch at noon, depart at 1:00 pm. That would get us back to Renton around 4:00 to 5:00 pm, pending traffic. With the ship leaving port at 11:00 pm, we'd have plenty of time. I never in my wildest imagination thought we'd be spending our Seattle time in this manner, but I wouldn't have chosen any other way. But what was I going to share as my devotional? It was late and I needed a devotional. Fortunately, along with my clothes, which Carlos had put in the car for us, was my Bible. I had been working on an article about why I considered myself a Baptist and my lengthy notes were inside my Bible. Shirley went on to bed but I stayed up and worked on my thoughts.

The next morning came earlier than imagined but with the room alarm clock ringing at 6:00 am, I crawled out of bed giving myself time to review my notes and us both time to prepare for the day. Making our way to the dining room, I recalled the frigid moment of the old barracks where we stood outside shivering, waiting for those wonderful biscuits, bacon and eggs. This morning we had windows opening to the beautiful mountains before us as we walked through the buffet line to help ourselves to a sundry of items from which to choose. Pastor Roy came in soon behind us and joined us. I could see his mother in his eyes. I mentioned how much she enjoyed this mountain as a young person and how much we enjoyed coming with our church group to the youth retreats. As for me it was life changing. I can honestly say I believe my youth group had a lot to do with shaping my faith and moving me forward in my journey. I was only a part of the Calvary group a short year and a half before we were transferred to Hawaii, but it seemed so much longer. However, those two trips to the Mt. Baker Youth Retreats are still very vivid in my memory. Roy joined in and shared that his mother Riva often expressed the same thing. Shirley shared her youth group always went to Stetson University for Youth Retreats and it was there that her future was in part directed to Carson-Newman. Shirley met a young man there by the name of Barnett. They too were both in high school, and as with Riva and me, experiencing a youthful heart experience. Barnett intended on going to Carson-Newman College and Shirley wasn't going anywhere. She came from a family that was dirt poor. But by a miracle of God, she got a full scholarship to a college and she chose Carson-Newman. Unfortunately, Barnett didn't quite realize the poverty from which Shirley came and when he witnessed it, it impacted him. Both of them ended up at Carson-Newman and it was there that God brought us together. God had his plan all along.

It was so strange for, in Shirley's telling that story, we realized we both had very similar, parallel storylines that ultimately led to us both to attending Carson-Newman and God's putting other significant people in our lives before bringing us together. And, uniquely God led us to other significant people who had successful lives. Barnett ended up being a very successful university professor but died in his late '60's of cancer. Shirley thinks often of her youth as I do mine and both of us are thankful for Barnett and Riva whom God put in our lives.

Well, time was flying and I needed to get my thoughts together for my Bible study. Around 8:45 am, Pastor Roy stood and announced for everyone to simply assemble with him in Meeting Room #1 at 9:00 am for Prayer Meeting. We finished our breakfast and made our way there. While there, the pastor asked us to share one blessing we felt this week. After so sharing, we then joined in and shared prayer requests, which Pastor Roy wrote on a piece of paper. We then broke into groups of four and were assigned to different parts of the room. Pastor Roy, requested each person take one of the requested prayer needs and be sure they were lifted up in their group, then, he asked that in the group we pray for 1) each other, 2) pray for the church, 3) pray for Renton, and 4) pray God will use the weekend to make a difference in our lives. At about 9:45 am, the pastor spoke briefly and then ask for us all to join him in a prayer, followed by our singing "Sweet Hour of Prayer." They brought in a table of coffee and pastries and we were invited to take a break before heading to the Chapel for our morning Bible Study. I'll admit I was somewhat nervous. I so wanted to glorify God in whatever I said to bring this beautiful time we had together in an uplifting close.

Finally, the hour arrived and it was time for the morning service. After several inspiring praise songs, led by the one who had earlier played his guitar, it was time for my devotional. I started off by first sharing the story of how I knew Pastor Roy's mother and my youthful crush on her as a young 14-year-old. I mentioned the times of our youth at Calvary, the Valentine's Banquet, the skating parties, my memories of the old Mount Baker Retreat facilities and how important the Mount Baker Youth Retreats were to my spiritual growth. I then spoke on why I am a Baptist. My talk was as follows:

I was saved as a young lad of eight years old under the teachings of my Baptist parents in Rossville, Georgia, 1952. As I sat in the back seat of a 1950 black Pontiac on a Sunday afternoon, while my pastor dad was visiting parishioners in the hospital, my mother leaned over the front seat of the car and asked if I loved Jesus and wanted to let Him into my heart. I confess I can't remember the date or month, nor do I recall a great rushed release of guilt over my sins. All I knew is that I did love Jesus and, from that day forward, mine has been a life of constant pursuit in attempting to live for Him, pursuing His Will, seeking His forgiveness, trying to obey Him, and wanting to glorify Him. No, I haven't been perfect and, no, I haven't been sinless and, yes, I have often wondered why I wandered into sin, if as an eight-year-old I was really saved. I didn't understand Justification, Sanctification or Glorification. I've let the carnal take me on side trips along my journey and I've been ashamed of my failings. But I always knew to Whom I could go for His love and His forgiveness and the older I've grown the more secure I've felt in His arms and the more I've felt the power of the Holy Spirit speaking to me and guiding me.

Once in my late 20's I made the decision I hadn't been saved. I looked at my life and seeing the sin I had let in it over my young years felt a Christian wouldn't have been that disobedient. I listened to an evangelist tell me that if I couldn't remember the exact moment, date and time of my salvation then I wasn't saved. I've heard preacher upon preacher proclaim that if there wasn't

a sense of change then there wasn't salvation. I went forward and confessed I was lost and was baptized again. The problem, I was an ordained minister, serving in a church position. I soon realized that action became difficult for the church to understand. It in part led to my demise on the staff of that church. Within a year I was asked to leave that church. I confess the order of the events during my short time at that church are no longer sharp in my mind. But the major crisis of faith it brought me is very clear. I've since gone back, and looking through a different filter of understanding, realized I did accept the Lord as a young eight-year-old but that growing in the faith is a life long journey.

The one remarkable date I do remember is October 23, 5:00 pm, 1971. Facing the deep hurt of a rejecting church, I sat in my church office overwhelmed by spiritual pain. I felt alone, rejected, isolated and shunned. I let myself get trapped into the emotions of a revival meeting. I mistook the Holy Spirit's calling to turn it over to Him. Instead, I mistakenly chose to confess my failings before a church by admitting falsely I was lost as one of their ministers. Sin is sin no matter how mankind may want to categorize them and they are all a disobedience to God and need His forgiveness. Sensing my pain, a member of the church felt my burden and called me to encourage me. She simply reminded me that there was nothing I could do to face my difficulties, but that I had to let it go and let God straighten it out. I remember it so vividly. I looked out my office window, eyes open, and from the utter gut level of emotions poured out my pain to the Lord stating, "Lord, I can't; but You can." I had to put my pride aside. I had to lay aside the fact I had a seminary education, was ordained and a minister in a church. I had to empty myself before the Lord. Across the room walked a shadow, it came to me and put His hand on my shoulder. At that very moment, I felt a release like I'd never felt before. I felt an emotional high, exhilaration unlike anything I had ever experienced. I walked burden free at least three days, three remarkable days before the carnal world reminded me once again how wounding it was and ready to spiritually murder me. Some would say I had been baptized by the Holy Spirit. I reject that. I think that for the first time I realized the full reality of His indwelling which had been there all along, I just wasn't ready or able to see it, or totally understand it. As a Baptist I fully believe that the moment you allow the Lord Jesus in your life, you have the indwelling of the Holy Spirit in your life; yes, even as an eight-year-old who may not fully grasp it and may not grasp it for several years to come.

As a Baptist, I believe that the Bible says that Jesus died for <u>all</u>. God so loved the world, not just the Christian, that He died for everyone and it is up to the person to accept or reject Jesus. If he rejects Jesus, then the atonement is not applied to the person and he will go to Hell. But, Jesus' sacrifice was not only sufficient for <u>all</u>, but intended for <u>all</u>, as supported by the following Scriptures:

- John 1:29, "The next day he saw Jesus coming to him, and said, 'Behold, the Lamb of God who takes away the sin of the world!'"
- John 3:16, "For God so loved the world that He gave His only begotten Son, that whoever believes in Him should not perish, but have eternal life."
- John 4:42, "and they were saying to the woman, 'It is no longer because of what you said that we believe, for we have heard for ourselves and know that this One is indeed the Savior of the world.'"
- 1 Tim. 4:10, "For it is for this we labor and strive, because we have fixed our hope on the living God, who is the Savior of all men, especially of believers."
- 1 John 2:2, "and He Himself is the propitiation for our sins; and not for ours only, but also for those of the whole world."
- 1 John 4:14, "And we have beheld and bear witness that the Father has sent the Son to be the Savior of the world."
- Romans 10:13, "For whoever calls on the name of Lord shall be saved [2-[https://carm.org/about-doctrine/did-jesus-die-for-everyone-my-calvinist-friends-say-no/]."

Second, as a Baptist I read in Ephesians 2: 8-9, "8 -For by grace are ye saved through faith; and that not of yourselves: it is the gift of God: 9- Not of works, lest any man should boast?" Just as Abraham was declared righteous because of his faith, not works, so we are so declared righteous by our faith.

Third, and most importantly, how do I as a Baptist, handle Ephesians 1:4, where Paul speaks of the "Chosen," in stating, "For he chose us in him before the creation of the world to be holy and blameless in his sight." This is at the center of the great debate. Well, let's look at the entirety of the text, verses 5-8, "In love [5] he predestined us for adoption to sonship through Jesus Christ, in accordance with his pleasure and will— [6] to the praise of his glorious grace, which he has freely given us in the One he loves. [7] In him we have redemption through his blood, the forgiveness of sins, in accordance with the riches of God's grace [8] that he lavished on us. With all wisdom and understanding..." I believe this is speaking of God's eternal plan for Christians, that is, for Christians to be made holy and blameless and to be conformed into the image of Christ. Christ alone is the Elect of the Father, and we are elect only by virtue of our connection to THE, one and only, Elect One, as an extension of Himself, being sown together with Him as the Bride of Christ, as part of the Body of Christ. Following the logic of that thought, I ,therefore, believe as a Baptist that Ephesians 1:5 states I am predestined to be adopted because I am holy, blameless and conformed to the image of God in the sight of God due to the Cross of Calvary. That connection came when I accepted Jesus as my Lord and Savior [3- https://bibleask.org/does-god-predestine-some-people-to-heaven-and-the-rest-to-hell/].

Fourth, what is Salvation and how did I make that connection to make Christ my Savior. Well, first let's define Salvation. According to the Baptist Faith and Message, "Salvation involves the redemption of the whole man, and is offered <u>freely</u> to <u>all who accept Jesus Christ as Lord and Saviour</u>, who by His own blood obtained eternal redemption for the believer. In its broadest sense salvation includes regeneration, justification, sanctification, and glorification. <u>There is no salvation apart from personal faith</u> in Jesus Christ as Lord [4-Baptist Faith and Message 2000]."

I believe in the Sovereignty of God. In His omnipotent love for me He died for me and set in motion from the beginning of time a process for my adoption into the Kingdom of God. I believe that He loved me so much that though He knew my imperfections and Sin, He was ready to forgive me when at the point of His wooing I recognized my need and desire to repent of my Sin, and sins, and ask the Lord to come into my heart to save me, justify me, sanctify me and set in motion my glorification. Although at eight years old I didn't fully understand all the undertaking of this nor exactly what all my sins were. But by His wooing He gave me understanding that I needed forgiveness for my separation from God. That in the future what Jesus did on the Cross was sufficient to forgive me for my past, present and future. I did understand that I needed to let Him into my heart, as simple as that was, that's when Jesus forgave my Sin, my separation from God. I simply wanted Jesus in my heart and He did the rest. All this happened when I became "In Christ" through the grace of His love by my step into faith via my acceptance and belief in Him as Lord and Savior. I did not save myself, only Christ could do that, but I had to recognize the time and point when I needed to do that, even at eight years old. I had to reach a point of my own accountability. That's what I believe as BAPTIST, but most importantly what I believe as A PERSON SAVED BY GRACE!

I closed by sharing the story of Allen who was my song leader at Powelton Baptist Church in Powelton, Georgia, my last pastorate. The church was one of the oldest churches in Georgia. It had its early beginnings back in the late 1700's, with Silas Mercer, its first pastor, the father of Jesse Mercer for whom Mercer University is named. In 1995, a handful of about 75 members were simply attempting to keep the church alive, although the town of Powelton had long since existed. We met every other Sunday. Allen was a Methodist but was faithful to this Baptist Church the Sundays we met. As pastor, I assumed Allen was secure in the Lord. However, one Tuesday evening my wife, Shirley met Sandra, Allen's wife in the grocery store. She shared that Allen was home in deep depression and concern. He had received the diagnosis he had heart disease and his heart was failing him, but most importantly he feared that he wasn't saved. Shirley rushed home and shared "you need to see Allen and see him soon." I got in my car and went straight to his home. There I found a broken man. I read him Romans 8:38-39: "For I am persuaded, that neither death, nor life, nor angels, nor principalities, nor powers, nor things present, nor things to come, nor height, nor depth, nor any other creature, shall be able to separate us from the love of God, which is in Christ Jesus our Lord." That night I found that none of his family had been baptized in believer's baptism and it thrills me to say that as my last act as their pastor I baptized that entire family. A few years later Allen went home to be with the Lord but I feel confident he went home secure. The point is God gave us each the opportunity to be secure. The question is, are you?

As I led in prayer, I could hear some tears and as we sang "Jesus Is Calling," some came to the front of the chapel and kneeled in prayer. After the prayer Pastor Roy, thanked me for the devotional and assured any who wanted to speak to him, or me, could do so. I left feeling the Holy Spirit had led me in the service and felt His presence there.

We all then headed back to our rooms to finish our packing and load the bus by noon. It gave us some extra time to walk the compound and enjoy the retreat area one last time before lunch. Pastor Roy caught up with me.

"Cal, I just want say, thank you. I've been down that road spiritually with you. We both know the pastorate can be challenging and the devil uses it to tempt us and defeat us if he can. My mom, (I knew he was talking of Riva) was there for me when I had those spiritual questions. She had a way of keeping me grounded. You can't imagine how much it means to meet someone from her teenage years who was a part of her early grounding. I know it was your mom whom God used to lead her to the Lord, but I can't help but believe those early months when the two of you were a part of the youth of this church, that foundation became a giant cornerstone of what each of you ultimately became in your faith. I am so glad God, in his infinite insight, led you to us these two days, it had to be a miracle!"

"Roy, you thrill my heart to hear that. All I can say is this stop over was indeed one awesome miracle."

With that we all headed to a wonderful lunch and with bellies full, loaded the bus for our three-hour ride back to Renton. Our ride back was just beautiful as we so enjoyed the scenery of the Cascades. Throughout the bus the buzz of conversation ranged from the blessing of the meetings, to the good food, to the beauty of the area, to reminiscing our younger years. I held Shirley's hand as this was such a memorable trip for us. I wasn't sure I wanted to get back on the ship. I was ready to head on back home. This was such a highlight of the trip, I'm not sure anything could supersede it. It was nearing 4:15 pm and we were approaching the outskirts of Renton. I must admit, I was rather tired from the long bus ride. I was ready to get on board and consider a nap. But by the time we got back to the ship it would be dinner time. As we pulled into the church parking lot, there was the limousine that brought us to the church, ready to take us to the ship.

Our driver loaded our luggage from the bus to the limousine. We went over to Pastor Roy.

"Pastor, I just want you to know that when God calls me home, I'm so glad that I had this experience as one of the potentially last times to visit this area and to have been a part of Calvary Baptist one last time. It was a significant part of my youth and now it is a significant part of my senior years. Thank you for your testimony, for sharing your mom with me once again and your church. I love you, brother. You and Calvary Baptist will be in our hearts from here on out."

"Dr. Meyer, it was an honor and a joy. God bless you."

With that, Shirley and I got in the Limousine and headed back to the ship. At this time of the afternoon, we hit the go-home traffic, but we were in no hurry. Crossing the floating bridge across Lake Washington, my mind went up the hill to Shorewood Apartment where we lived those years early when I was a lad of 14 years old. I recall my mom's lasagna dinner she prepared for the officers in Dad's outfit. I recall going down to the shoreline and playing with my homemade boat, noting the hydroplane races were annually held on Lake Washington. I recall the Sunday morning getting up early to deliver the Seattle Times in the apartments. Then as we came into the Seattle skyline I remember the ferry trips to Bainbridge Island. My mind was abuzz with memories. The time to the ship wasn't long at all.

Finally, the silhouette of the MH MKaddish appeared. Arriving at the port, the driver assured us our luggage would be delivered to our room. It was nearing 6:00 pm and I was a bit hungry. We had eaten lunch at noon. So we headed up to the buffet, "The Heaven's Abundance." We had so much good food at the retreat, I wasn't sure what I wanted.

Shirley spoke up. "You know I think I'd like to have just a hamburger and fries and perhaps some chocolate cake for dinner."

Outside the restaurant was a hamburger bar. We decided to go out on the deck, although a bit chilly and enjoy a simple hamburger, fries and soda, while viewing Mt. Rainier in the distance. However, I did recall that the very first meal I had as a young boy in Seattle was the night we arrived back in 1956. We pulled into a simple diner and for the first time saw "Fish and Chips." I never heard of that before! I thought I so wish I had ordered that, but I wasn't sure they had that in the restaurant. None-the-less, I was full now and really couldn't eat anymore.

While eating, the public address system announced the following:

"Ladies and Gentlemen. The MH MKaddish will be leaving port at 11:00 pm. For anyone wishing to make trips to downtown Seattle, the Space Needle or the Fish Market may board busses at the front of the Port Building at 7:30 pm. They will return by 10:30 pm. There will be four available busses to make the trip. If you choose to do so, please remember to stay with your group and return with your bus."

I was tired, but this may be the last time to see Seattle.

"Shirley, let's try it."

Shirley responded, "Okay."

We finished our meal. Went to our room and got our warm coats and were at the dock by 7:30 pm. We were one of the first, so we got on Bus #1.

To our surprise, there were 200 or so people that wanted to do the same. I guess the rest were still out on their tours. All the buses were filled.
"Ladies and Gentlemen. The city of Seattle has been kind enough to keep the Monorail open late tonight for you to experience the Space Needle. We will go to the center of town where I will let you off and there you may board the Monorail. Tickets for the Monorail may be purchased at the Monorail station and tickets for the Space Needle are at the base of it. You will have one hour to get to the Space Needle, enjoy it and must be back on this bus by 9:00 pm. Remember you are Bus #1. I am passing out to you Name Tags for you to write your name. The tag already has the name of the ship."

We were kind of excited. I really did want to see Seattle again. Though tired, we headed out into the city lights and toward downtown.

Arriving at the downtown Monorail Terminal, the four busses unloaded and we filled the monorail. Its terminus is the Space Needle surrounded by the old 1963 Seattle World's Fair complex which has been turned into other venues. I recall the days they were building the Monorail, as Mom and Dad had just been re-stationed at Fort Lewis in 1961 and on our few trips to Seattle we witnessed the building of the Monorail and the Space Needle. I wonder how many on this ship can share that!

Though Shirley and I had been to the Space Needle on previous trips to Seattle, it was always a delight. I guess the memories of seeing its being built, the view of Puget Sound, etc., it is something of a wonder. Anyway, my mind was taking over and I wanted to see the night over Seattle. We walked the short block from the Monorail to the base of the Space Needle, waited in line and paid our fee to ride the elevator to the top. As we did, we felt a little shake.

"What was that?" Shirley asked.

"I don't know?" I was a bit concerned but after all we had been on a bus all afternoon and we were tired. But then it happened again. None-the-less, we traveled to the top and saw the beauty of the city lights. I could see what was old Fort Larsen in the distance, as it sits on a hill overlooking Seattle. You can see the lights from it. It is now a part of the city. I recall the officers' picnics we had there. I recall with great fondness the joy my dad had in being stationed there. I believe it was truly the highlight of his career even though it was his second assignment in the Army. Then it happened again. We turned and looked and I thought I saw a yellow glow coming from the Mount Rainier area. Surely, Mount Rainier wasn't about to blow, as did Mount St. Helens.

"Ladies and Gentlemen, there has been a small earthquake near Mount Rainier. We must ask you to vacate the Space Needle and return to your ship." This was a public address we just heard. It wasn't our imagination.

In an orderly fashion, Shirley and I, along with the other passengers, headed to the elevators, and eagerly arrived at the base. There the busses were waiting for us. We immediately went to the ship. It was worrisome in that I had always heard that, if Mount Rainier blew, it would devastate Seattle. I had experienced a small earthquake once when I visited Mom and Dad during one of the Christmas visits from college. But it was just a small shake, nothing came of it. Perhaps what we felt was just a small earthquake and that yellow glow was just my imagination. I don't know. But one thing for sure, I didn't want to be on the top of the Space Needle if Mount Rainier were to become a Mount St. Helen!

We arrived back at the ship and just as we boarded, although it was only 10:00 pm, they
were beginning to haul anchor.

"Ladies and gentlemen, this is your captain speaking. Due to the fact there has been a small earthquake in the area, we are simply taking precautions and debarking early. We have everyone on board. Please be assured there is no need for alarm."

That wasn't particularly settling but I was tired and we went on to bed. When we wake up, we should be out to sea.

Chapter 11: Alaska

We awoke the next morning and, indeed, were out to sea heading toward Juneau. We had been there before. It was always beautiful. But after 12 days, I'll admit, I was getting a bit weary. Oh, that's not to say the trip hadn't been enjoyable or full of surprises. I was just getting tired. Then the public address system came on,

"Ladies and Gentlemen, this is a reminder our Chapel Services will be held in **Heaven's Gate**, at 10:00 am. Our speaker this morning is one many will recognize. Please come to be blest."

Indeed, I was eager for the morning service. I had already been blest by our time in Seattle, rather Mount Baker. Though tired, we meandered our way to the breakfast buffet on top deck. I wondered why nothing was further said about the small earthquake near Mt. Rainer last night, but there was no mention of it by anyone. I suppose it was only a quiver of a shock, like the one I felt back in the '60's when home from college. The yellow light I thought I saw had to be simply a coincidence of some city light I was seeing. We never heard anything further about it.

"May I sit with you?" came a soft voice. We looked up and Shirley jumped up out of her seat. It was her sister!

"Dot, what are you doing here?"

"Oh, they brought me on board in Seattle. I flew in last night."

We were both a bit stunned in that the Christian atmosphere of this ship didn't really seem to fit a Jehovah Witness background. We truly didn't know where to start. The last we heard from Dot was anything but welcoming. She and Shirley broke relationship years ago after Dot become a Jehovah Witness. Through the years we tried to establish a relationship but nothing really worked. She had an influence on our children that burdened us beyond words. She more or less became the Pied Piper of our family. For whatever reason our children and their children were drawn to her. It crushed us! But our prayer through the years has been to bring Dot, our children and grandchildren back home spiritually.

Dot's husband, Jim, whom we all loved, passed away just over a year ago. We were hopeful Dot would reach out to us, but it didn't seem like it was going to happen. Now this.

'Shirley, I'm here to bring you home!"

"What?" Shirley said in surprise.

"You see, I'm here because the Lord sent me. I've never been on an Alaskan cruise and I know you have, so I want to enjoy this one with you, then I want to go home and take you with me."

That all seems a bit ominous to us. I felt a bit uneasy and I could tell Shirley did as well.

Dot went on. "Things have changed and as we enjoy the next few days together, I'll share that with you. Simply, I want you to know I've found the Lord again."

A bright glow came over Shirley's face as though she had seen and felt the presence of something holy.

Shirley and Dot continued to talk, Shirley asking about the family, what her intent was with the house and what she was doing in her life spiritually. I think we were both so overwhelmed by the impossibility of seeing Dot there and what she was sharing, it was hard to take it in. We did intend to eat some breakfast, but I don't remember what, who cared?

It was time for services. Shirley asked Dot, "You are coming with us, aren't you?"

"Certainly," she replied.

We arrived at **Heaven's Gate** and entered as a quartet came to the stage. I loved the Specks from when we traveled on the Alaskan cruise with Charles Stanley, and I also loved my good friends from Liberty days, the Pantanas. One of my favorite songs by the Specks was "The Race." Would you believe that was being sung as we entered the auditorium. We then started to sing "Heaven Came Down and Glory Filled my Soul..." The morning was getting better and better. I noticed Dot was joining in. Then, finally, the captain got up and said,

"Ladies and Gentlemen, it is my honor to introduce to you a pastor whom many of you have known well, a pastor who has preached to millions. He needs no introduction. Would you welcome the Rev. Dr. Billy Graham!"

This couldn't be! Billy Graham is old and doesn't travel anymore. This can't be! He's a saint now. The last I saw him in real life was back in 1987 when he held a crusade at Williams Brice Stadium in Columbia, South Carolina. Shirley and I were counselors for that crusade. When Dr. Graham arrived on stage, it wasn't the 99-year-old man we were expecting, but rather the younger 60- year-old version we last saw in South Carolina. Awed beyond words, we felt we either missed something in the news, or perhaps had dreamed it, but then Dr. Graham proceeded to talk.

"This morning I want talk to you on 'Hope.' A saint always looks for hope. Let's turn our Bibles to 1 Peter 1:3-6. Read along with me from Bible Gateway's Commentary."

Dr. Graham proceeded to share the following message on hope, with the outline provided us as we entered the auditorium.

OUTLINE FOR THE MORNING MESSAGE

"³ Blessed be the God and Father of our Lord Jesus Christ, which according to his abundant mercy hath begotten us again unto a lively hope by the resurrection of Jesus Christ from the dead,

⁴ To an inheritance incorruptible, and undefiled, and that fadeth not away, reserved in heaven for you,

⁵ Who are kept by the power of God through faith unto salvation ready to be revealed in the last time.

⁶ Wherein ye greatly rejoice, though now for a season, if need be, ye are in heaviness through manifold temptations:

King James Version **(KJV)**

- What is that hope? It is more than not spilling coffee in front of your provost and on an expensive conference table!
    - First, it is hope built on the fact Jesus resurrected from the dead. Let me read from Charles Spurgeon:

- **COMMENTARY – SPURGEON** - Our first birth brought us into sin and sorrow, but our second birth brings us into purity and joy. We were born to die; now are we born never to die, "begotten again" unto a life that shall remain in us for evermore, a life which shall even penetrate these mortal bodies, and make them immortal, "by the resurrection of Jesus Christ from the dead. How full of grace every sentence is! He blesses God because God has so freely blest us; and he abounds in thanksgiving because he sees that abundant mercy, by which believers have been begotten again — born again — made, therefore, children after a new sort, and so made heirs of an inheritance very different from that upon which we enter by nature "an inheritance incorruptible, and undefiled, and that fadeth not away."

Folks that's Hope! - A hope that is built on being "Begotten again"
- Second, it is hope that never fades away.
    - It's a hope built and a salvation that will never be taken from us.
    - It's a hope that is built on the promise of God as revealed in His Word.
    - 1 Peter 1:23-25: Having been born again, not of corruptible seed but incorruptible, through the Word of God which lives and abides forever, because "all flesh is as grass, the grass withers and its flowers falls away, but the Word of the Lord endures forever."
- Third, it is hope that is realized by the power of God through faith.

- - Why? Because He gives us the fruit of the Spirit, Joy, when we turn to Him in faith.
    - Why? Because He gives us full free grace.
    - Why? Because He gives us full abundant mercy.
  - Fourth, it is hope that rejoices when we are surrounded by trials.
    - Paul put it in words, "as sorrowful, yet always rejoicing; as poor, yet making many rich; as having nothing, and yet possessing all things." (2 Cor. 6:10).
    - We can rejoice in trials because we know it is but a short time.
    - We can rejoice in trials because God can use such efforts to purify and teach, *i.e.,* Job.
    - We can rejoice in trial because we know it will bring honor and glory to God in ways we could never imagine.
    - It could be that trial that saves that special someone from eternal hell [1-Herschel Hobbs Commentary-Lifeway.adults]."

He then shared, "I know there are those in this auditorium who have given up hope in their lives. They've pursued other avenues than Jesus Christ to find it. They lost hope in their children. They've lost hope in their jobs. They've lost hope in their mates. They even lost hope in their church. But I stand here this morning to tell you Jesus Christ is the hope you live for! A saint knows in his heart who is the core of his hope. Let me say this morning, I believe the time for His Second Coming is near. We need to look for it in the spirit of Hope! We need to look for it as we look up to Heaven and praise the Father who made it a hope that:

- Is built on the living, not the dead.
- Is built on the permanent, not the temporary.
- Is built on the power of God, not our simple wishes for it.

- Is built on the endurance of trials, not the pain of grief.

We can all sing joyously "My Hope Is Built on Nothing Less than Jesus' Blood and Righteousness."

I'm so glad they provided us an outline. It is something I can take with me. I noted that Dorothy was writing on hers as Dr. Graham was speaking. It was a message I would have loved to speak.

After the service, we looked for Dorothy again to consider our day. This was a day at sea, and I know Shirley and Dorothy wanted to be together. But to our surprise, we turned, and she was no longer there. What about the days she was going to spend with Shirley? What about taking Shirley home with her? I must admit I was confused. Dr. Graham's age, seeing Dorothy, now not present? I'm either losing my mind, or we're experiencing miracles of imagination beyond belief. However, it's not just our imagination, but the hundreds aboard this ship.

We had been on cruises to Alaska at least three other times and I'll admit Alaska is always beautiful, but I'm not sure we're needing a simple typical Alaskan cruise tour this time around. We've stopped previously in Juneau and have seen the salmon hatchery, gone out to see the whales and the Mendenhall Glacier. We've been to Skagway and rode the White Pass and Yukon Railway Train up the Mountain. We've been to Ketchikan and saw the Totem Pole Village, as well as the Lumberjack Show. While awesome when we first experienced all of them, routine never lives up to the first hype over them. Besides that, based on the unusual experiences we're having, I'm not sure we want to go through the motions of doing those things again. Shirley looked at me, as I did her, and we almost simultaneously said, "I think, I'm ready to go home." About that time, Carlos showed up and said:

"Dr. Meyer and Shirley, we understand you're ready to go home."

"Well, yes, how did you know?"

"We knew it from your heart."

"Let me share that we have some other surprises that may excite you. We're going to change your Itinerary a bit. All are complements of Dove Cruise Lines. Your trip isn't quite over but we have some new adventures for you."

Looking rather aghast, and not sure we were ready for more, I said:

"Sure, I guess so. What next?"

Upon which Carlos responded. "Well, first, we're going to have you leave the ship in Juneau and we will take you and your belonging to the airport. We're going to fly you to Anchorage and from there you will take the train to the Denali where you will spend a couple of nights. Upon leaving there we intend on flying you back to Seattle and then fly you back to where you two began your marriage, Florida."

Dorothy was right, she was taking us back home!

Well, as our itinerary showed this was November 10, our 13th day on the cruise. This meant we'd dock in Juneau tomorrow and fly to Anchorage for our trip to Denali. We were rather excited. Though saddened to some degree to leave the ship, particularly after all the miracles we had experienced, we were a bit sea-weary. And, as expressed, we had already been to Juneau and the inner passage three other times. Shirley and I eagerly packed our bags for leaving the ship and for the continuation of our journey by plane and rail. We spent the rest of the day just sitting on the inner deck, viewing the ocean and beautiful scenery as we traveled. The night program would be a special music presentation by a mystery guest. We were eager to find out who. In the meantime, we decided to spend this final night on board at one of the other restaurants on the 6th deck, either **Jacob's Well** or **the 5000**. Did I want fish or a steak? Ah, I remembered I always loved lobster tail and I heard **the 5000** served it.

We made our way to **the 5000** and indeed they had lobster tail with shrimp on the menu. I ordered that and Shirley had salmon. Noting this would be our last night on board, we wanted it to be a special meal. About 7:30 pm we made our way to the auditorium, **Heaven's Gate,** eagerly awaiting our special guests. To our delight it was Sandi Patty. I remember her from our days when I was principal in Columbia, South Carolina. She was sponsored by Columbia Bible College to sing one night. Oh! What a voice! Oh! The duet of her and Larnelle Harris, it took you right to Heaven's Gate, particularly "I've Just Seen Jesus." What a night of bliss and blessing! To our delight, after the program, Carlos came up and said, "Would you and Mrs. Meyer like to meet Ms. Patty?"

I was rather dumbfounded. Sandi Patty has been our singing heroine for years. She was the one we weaned our children on during their early high school years. She was the one who inspired me many times as I prepared my messages to preach in my bivocational churches. We reached back to the late '70's and early '80's. Oh, my, can this be happening?

A few of the ushers came down to where we were sitting and took us to a side room off the stage where we and about 10 others had a special audience with Ms. Patty. Sandi encouraged us to sit. We were in a small semi-circle where we could actually have conversation with her. I couldn't help but share how she had been such a blessing to us and our family through the years. Sandi, as she had done in her early performances, often shared her personal side and it wasn't long before we all felt we were with a friend, not just an admired entertainer. Then it happened.

"Dr. Meyer, I just want you to know your children did return home spiritually." Sandi Patty had just revealed a personal prayer of mine through the years. How did she know? She smiled and as I returned the smile, she pointed her finger toward Heaven. I don't know Sandi Patty personally. This is the first time I've had any opportunity to meet her. How could or did she have such insight into our greater spiritual yearning? Another miracle? I do know that coming from her, I felt a hair-raising chill overcome me, as though I had just experienced a really extraordinary event that grabbed my senses.

We didn't get to have any other personal discussion with Sandi as the evening came to a close and our time with her ended as she excused herself graciously. We all left feeling we had been in the presence of a powerful saint of the Lord.

With the evening of song, worship and miracles coming to an end, Shirley and I returned to our cabin, finished our last-minute packing and prepared ourselves to leave the ship early in the morning.

Morning came quickly enough. We left our luggage in the room, assured it would be picked up and taken to the airport. We went to the restaurant on the upper deck for our final breakfast and in some ways began to feel a sense of regret for leaving the ship. As we enjoyed my last plate of wonderful French toast and my second cup of coffee, Carlos came by and shared that all was ready for us to debark the ship. With our previous stop, on other cruises, I don't recall exactly where the airport was located. I must assume it was on the way outside of town on the way to the Mendenhall Glacier. I do remember that was the only four-lane highway we ever traveled on any of our stops in Alaska and it would clearly be the most probable location for the airport. Sure enough after leaving the ship and town, our limousine drove us in that direction and soon we turned to the right heading toward the airport. As we left the car, the driver, a staff member from the ship, gave us our tickets.

He pointed us to the entrance of the Airport Terminal and said, "Dr. and Mrs. Meyer, your flight is Alaskan Air Flight 3, Juneau to Anchorage, leaving at 10:30 am." I looked at my watch, noting it was right at 9:30, giving us a few minutes to get through security and aboard the plane.

"What about our luggage?" I asked.

"That has been taken care of. You will see it tonight in your room at the Denali Hotel."

My, oh, my! They did indeed take care of us. Shirley and I went to the security area but we were whisked through a special line, once they saw our passports. Apparently the cruise company had even taken care of that for us as well.

We arrived at our gate with 30 minutes to spare but it wasn't long before they began boarding the plane. It was a small commuter jet, carrying 30 to 40 passengers. We looked around the seating area and noticed the plane apparently was going to be full. I looked over in the far corner of the area and I could have sworn I saw Dorothy, Shirley's sister.

"Shirley!" Nudging her. I pointed to the area but Dorothy was gone.

"What?" Shirley inquired.

"I thought I saw Dorothy or someone who looked like her."

"Oh, you're just imagining things."

My mind is clearly playing tricks on me, but why not? I have seen more than imaginable on this trip already.

Once onboard, we went through the typical safety procedure. And, as I do every time we fly, I pray for God's traveling mercies. I'm okay, once we're in the air, but for some reason I get rather nervous at take-off. I used to love to fly, but I rather dread it now. I don't know if it all the TV shows about airplane disasters we've recently watched or the hassles of going through security, or the hassle of now carrying our CPAP machines, or the uncomfortable seats, I just really don't like to fly anymore. However, we were now in the air and looking down over Juneau and the glacier was beautiful as we headed toward Anchorage. I knew it would be about a two-hour flight, just enough time to relax and enjoy the view, have some orange juice and a cookie.

It was a beautiful flight. I'd never seen Alaska from the air. Upon landing, a gentleman, with a sign "Dr. and Mrs. Meyer" was awaiting us as we left the security zone.

"I'm Dr. Meyer."

"Hi, Dr. and Mrs. Meyer, I'm from the Dove Cruise Lines. Carlos contacted my office. My name is Richard and I'm here to escort you to the bus that will take you to the train."

"Train?"

I had forgotten about the scenic train and I wasn't sure that it ran out of Anchorage."

"Yes, you'll have about a two-hour ride on the bus. They will stop for lunch on the way. Then you'll board the Alaskan Scenic Train to Denali."

I must admit I was excited. I then looked at Shirley with my big grin but then in the near distance something caught my eye. It was Dorothy again. I'm sure of it. Again, I tried to get Shirley's attention but before I could, Dorothy had disappeared. By now it was going on 1:00 pm and after about a 30-minute drive across town, we boarded a very nice scenic cruiser bus for the trip to the train.

I had a lifelong dream of riding this train. As shared, Shirley and I had been on the Alaskan cruise three other times, this trip made the fourth, and all were in the Inner Passage. This was the first time we had the opportunity to do an inland tour. The bus finally arrived at the train station and boarding was to commence within 30 minutes. In actuality, the train was scheduled to depart at 3:00 pm, Alaskan time, arriving at Denali around 6:30 pm. Talk about timing! It had all scenic windows. Knowing we had a three-to-four-hour trip, we settled into our seats. Our tickets had been given to us by our cruise driver before boarding the bus. The conductor soon came by to collect them and shared that the dining car was to the front. I wasn't sure if dinner was awaiting us at the Inn, but I was hungry. After the train departed, the announcement came on that the dining car was open. I wasn't sure if they meant sandwich car or dining car. But we headed in that direction. When we entered, it was delightful as all the tables were draped with nice table cloths and fine dining ware.

We sat, looked at the menu and realized we could order anything from steak to hamburger. The waiter came by and handed us an order card. Shirley and I looked at each other and knew each of us was hungry, we saw they had what Alaska was known for, salmon. Shirley had it last night, thus she chose a small steak. We made our order. Both of use ordered broccoli, mashed potatoes, and iced tea. All the while we could look out the windows and see the beautiful countryside of Alaska pass by. As we sat there awaiting our meal to arrive, someone tapped my shoulder. I looked up and I couldn't have been more overwhelmed. Shirley almost screamed. It was Dorothy.

"Dorothy?" I spoke in some excited tone, somewhat overwhelmed but clearly confused. Shirley got up from her seat and ran to hug her. Were we seeing things? Was this for real? What about on the ship?

"I thought I saw you at the airport and also around the bus."

Dorothy, replied, "You did, but I wasn't prepared to see you then. I waited until now."
We sat down and Dorothy pulled out a seat.

"We've ordered. Would you like to order?"

"No." She answered but then continued, "Jim's here."

This was way too much. Jim passed away just a few months ago. It was one of our greatest heartbreaks. Dorothy and her family forbade us to go to the funeral given her faith was such they would not tolerate our beliefs even present there. It didn't matter we were family; we weren't welcomed. It hurt and hurt badly. Jim was Shirley's brother-in-law for 62 years and she grew to love him. As Dorothy and Jim were married young, Shirley grew to accept Jim as her brother and loved him dearly. It wasn't until Dorothy accepted a religion that was so foreign to our beliefs that she turned against us. That too hurt and hurt through the years. Jim tried to rise above it but he loved his wife and family and ultimately succumbed. We just never thought we'd be banned from his funeral. Thus, seeing Dorothy here and now on this trip of miracles just seems so out of place, or is it?

Soon our meal arrived, but we weren't all that hungry. Dorothy got up.

"Where are you going? I inquired.

"I need to meet Jim. We'll see you later."

Suddenly she was gone and out-of-sight. Did we see another aberration?

We settled down to our dinner but weren't all that hungry after all. Things are happening way too fast. Our lives have been a history of that. Our kids have grown way too fast. We've grown old way too fast. Life around us has changed way too fast. We finished our dinner and headed back to our seats.

Finally, arriving at the station, a small bus was awaiting us to escort us to the hotel. We were way too tired to do anything, but go to bed.

The next morning, we arose to a beautiful sunrise over the Denali Mountains. Since President Obama changed the official name from Mt. McKinley, I'm still confused. I still like calling mountains by the names given them in my historical upbringing. It seems everything we grew up learning has been changed. Depending on one's politics, street names, school names, buildings, etc., are changed. And, heaven forbid, if someone has a disdain for something historical, that has now been considered reprehensible. I fear it won't be long before the Bible will be considered censored material. Oh, well, I didn't intend to turn this into a sermon. I just want to enjoy the mountain.

Soon we heard a knock on the door and an envelope was slid under it. Opening the door, we found no one there but we opened the envelope. It was our itinerary for the day and our tickets for our coach and tours. Noting this is fall and into November, all the other cruises have long since stopped. Thus, we're already finding snow, cold and ice. I'm surprised we made it this far. But as we've found miracles never cease to happen. Our itinerary had us scheduled for a 10:00 am coach ride up to a major ranger station and overview. We were already seeing a lot of snow as we did on the train. But I figured these folks knew what they were doing. The hotel wasn't packed but it was full enough. We, thank goodness, had bundled some warm clothes.

After a hearty breakfast we went to our room, got our tickets and coats and headed to the foyer to meet our coach. There were about 40 or us ready to board. Our driver, with a female associate, was there to welcome us before we boarded.

"Ladies and Gentlemen, Welcome to Skybound Tours. As you can tell we have a beautiful morning for our tour. There has been a snow overnight and there are some avalanche concerns up the mountain, but well beyond our destination. You're going to see some views our typical tourists never see, given this is not the typical tourist season. I have on board some fruit juices and a variety of pastries. My associate will be traveling through the bus from time to time to assist. We have lunch awaiting you at the ranger station. Our tour will be about five to six hours round trip."

His associate then spoke, "Hello, my name is Faith and if I can be any service on the trip, let me know. I will serve as your tour guide and give you information about the mountain, its history, geology etc., as we travel and as David, our driver indicated, I'll be serving juice, cookies and pastries as we travel."

We left the hotel rather excited. It was cold and brisk, but the sun was out and the roads were clear. We made our way toward Mount McKinley. The snow was thick on the hills. It seemed so soft and glistened beautifully. Trees were covered and looked like silhouettes of various art forms of white covered shapes. It felt refreshing and a warmth of wonder covered our spirits. I was so glad we decided to leave the ship and experience this.

Faith soon came around with a canteen of hot chocolate, first providing us cups. It was so natural. She poured carefully and although each of us got about half a cup, it was sufficient to warm our souls and melt our hearts even more into the moment. She then sat in the front seat and proceeded to inform us of the geographic dynamics of Mt.

McKinley and the history of its naming. Of course, most of this can now be found on Wikipedia. Given today was Sunday, November 13, I felt it was much like a worship experience. Faith indicated that once we arrived at the ranger station, we would have a brief Sunday worship experience, indicating David, our driver, was a minister and would be sharing with us some Scripture, a brief devotional and leading us in some singing and prayer, all of this after lunch. I thought it most fitting. The entire trip was simply awesome.

After about two and half hours, or so, with it reaching nearly 12:45 pm, I was getting hungry and ready to get off the bus to stretch my legs. Shirley, always having trouble with her legs swelling when on long rides, was clearly eager to get up and walk around. We soon saw the Ranger Station and the mounds of snow from the shoveled parking lot. David drove us to the door. We all deboarded the bus and were escorted into to a large room with a beautiful full-frontal window looking up toward the peak of Mt. McKinley. It turns out our lunches were all on the bus with us. Faith, David and the rangers unloaded the boxes of sack lunches the hotel sent. We were delighted to see boxes of packed turkey, roast beef, or chicken sandwiches with a selection of relishes and condiments to put on them. There was also a selection of chips, small containers of macaroni, fruit cups and bean salad. For beverages, they had anything from soda to lemonade to tea. In other words, a good ole winter afternoon picnic. The ranger station also had a selection of hot chocolate, brownies and cookies, which I assume Faith also had on the bus. Once everyone was in the room, the food unpacked onto the tables, Faith gave us some simple directions about lining up and getting our food. David then led us in a blessing. There were several round tables to sit at and enjoy our meal and fellowship with our passengers.

It wasn't a steak dinner by any means but if filled the tummy and the sandwiches were good. It met our need. I knew that night we'd have full benefit of the motel restaurant and be able to order a meal fit for a king. Having enjoyed the meal with time fleeting, the view breathtaking, Faith stood near the front of the room and asked for our attention. She introduced David. David was a local pastor who drove for the hotel. He was bivocational and was a lifelong Alaskan. Upon finishing his tour with the Air Force, he felt the call to return to his native Alaska to be a church builder. He worked in a local village, with his wife and family. He had three kids, ranging in age from 6 to 13. David and I had something in common, we both attended Southwestern Baptist Theological Seminary for our theological training. I was thrilled to meet him and hear him preach.

On this particular morning, he spoke on how life throws at us the unexpected. He shared the story of when in seminary he had the opportunity to consider pastoring a full-time church in Tennessee. His wife, being a native Tennessean, was eager to return home. However, in his last term at seminary, they had a mission trip scheduled for Alaska. Given he was raised in Alaska, his home being in Fairbanks, he was eager to join that mission team. He thought it was just a late spring mission trip. But when he arrived and saw the need and the Area Director of Mission laid it upon David's heart to return and build a church, David couldn't escape the tug. But how was he going to tell his wife? How would he deal with her disappointment? At first David attempted to ignore it. Then he tried to rationale a calling to the church in Tennessee. But then he remembered Jonah and how God just wouldn't give him rest. At first, he didn't tell his wife when he got back home. He didn't want to deal with it. For a few days he thought it would just go away or at the very least he'd lose interest. Then one day the church in Tennessee called and wanted to set a date for an interview with the pulpit committee. His dean had highly recommended him. He, after all, had sent them his resume'. He had to deal with it. He either had to go ahead with the interview and chance misleading the pulpit committee as to his commitment or he had to decline. His heart was heavy. The words wanted to come out to ask for more time, but he knew the answer. About that time his precious wife came to the phone and could sense his agony. She knew his spirit was in a battle. She touched his arm and whispered, "It's okay." It was like an angel of the Lord came and whispered, "Alaska!" He declined the offer to Tennessee and that night he and his wife sat in prayer as David shared what God had done on that mission trip. In tears, she responded that she knew God had been dealing with him and that wherever God led him, so He led her. She was disappointed to be sure, but the Holy Spirit has been dealing with her heart as much as He had David's heart.

What David did not know was that his wife, Sarah, had been reading Job and came upon Job 10. She read Job's prayer and was reminded of how great God is. She also looked at her own life and had come to understand she was selfishly attempted to tell God what she expected of Him rather than let Him lead them. Then she read Job 10:9 "Remember, I pray, that you have made me like clay..." The unexpected happened, God led them back home to Alaska and their work in that little village, though arduous, is impacting souls. It reminded me of our call out of seminary. It was such a similar story to the calling I had to pastor a little pioneer church in Grand Rapids, Michigan, a place where we had no intent of living. But on a mission trip God opened the door for me to pastor that little church in that pioneer area for Southern Baptists and it was there we adopted our first son.

While David's message struck such a personal chord, it was one that took us down the road of many fond memories of years past. David concluded his sermon by reminding us that in each of our lives we can expect the unexpected but it's not the situation that has to determine our reaction but our willingness to be clay in the potter's hand when that situation occurs. In David's life it brought him to Alaska and in many ways brought him back home, both physically but also spiritually. For us, our situation started a journey. A journey as parents of a little three-year-old that would be the son to bless us with his love into our senior years. It was also a journey in understanding God's unfolding call of my life on the vocational call as an educator and ministry of a bivocational pastor for which I would spend my next 43 years.

CRACK!!!!!! Came a loud sound that vibrated throughout the entire building. We all felt it and suddenly the lights went out then we heard all the sounds of fans, blowers and anything mechanical stop. We had daylight but it was clearly darker in the room. We all looked stunned, as did David and Faith. We noticed the rangers scurrying to the windows and then to the mechanical rooms. In the distance we heard one of the rangers attempting to call on his cell phone.

"Hello, Ranger Station Central. This is McKinley One. Hello, Ranger Station Central. This is McKinley One." Apparently, there was no response.

"Ladies and Gentlemen, we apologize for the inconvenience. We have lost all power and from the sound we fear there has been an avalanche nearby. We cannot reach Ranger Station Central, meaning we think a tower has been damaged or taken off-line. We are investigating and will let you know as soon as we find out something. It is our hope to get you back to the hotel as soon as possible."

Two of the rangers got in their SUV and headed down the road from which we had traveled. However, they arrived back in about thirty minutes.

"Ladies and Gentlemen, we regret to inform you there has been an avalanche approximately ten miles down the road and it has completely covered the road. There is no way to get through. We fear there has also been one up the road as well, which means we're rather blocked in. We are unable to contact anyone outside. However, the staff at the motel is aware of your destination and we're confident they also know of the avalanche by now. We have plenty of provisions and we have wood for the fireplace if that becomes necessary."

Well, this meant a bit of a delay to our plans but none of us felt any particular danger at the moment. Soon another crack but this one sounded much closer. The building shook. We ran to the window and with horror in our eyes we saw an avalanche pass across the road some 500 yards from the building. It was on the road heading upward, the same one that had the road blocked even further up. Now with the roads blocked in both directions and avalanches falling around us, we knew we were desperate.

Again, but with much more intensity, "Hello, Ranger Station Central. This is urgent! Ranger Station Central, this is an emergency." The ranger continued to attempt phone calls, but we all knew it was hopeless. Until someone who could do anything about it and realize we were missing, we were isolated and without hope of getting out.

David called us together around the center of the room. He stated, "Ladies and Gentlemen, we need to pray." He then led us. "Father in Heaven, you see our plight. We are helplessly isolated and surrounded by avalanches. We feel so fortunate that as of this moment an avalanche has not yet hit our station. Lord, we pray You will hold the snow back, keep us warm and give us the strength to overcome our fear. We know our safety is in Your hands. Help us to endure however long it takes for us to be rescued. Jesus we need a miracle and we know You can provide it. But whatever Your Will is we ask You for the grace and peace to accept and understand it whatever it is. May we be a comfort to each other and family to each other as we face the time before us. We love You, Lord Jesus. We place our lives and our spirits into Your hands. In Jesus Name, Amen!" We all joined in on the "Amen."

Of course, we all had questions and wanted answers but needless to say no one had them. All we could do was wait, hope and have faith. It struck us that we may have a crisis concerning water.

I asked, "Do we have enough water? Water to drink? What about the bathrooms?" I truly didn't want to create further anxiety.

I saw the alarm in the ranger's face. "We may have a problem depending on how long it takes them to rescue us. If necessary, we can melt the snow for drinking water. We typically have reserved water from rain and brought in water during the spring and summer. But as winter approaches, we have a reserved system. With us on the advent of our winter, which is low as this was to be our last tour. As for the bathrooms, we need you to treat that sparingly. We'd suggest use one bathroom for stool and as they do in some third world countries. Put your stool in toilet paper and then put it in a plastic bag which we will provide. We have storage for those for several days. If we get to the point of needing water for the other toilet, we'll melt snow for the urine toilet. It is on a septic tank system but can get blocked up. At this point, I think we're good for at least two days." That didn't really satisfy us, but it at least encouraged us to some degree. None of us hoped it would take more than two days to rescue us.

We settled back pondering what to do next. There was a chill in the air. One of the rangers put logs into the fire place and started a fire. It began to remove the chill. We wondered just how much chopped wood they had in reserve. I didn't dare ask. However, there were some trees surrounding the station that I suppose we could chop down, if needed. It soon began to get dark, but then the emergency lights turned on. Again, how long they would burn, we weren't sure. Another ranger went out and started a generator. A generator? Why didn't they tell us? It gave us some additional heating and they used it for the emergency lighting, thus turned off the lighting run by batteries. We also began to check our food supply. It seems there were some left over sandwiches and chips from lunch, but not much. However, the ranger station did have a small food closet with some canned foods for about four people, meaning about eight cans of food. None of this was going to last long with our 40. Some folks began to bring forth some snacks they brought with them, a few crackers and candy bars here and there. We laid it all out on the table and figured that with rationing, we could cut the leftover sandwiches, spread out the chips, water down the canned foods and maybe feed a cup of some kind of food about twice a day for two days. After that, we had no idea unless we got rescued. We're indeed in for a wilderness experience and truly needed a miracle.

We settled in. We weren't sure if we should sing, pray or simply talk to comfort each other. David seemed to be our designated leader or one of the rangers. Finally, one of the rangers spoke.

"Ladies and Gentlemen, I would suggest you prepare for the evening. We probably need to save our food for tomorrow. Let's use our coats, the few blankets we have, as well as the ones we have from our supply. I would suggest you get into groups of four to six. Get as close as you comfortably and modestly can to conserve body heat. We'll keep the heat on as long as possible by we're going to stage it with one hour on and then an hour off initially, until we see how long the heat remains. I would suggest you consider your use of the bathrooms in groups so we can insure everyone has access and remember we need to flush sparingly. Once you're in your groups I will number you and we'll access the bathrooms by sequential number, once everyone feels they are ready. Any questions?"

One spoke up, "Sir, do you have any idea what we're looking at in terms of potential rescue, dangers, hours, etc.?"

The Ranger responded, "Just call me Jim, we're all in this together. No, I can't give anything definite. Ranger Central knows we're up here and expect us back this evening, if not this evening, then to report tomorrow morning. But most certainly, they are aware of the avalanche. I'm confident the Hotel administration is expecting you back, so you can be assured someone will be looking for you if they haven't already begun. Getting to us by the highway is pretty well impossible; thus, I'm hoping they'll be sending helicopters. However, they don't want to risk other avalanches and what we don't know is how unstable the snow is above us. But you can believe they'll take every precaution before they attempt anything."

Another raised his hand. "Jim, I'm on heart medicine and I didn't bring it with me. I can't go more than 48 hours without it." Others raised their hands indicating they too were on prescription medicines, all of which were left at the hotel. This only added urgency to the emergency.

We gathered in our groups and suddenly one lady broke into song, singing "My Jesus, I love thee I know that art mine." Others one by one joined in "For Thee, all the follies of sin I resign; My gracious Redeemer, My Savior art Thou; If ever I loved Thee, my Jesus, 'tis now. I love Thee because Thou hast first loved me And purchased my pardon on Calvary's tree; I love Thee for wearing the thorns on Thy brow; If ever I loved Thee, my Jesus 'tis now."

David, then broke into prayer, "Lord Jesus, we come to You. You know our plight. While we feel lost, we know we're in Your hands and in that we can never be lost. You found us on the cross. You've taken us from our darkest moment, and this is pale compared to that moment. You made the mountains, and we know You can hold them still. We trust that the one who stilled the water will still the snow. Guide us through the night. Give us warmth and rest. We pray our rescuers will find their way to us soon. We place ourselves into Your hands." With that there was a collective "Amen."

In our group were two other couples. We found there was Jacob and Sarah Sadler, as well as Carl and Betty Hunter. For whatever reason, both names seemed so familiar to me. We began to get familiar with each other. I introduced us. The Saddlers lived in Alabama and the Hunts were from Georgia. Unique in that at the time we were from Tennessee. We made up the Southeast group. It was tempting to talk football, but the atmosphere really didn't support that, nor would the ladies feel comfortable with that. I mentioned that somehow both their names seemed so familiar. I began asking about their past. I found that Jacob was an army brat just like me. I knew it. His dad and my dad were at one time stationed together. It had to be either Hawaii or Fort Lewis, Washington. However, if Hawaii, Jacob and I would have been in high school together and I would have known him. He wasn't. So it had to be Fort Lewis. It turns out his dad was also a Chaplain. I knew it. Chaplain Sadler and my dad were good friends, and good fishing buddies. I was in college at the time, but I recall meeting his mom and dad when we first arrived at Fort Lewis, in the summer of 1961, before I headed to college that fall. They hosted us for a brief time until Dad got post quarters. I never knew Jacob, but I recall meeting them. Dad spoke of Chaplain Sadler fondly. Dad had some tough times with a commanding officer that had a conflict with Dad. Dad got a less than stellar efficiency rating from him and while it didn't destroy his career, it kept him from promotions far beyond what it should have. Chaplain Sadler was a moral support to my dad through those rough times. I shared that with Jacob, and he almost broke into tears, sharing that his dad was killed in Vietnam. I was so taken back by that. My dad never knew that. But it brought back good memories of better times.

As for the Hunters, I discovered they were lifelong residents of Fort Oglethorpe. O my! Another coincidence. I asked if they knew of the little community church that sat on the edge of the circle which was once the old original Army post. Carl and I were about the same age.

He responded, "Yes, as a matter of fact, when I was a child, my mom and dad went to that church. My dad was a deacon in that church."

I asked, "About what year was that?"

"Oh, somewhere between 1950-1955." Carl attempted to recall.

"Really. Then do you recall a Pastor Meyer?"

"No, but I recall going to revival and before services each night, the evangelist would ask the children to come to the front and cite memory verses he gave us the night before. If we got them right, he'd gave us little toys he bought at some bookstore."

"Carl, I recall the same thing. That was during the time, my dad was pastor. I was saved during that time!"

"Well, Cal I don't remember you. I know my dad wasn't happy at home during that time as he'd be so angry at times. But I remember his taking up the offering every Sunday."

What I didn't tell Carl was that during my dad's pastorate, they found some money stolen from the offering plates and it was later found out that one of the deacons was taking the money. At first, they attempted to blame my dad and it was such a difficult time for him, but in the end the truth was discovered.

"Whatever happened to your dad, Carl?"

At first Carl was a bit uneasy in talking about it. "Dad wasn't right spiritually for years. I knew it, we all knew it. He loved to play church, but we knew something wasn't right. Something was wrong with his spirit. He never read his Bible, never really talked about Jesus or even loved Jesus, particularly in those early years in my life. I guess that's why your dad and that little church is rather fuzzy in my thinking. He was into the trucking business. He was in management. He thought he should run everything just as he ran those trucks. He thought he should control his home life and his church life the same way. I don't think he had really accepted the Lord as his Savior. He made good money and often had a pocket full of change as I recall. We never knew why."

I knew why and it was becoming clear what had happened to that offering. But knowing my dad, he would have forgiven Mr. Hunter.

"Well, what happened?"

"Well, one day, he decided to check on the operations at the terminal in Alabama. He caught a ride with one of the loaded trucks going to that terminal. They left after lunch and would be heading toward Birmingham. This meant going over the mountains. This was before I-24 and I-57. They made it through Chattanooga fine and on their way down to Birmingham, they hit a major thunderstorm. Mind you this was back in 1950's with a mix of four-lane and two-lane roads. It was a four-lane they were on but the visibility was poor. All the sudden the traffic came to a halt as some driver decided to put on the brakes and come to a crawl in the storm. With visibility as it was, people began pulling off onto the narrow shoulder. Dad was in the passenger seat. The driver saw the tail lights of cars in front of him, but he was too late to stop. He had been going 55 mph, but even so he couldn't stop. His instinct kicked in and he pulled the rig to the right, but unfortunately, on the shoulder was another rig loaded with building materials. Dad's truck hit the rear end of that rig going at least 50. It literally smashed the cab flat, crushing my dad into the back of it and killing the driver. Dad was hanging onto life, barely. His ribs were crushed. His neck broken. He had almost every bone in his body broken. It took the jaws-of-life to pull him from the wreckage. There was no way he should have lived."

"Carl, I am so sorry. What happened?" We were all intrigued.

"Dad was rushed back to Chattanooga to the hospital. He was in a coma. His brain was swollen. The family was called in. It was 1956. We never expected to see him alive again. They did emergency operations on whatever they could of his broken bones, to reduce the brain swelling, etc. For a short time, he was on life support but once the brain swelling went down, they found he could breathe on his own. He was in a coma for almost six months. People prayed for him. Mom had left that little community church. A new Baptist church started in town and she started attending it. There that church family surrounded her and our family with love. During that time, they came to the hospital night and day. They brought food and were there for our family. Then one afternoon, with Mom by my dad's side, he opened his eyes. He looked over at her and called her name. She couldn't believe it. She loudly called back his name. Then she screamed for the nurse, who came running. Everyone was so excited. It was the start of his recovery."

We were all so involved in this story that time was passing by quickly. "How long did it take him to recover."

"Well, Dad was in the hospital at least another six months. He had several other surgeries as well as a lot of therapy to go through. No one was for sure if he'd walk again. He finally was released home but in a wheelchair with months of therapy ahead of him. He had at least another year of recovery facing him. But during that time, another recovery was taking place. Dad began to go to church with Mom. His heart began to change."

I began to see the story of two men, both in my dad's life. One who was a friend and the other a foe. One died early in his life but stood by my dad in times when things were tough for him. My dad eventually got his promotion, but not without a lot of heartache and self-doubt. God protected him. Had he been in today's Army, he would have never been allowed to stay. However, time and time again we saw the handiwork of God protecting him. Dad took on jobs that normally were slots for men of much higher rank. Finally, in Belgium the Commanding General saw potential in my dad and wanted to make him post chaplain. However, it was a slot for a field grade officer, meaning Major and up. After the General reviewed Dad's record and disagreeing with the evaluation of the previous superior, he flew to Washington and brought back Dad's promotion to major, thus qualifying for the Post Chaplaincy the General wanted him to serve. It was Jacob's dad that inspired my dad and I shared that with him. I felt it was a miracle God allowed Jacob and me to be together that night.

As for Carl's dad, well, he was at the heart of one of my dad's greatest heartbreaks. Dad saw a man fighting God and sinning against God, a man stealing from God. I couldn't tell Carl that. I so wish Dad was hearing this story now. But somehow, I gather he knew.

Carl went on, "One night the pastor preached on 'Forgiveness.' I saw tears in my dad's eyes and soon sobbing. He was still in a wheelchair. He heard how God forgives and forgets. Dad for years had been unable to forgive himself. He had been so cold against God. Then this accident. He knew he should have died that night. Everyone told him it was such a miracle he lived. There was no explanation for how he survived. Dad knew that. But he realized God had given him a second chance. At the invitation, he wheeled that chair in the aisle and as fast as he could he rolled it to the altar. Weeping and sobbing loudly, everyone could hear, 'Father, forgive me, forgive me.' The pastor prayed with him and Dad admitted that, for the first time, he was allowing Jesus to become Lord of his life and as soon as he was physically able, he wanted to be baptized."

By this time, there were tears in all of our eyes. "It took Dad another eight months of difficult therapy to be able to do things without the wheelchair, sufficiently enough that he announced to the pastor he was ready to be baptized. Dad became a changed man! He not only became a regular attender in church and Sunday school but he was there when they needed any kind of volunteer work he could do. Dad also began to tithe. What we also realized is that he began looking for Mission Projects he could help support. Dad read his Bible regularly and had his Morning Prayer time. This was the dad I came to know the rest of my life. He never again accepted the role of Deacon, although nominated several times. He always said he just didn't feel qualified and that he would serve God in other ways and, that he did."

Carl then shared that his dad died some twenty years ago, a faithful servant of the Lord. I must admit I was so blessed by this story. I knew this would have been such a blessing to my dad. I guess I've learned that we may have a passing part in people's lives but never see the potential miracle God intends for them.

What more could anyone add to the evening. We felt blest, but then our attention again turned to our predicament. We noticed other groups beginning to shut down and going to sleep and, thus so did our group. We tried to get as comfortable as we could. We felt the uncertainty of our situation but, at the moment, rather resigned to the fact all we could do was wait.

I dozed off. It didn't seem long before I felt a tug on my coat. I looked up and it was, no, it couldn't be, it was Jim Rewis! Jim died five months ago. He wasn't in the group. He whispered, "follow me." I got up and did as he said. We went out the door into the snow. This wasn't right.

"Jim, where are you taking me?"

"Don't worry Cal, I want to show you something." He pointed down the road. He left and I followed his direction. I saw a spot that seemed a bit unusual. It seemed to be the opening of an old snow shed. I walked toward it and couldn't see far, but it seemed clear. I went back to the station and found everyone asleep. I wasn't sure what to do. Oh, well, I thought, I'll mention it in the morning.

I awoke the next morning and either felt I had been dreaming or sleep walking. Surely Jim Rewis did not come visit me in the middle of the night. I didn't want to make a fool of myself by talking about it. I kept quiet. The rangers came around asking how all of us felt. Of course, we were still very worried. The heat was off, as the rangers were attempting to conserve whatever fuel was left in the generators and the wood. It was snowing outside. The sky was as gray as ever. It didn't seem there was any hope we'd be rescued this day. Snow surrounding us, the prospect of more coming, another avalanches a real possibility, all seemed so hopeless. We took a few of the food items and shared them among ourselves, conservatively. I had to ask. I had nothing to lose. So, I approached a ranger.

"Sir, I don't mean to meddle. But is there a possibility that there might be an old snow shed down the road?" He looked puzzled.

"Well, yes, years ago there used to be an old logging, clog-wheel-type train that used to come up the mountain. There was an old lumber camp further up. But it has been closed for years. They had a snow shed down the road, but it was deteriorating and unsafe and so they boarded it up and left it abandoned. It is back in the woods off the road. How do you know about that?"

"I had a dream, I think, last night, and saw it in my dream. I walked toward it and found it open. It looked clear. I wonder where it might lead to."

The ranger looked astonished. He got with the other rangers, then came back to me.

"We'll check it out."

A few of the rangers left and we saw them travel down the road, I thought I had traveled last night. After about an hour, they returned, faces red, but somewhat excited.

"The snow shed is clear from one end to the other. It's a bit of a walk and may be a bit unsafe but we got through to the other side. It seems the avalanche went right over it, covering it, but in so doing left a snow cave. Once on the other side, there is an open section of the highway. I called Ranger Central on the other side and they will have helicopters waiting for us in two hours. They are willing to chance it but, they can get in and out if the weather clears. The forecast is for the snow to stop within the hour. We need to prepare for the walk."

Fortunately, since this was only supposed to be a day tour we had only the clothes we had worn on the trip. The rangers advised us to stay close together and to remain in our groups of four. His concern was any shifting of the snow and any cracking of the old timbers as we walked through that old snow shed. The rails had long been taken out. We began our walk and soon came to the snow shed. It was just as I had dreamed, or saw it, last night, just as Jim had shown me. The ranger asked that we not speak or make any noises for fear any sound would cause vibration. We began to enter slowly and walk carefully. We looked all around us. We could see the old timbers. They looked ancient and ready to give way any second. We saw the snow bank to our right. It was a sheet of packed white snow. We realized we could all be buried under it in the blink of an eye. One by one we began to hold hands. Fear did grip us but we continued, wanting ever so quickly to get to the other side. Then suddenly, a lady in front of us sneezed. We all froze where we were. We heard cracking. We stood there. Some snow began to lightly fall upon us. We stared at the ceiling. After a minute, or so, the ranger motioned for us to continue. We knew the lady was embarrassed, but needless to say, it wasn't really her fault. We were all so gripped with fear, it is a wonder our emotions didn't explode into screams!

We looked forward and soon began to see daylight at the end of the tunnel. You know, that is exactly how it is when one finds the Lord. Our lives are in a dark maze of confusion and loss. I've recently read of the movie stars who have taken their lives with drugs and who have given up. We have a church friend whose husband committed suicide three years ago, a former Sunday school teacher. He just arrived at a point he gave up hope. It devastated his family. I recently read that if considering retiring one needs to have a plan to replace the loss of significance, the loss of routine, the loss of value to others, the new roll within the family. I've found all of that true. At the age of 75 everyone considers you "over the hill." Uniquely you're on everyone's charity list for donations, but no one considers you valid enough to be of importance in significant roles. That, sadly, is not only true in the world, but so often in the church as well. To that end, so many my age are so willing to give up, as did our friend's husband, just mentioned. You feel lost, in a dark tunnel with the world ready to crack and bury you. But the Lord comes along and says, "I still love you and I still have need of you. It may not be as you once were. It may be bagging groceries at a food bank, or teaching a Sunday School Class in a low-income housing development, or giving a devotion to a center for men with emotional issues. But you are important. Look at the light at the end of the tunnel and you will see Me standing there waiting on you."

We finally reached the end of the tunnel. We had cleared it. The helicopters had not yet arrived. The rangers got on their phones.

"Ladies and Gentlemen, the helicopters are on their way."

We stood watching for the miracles that were to rescue us. Soon we heard the rotors fluttering in the distance. Then four copters came over the ridge. They were Coast Guard copters and each able to carry about 10 of us. As soon as they landed, we heard a loud crack in the tunnel and a huge cloud of snow coming from it. The tunnel had indeed given way with the loudness of the helicopters.

We were whisked off over the hills and could only see snow for as far as we could imagine. The ranger station was nowhere in our sight. They took us to Ranger Central where busses were awaiting us to return us to the hotel. We had indeed experienced a miracle!
Once back at the hotel, both officials of the hotel and the ship were there to greet us. It is apparent all were deeply concerned we had been lost. Most were concerned we were dead. All I wanted to do was go to our room, get a good sleep, pack and head home. I'm sure I was not ready for any further adventures. We were all offered the opportunity for a nice meal but I dare say most of us simply wanted to sleep. When we got to the room, a bevy of sandwiches, chips and soft drinks were awaiting us to eat at our leisure. The staff knew we weren't in the mood to do further socializing.

About 7:00 am the next morning our phone rang. I wasn't expecting a call.

"Hello, Dr. Meyer."

"Yes."

"This is Carlos, calling from the Lobby. The Captain asked me to meet all the passengers who had special arrangements to exit the ship to gather in the lobby around 10:00 am. Have your bags packed as you will be checking out. You might want to stop by the restaurant for some breakfast before reporting to the Lobby." Stunned and still half asleep. I said, "Sure, okay."

I'm not sure what I agreed too, but I got Shirley up.

"Hon, that was Carlos. They want to meet us and other ship passengers in the Lobby around 10:00 am."

"10:00 am?" she said with some question and amazement. "Passengers, what other passengers?"

We both never understood we were among several passengers who left the ship for this side trip. It seems our encounter on the mountain was with fellow passengers, or was it?

We got up, got ready, packed and headed down to the restaurant with luggage in hand around 9:00 am. We were ready for some breakfast. To our joy, we found the restaurant full. It seemed the entire hotel got the same message. We found a table; it was a breakfast buffet, had our blessing and proceeded to the buffet line. We weren't quite sure what this was all about.

As we looked around, we found as much confusion as we felt. We found a smaller group of passengers who clearly weren't with our group. They apparently arrived before we did but were on excursion as we arrived.

We found a table with another couple.

"Hi, I'm Cal and this is my wife, Shirley. We're the Meyers. Well, we're Meyer, but as Shirley always says, we're Meyers when there are two of us. May we sit with you?"

"Sure, we're Bill and Sarah Bailey from Columbia, South Carolina."

"You've got to be kidding. I got my Ed.D there at USC. My mom and dad are buried there. You do seem so familiar."

"You do, as well. My wife's parents were Frankie and Tommy Morris. He used to own the old Farmer's Market."

"You've got to be kidding. When my dad died, Mom and Frankie were the best of friends. Frankie did so much to get mom through her grief. Sarah, I'm not sure if you remember but I saw my very first TV at your house. I considered you the wealthy family. When my dad was in Korea, your mom and dad invited us over to your house after church for ice cream and you had a TV. It was there I saw my first TV!"

Sarah didn't remember but went on, "We were blessed financially. I do remember your mom as my mom talked about her a lot, particularly in her latter years. I know they hung out together quite a bit after your dad died."

"Another memory I have is when my dad returned from Korea, your mom and dad had a big BBQ in their backyard and invited all the family and many friends from the business. It was a warm afternoon, as summers in Columbia tend to be. What I remember most, sadly, is getting sick on some warm watermelon. But I still think of that as a great day and have such fond memories of your parents. Tell me what happened to your mom. I know your dad died several years before your mom did."

"Well, as you know when your mom started having strokes and couldn't get around, she and mom finally slowed down and finally each became so agile neither were able to see each other. I heard your mom was put in a nursing home and sadly we had to do the same with mom. Mom died in 1999."

"You know we've always thought about your family. After we graduated from Carson-Newman and were heading to Florida to get married, we stopped in Columbia on the way. Your mom would have nothing else, but for us to spend the night with her and your dad. I don't remember seeing you though Sarah as I think you were still at college at that time."

"No, I wasn't home then. Mom and Dad were going through some rough times. Dad had begun to leave church out of his life and his business took over his entire time. Their marriage took some hits and Mom went into a shell, spending more and more time finding happiness in things. It wasn't until later that she began to find her way back when your mom came back into her life. That, I think, was when she began to find her way back to some degree, spiritually."

You know I needed to hear that! Here we were at breakfast, awaiting directions for our next part of our journey and our past comes back to us. What a coincidence that we saw the Baileys! No! What a blessing. No! What a miracle!

After that wonderful experience, we headed to the Lobby as it was nearing 10:00 am. There stood Carlos. We were two of a bus load of passengers. Soon Carlos came forward and beckoned us to listen carefully.

"Ladies and Gentlemen, we have a bus waiting for you which will take you to the Anchorage Airport. We are flying you to Orlando, Florida, where you will meet the MH MKaddesh in about 11 days. If you recall, you left the ship on November 11, with today being the 15th, you will have until the 26th when the ship is ready to depart from Cape Canaveral. In the meantime, we have personal itineraries for each of you to enjoy unexpected blessings."

Unexpected blessings! What in the world does he mean? Anyway, we all got in line to board the bus for the several hour trip to the airport. I wondered if we did the right thing in leaving the ship. We missed the sights of the Inside Passage of Alaska, but then again we've been on that trip with three other cruises. I missed the Panama Canal, but then again I saw the canal when I went on the mission trip back in 2015 with our church. I clearly didn't miss all the days at sea. We got our fill of that on our last cruise to Hawaii, hitting a storm on the way back. Shirley suffered vertigo for years following that experience. I found that cruising is a lot like Forrest Gump's famous statement, "Life is like a box of chocolates. You never know what you're going to get." Well, this trip has certainly been full of surprises! The last few days most clearly so!

With luggage boarded and everyone in their seats, the bus pulled away from the hotel. It was a gorgeous morning. We were ready to leave and eager to board the plane to much warmer weather and those "Unexpected Blessings."

Chapter 12: Unexpected Blessings

We arrived at the airport around 1:00 pm and realized the entire bus was boarding the same plane. Carlos went on the bus with us and escorted us to our gate. We entered an entrance that took us directly to the plane, no security, no checking of our luggage, nothing. That, in itself, was an unexpected blessing. The plane appeared to be a Boeing 737. We had our own entrance to the Jet way. Before boarding we heard the following announcement:

"Ladies and Gentlemen, you do not have assigned seats but as you board you will find there is plenty of room and we are allowing you to choose your own seating. We are boarding married couples first so that they can find seating as a couple. Once on board, we will take off immediately. Keep in mind we have a five-hour difference between Alaska and Florida. Given this is an eight-hour flight, our anticipated time of arrival will be approximately 2:30 am. Lunch will be served on board, with available snacks throughout the flight. We have hotel arrangements for you once we arrive."

Once on board we noted the entire 737 was business class and seating was indeed comfortable for all. Shirley and I were some of the first on board, particularly given our handicap status (Shirley's lack of cartilage in her knees and shoulders, as well as my arthritis in my hips have insured that). We chose seats just in front of the wings and sat back for a rather lengthy ride. We knew that by the time we arrived we'd be exhausted. Flight has not been our forte in recent years. Shirley's ankles swell when sitting for long periods of time and normally going through security is a nightmare. At least we avoided the latter.

The plane's engines revved up; we began to move. That, to me, has always been exciting. Soon the steward came over the PA system and reviewed the typical safety procedure, reminding us we also had ear phones for listening to music. I also noted we had a screen available in front of us, each of us having our own private screen for viewing movies. We began to roll past the terminal on down the tarmac to the take-off runway. There wasn't any traffic ahead of us, thus we rolled rather quickly to our take off. Once there, the engines went into high power and we felt the surge of power taking us speedily down the runway, soon the front lifted, wheels off the ground and the ground below us ever further from us. We could see snow laden mountains for miles. Given it was November, I imagine we'd see nothing but snow as we flew over Canada down the northern US across the middle part of the country into the South and Florida. I didn't imagine we'd see anything green or bare until we came across the middle part of the country southward. Even in Tennessee it gets into the 30's in November. I'm a fall/winter person and love the snow, particularly during the holidays. And this is the holiday season.

It wasn't long before the steward and stewardess began pulling out the dinner carts. Notably they were wearing the same kind of uniforms as those seen on the MH MKaddesh. This obviously was all part of the same tour program. The captain came on the PA system:

"Ladies and Gentlemen. Welcome to flight #7 to Orlando. We anticipate clear skies most of the way. We will be flying over Canada, crossing into the United States through Washington State taking a southwest path across the country through Missouri, Tennessee and on to Florida. Our flight time is expected to be right at eight hours. We do expect to arrive on time at 2:30 am, Eastern Daylight Time. At this time, our steward, and stewardess, whom some of you may recognize from our ship the MH MKaddesh, will be serving you lunch."

Oh, my! I know this is going to be a late day. Traveling these time zones is truly going to take a toll on our body clocks. The take-off went smoothly and I felt a sense of relief we had finally left Alaskan space and were heading home. Well, at least, to a part of the country we once called home. For Shirley it was for sure home, having spent much of her childhood in Central Florida and being the place where she gave her life to the Lord. As we approached our cruising height of about 32,000 feet, everything below was so small, but white.

As we flew over the Cascades and Rockies my mind wandered back to the days of my youth once again. I saw the white below me and remembered the week of our visit with our friends Major Harper and his family as they came by way of Seattle on their way to Japan. They, too, were scheduled to take one of the last Army Transport Ships used to carry men and families to their next station. They were assigned to the General Freeman. At the time I never had any idea our next travel would be aboard the General Gaffey on our way to Hawaii. All I knew was how I so envied them as we said our goodbyes the day they boarded the ship. However, the week before we took them around the area I was amazed at the beauty of it all. We traveled up Mt. Rainier and was overwhelmed by the height of the snow that had been plowed by the sides of the road, the Welcome Center and main hotel. We're not talking six to eight feet; we're talking 12 to 15 feet high. The sun was out and it was simply inspiring! You know, as I looked from 32,000 feet above, I couldn't help but wonder. How could a people with all of God's awe-inspiring creation surrounding them not be continually in reverent fear of Him? I thought of the politics of our day where mankind now murders babies, legalizes marijuana, takes "So Help Me God" out of our oaths, allows atheists to steal prayer away from our children, deny the Bible in our schools, will attack a man for following his faith and yet we live in a country where we sing "America the Beautiful." I can't help but see the miracle below of God's love in providing such a wonderful creation but at the same time the tragedy below in the hearts of so many, particularly our political leaders. However, while contemplating this, I am reminded that one day, just as I am in the air now, I will meet Him in the air and be with Him for eternity. An eternity more beautiful than anything I can imagine! An eternity of living in relationship with my Lord and Savior Jesus. An eternity of blissfulness. Just as I so wanted to sail on the General Freeman that day with the Harpers, one day my ship will set sail for Heaven. That is the miracle God has shown me in this flight.

Well, so much for daydreaming but that's what this flight is all about, living our past and seeing it a bit more realistically than we dreamed it would be. I can't help but think about America as it was back in the '50's when I had simple dreams of just being on a military transport to Hawaii. But today cruising is the common man's vacation. Everyone can do it. It's inexpensive, comparatively speaking. They have multiple cruise line ships that are two and three times the size of the General

Freeman and General Gaffey. Yet, still, when the cruise on the MH MKkaddesh came along, we didn't hesitate.

But there is something inside that clearly tells me this will be the last cruise. I look over our experiences and our country and there is a fear that grips me. Not a fear of dying so much. I know that is coming. The older I get the more my heart and mind is relaxing to the anticipation of it. Oh, that isn't to say I don't want to live as long as possible, but when the day comes, I do believe I'll be ready. What I fear is the destructive forces I see taking over our wonderful Republic. Right from wrong is no longer discernable. This generation has forsaken God and the church has lost it impact on the nation. It is evident God has removed His blessing from us! Yet I do believe it is the presence and witness of the remaining saints that keeps us yet alive and continues God's longsuffering endurance with us. But America's heartbeat is slowly, but surely, showing signs of an imminent final terminal heart attack.

As I look below at the magnificence of God's beautiful creative order, I don't understand how hard it is for mankind not to have God in it. Crossing the Rockies, down over the Midwest, passing the great Mississippi on toward Florida, you see so much diversity of nature that only God could design.

I still remember my first time at Yellowstone National Park, at age 12, and the awesome feeling I had when I saw Old Faithful shoot her stream of hot water into the air and realizing she did it consistently hour by hour. My fondest memory was riding the Great Northern out of Seattle to Chicago on my way to my freshman year at Carson-Newman as a young 17-year-old. The sights and smells of the train and traveling over the Cascades on past the Rockies truly titillated my mind helping me to cope with what was a sense of great fear of leaving Mom and Dad behind. Though long forgotten, I now recall the day we drove past St. Louis as Shirley, and I left seminary in Texas to accept our first pastorate in Michigan. There was no Arch. It was just a rather typical city filled with the haze of industry. We'd later come back to live in that city as a college professor and ride to the top of that Arch to view the city from a clear and impressive view. My flying over my past does bring back of lot of memories and, I suppose, reminds me of a lot of past blessings God personally allowed us to live.

The one thing I'm beginning to learn in retirement is that the past is there to enjoy but one can't stay there. I've come to realize that God blest me in my career and it was only by His grace that I completed it to the point of retirement. But to expect that the same blessings I had in my career will continue into my retirement was not the intention of God. God had a point in His guidance of me in my career. I look back and I realize there were a lot of miracles that God provided to enhance my career, to keep me from destroying myself at various points in time and institutions and with various people. He took me into and out of circumstances that were way beyond my control. In retirement I have expected God to continue to act the same, but He's let me know His actions now are to meet the needs of my retirement years. For example, as a college professor I've long lost the dynamics, intellect and skills required of me to return to the roles I once held. Not only that, but several years into retirement has also seen changes in technology, media and social attitudes that no longer coincide with who I am, or what I'm capable of doing. That doesn't mean I'm ready to be put out to pasture, but it does mean I have new roles to serve. Perhaps not with the same social status I once held or with the same energy once required, but God has new challenges with new blessings awaiting me. As I cross this land, I've basically gone backwards returning from new adventures to remember old adventures and opening my mind yet to what the future, in God's Will, holds for me.

"Ladies and Gentlemen, please note the seat belt sign is on, we are now in the landing pattern for Orlando. We should be arriving in approximately 20 minutes." My! That was fast! I guess through the daydreaming, snoozing and enjoyment of the scenery, it went fast. Not to mention it is nearing 2:30 am and I am truly tired. I'm ready for bed. I wonder what awaits us upon our arrival. We saw Dorothy and Jim, so we thought, in Alaska and they gave us a hint we'd see them again. But Jim is dead! Florida is Shirley's home and has never been the point I can call it so. Oh, we've had our memories there to be sure; my pastorate at Bethel Baptist, our times with friends at the Auburndale High football games and even the family times with Dorothy and Jim before she got caught up in the Jehovah Witness cult. Shirley still celebrates October 19, 1952, as the date she, her mom, Dorothy, Roy, and Emmit arrived in Florida to escape the poverty and alcoholism of her dad, before he was saved. Shirley was saved there at Lena Vista Baptist Church. Had it not been for Florida, there would have been no Carson-Newman in Shirley's future and no Shirley in my future. I need to remember October 19 is an important date for me, as well.

Sure, enough just as announced we were over the lights of Orlando and landing. As we taxied down the runway toward the terminal, the stewardess came over the PA system.

"Ladies and Gentlemen, once we get to the gate, we ask that you keep your seats. You will be met at the gate by staff from the hotel. We have rooms reserved for you and a bus is waiting for you. You need not worry about your luggage; it will be delivered to your room. As it was planned, we arrived on time. The time is 2:30 am, Eastern Standard Time. Please keep your seat until the captain turns off the Seatbelt sign and we open the door."

Wow! Am I tired and I definitely feel like we're being treated first class. I am wondering if Jim and Dorothy will be greeting us, or for that matter anyone from the family?

Chapter 13: Home?

It was late afternoon, and I was ready to get to the hotel. To my amazement there was no one waiting for us, much less Dorothy and Jim. I suppose I had built up an expectation that some unexpected miracle might happen, and they would appear. When we left, things were so distant between us. Dorothy refused to let go of her dogmatism in her non-Christian faith. It had gotten to the point she refused to even allow Shirley to visit her at her home when we visited Florida. But we kept hoping. The busses picked us up, our luggage had indeed been loaded and, off to the hotel we rushed. I wonder where they'll take us. There are so many Fantasy Worlds around Orlando, surely, we're not going to stay at Disney World or Universal. Nope, our busses headed out of the terminal down I-4 past Orlando, Universal, Disney World and on toward Lakeland and finally to a private resort known as "God's Peace." Shirley and I had never heard of it before. It wasn't on any map.

We pulled into the campus and there stood a beautiful ornate white, three-story hotel, all lit up with a line of porters, maids and staff awaiting us. Finally, a kindly gentleman came on our bus.

"Ladies and Gentlemen, Welcome to God's Peace. You will be our guests for several days until the MKaddesh arrives in port at Cape Canaveral.

Well, it looks like we're going to be here for about two weeks as it is now going on November 13th and the MKaddesh won't dock in Cape Canaveral until November 26. My! Oh, my! What are we going to do in Florida for two weeks? I began to clearly doubt our decision to depart from our planned itinerary as it has certainly proven to be anything but normal. Now we have two weeks of uncertainty and Florida has never been the place I considered home or particularly enjoyed. But it is November, and the heat won't be as pronounced.

After the pause on the bus, we were all ushered to the foyer of the hotel. There was a bus load of about fifty of us. Apparently more than those of us who experienced the fright of the Ranger Station were to experience the next two weeks together. Couple by couple were given their keys to their rooms in what was a very luxurious hotel. The Registrar then said, as she had apparently told each couple,

"Please be in the Main Dining Room by 8:00 am. We'll have a nice buffet breakfast awaiting you with a special guest who will give you additional instructions." She then smiled and said, "Have a nice sleep and God's peace!"

But what about dinner? It was going on dinner time, and I was tired, but I needed something to eat.

"What about dinner?" I asked. Our last meal was earlier today on the plane.

"Oh, I'm sorry. I should have mentioned. There are sandwiches, fruits and various drinks and delicate delights in your rooms. We just assumed you would see them and partake as you wanted. We figured you'd be too tired to want a formal dinner." I thanked the registrar, with a bit of embarrassment.

We got to our room and indeed there was a food cart with a lot of fruits, nice sandwiches, desserts and drinks. After filling myself, I was almost too tired to get ready for bed.

It seems like I barely brushed my teeth and got into my pajamas before the phone rang. I thought my goodness who would call at this hour. Not only that, but it was now 7:00 am and it was a wakeup call from the front desk, a wakeup call I didn't request.

"Good morning, Dr. and Mrs. Meyer. This is your Wakeup Call to remind you that you have breakfast in one hour in the Main Dining Room."

I rushed Shirley up and we both hurried to get cleaned up, ready and prepared for breakfast. I was at first a bit annoyed, but this was on their dime, and they have been so good to us. Who was I to complain?

Our room was on the third floor with the most gorgeous view of a lake and that morning a glamorous sunrise one could only imagine. We headed to the elevator, somewhat groggy with sleepiness only to find others the same way. But yet we all were peaceful and eager to see what awaited us. We walked into the huge dining area, with round tables adorned with absolutely some of the most God-given floral arrangements. There were a variety of flora with many different colors. It looked like a room of rainbows at each table. To the right was a long buffet table, as there was to the left. A hostess gave us a number and then beckoned us to find a seat. There were at least 10 tables, with at least six seats each. Our number was #7. Thus, we sought out Table #7. We wondered whom we might get to sit with, given we met several in our ordeal at the Ranger Station. Well, if I remember correctly there was David and Sarah, but I don't remember their last name. Then there was Jacob and Sarah Sadler, and Carl and Betty Hunter. Our lives seem so intertwined in some way. I do wonder if any of them would be seated with us. Surely, there was a reason for our being given Table #7. At least four others were assigned the same table. Were we looking for someone we had not known, or someone who had connections to our past, as many on this trip have?

It wasn't long before Richard and Connie, Shirley's nephew and his wife, walked in and sat at our table. Then shortly following was my brother Dan and his wife Jan. I couldn't believe it! These were all people we knew, a part of our family. Neither Dan nor Richard knew each other and had literally nothing in common. They were as surprised to see me as I was them. All they knew was they received a vacation package from God's Peace Resorts for an all-expenses paid five-day experience. And miraculously they were available this time of the year. They asked what I was doing here. I attempted to share the best I could that we were on a cruise, but had a layover at God's Peace before rejoining the ship in two weeks. But for the sake of me I had no idea what Richard, Connie, Dan and Jan would be doing the next five days that would include us. It wasn't long before we found out.

"Ladies and Gentlemen, Welcome to God's Peace. My name is Nehemiah, I'm here to share the reason why you are here and explain foundations you will be building together for those who have been sent here as a part of the cruise."

Wait a minute! Did he just allude to the book of Nehemiah and the rebuilding of Jerusalem?

He went on to say, "But first, let's have our blessing and enjoy our breakfast. Some of our guests must be leaving within a couple of hours." Nehemiah then asked all to bow our heads and he prayed, "Heavenly Father, we come to You submissively, knowing our lives are bound together by You. Our past ties us intrinsically to our future, but sometimes we must travel it again to see just how marvelous Your plan is. It ties us by people and events and human emotion. But may we see the larger means by which You use it to take us to realms we never imagined. Now, bless the food and may we always be grateful for Your bounty. Amen!"

Well, I must say that was an unusual prayer!

"Now, Ladies and Gentlemen, please feel free to go to the buffet tables and enjoy your meal. Before you go. I need you to know all of you were brought together because of your common bond. See if you can identify it. It will be important for you to build a purpose of communication."

Common bond? Well, of course, Richard is our nephew, Connie is his wife, Dan is my brother and Jan is his wife. Other than that, I see no common bond between Richard and Dan. Richard and Dan both served in the Air Force, but I didn't. I get it that the wives are here as one with their husbands and to be on vacation with them. Dan and I are Baptists, but Richard is Church of Christ.

Oddly, we all went up to the buffet with our wives and did little communicating on our way and back to the table. I'm not sure we were really into this game. Once back, I remembered the one time Richard and Dan met. Our Wedding back in 1965! Both were about the same age. Dan was my Junior Best Man and Richard was our Ring Bearer. It hit me and I asked if either remembered meeting each other. They had not. But it opened the door to conversation as I began to share how thankful we were for Roy, Richard's dad, Shirley's brother, who loaned us his car the night of the wedding to drive from the church to our hotel and then we drove to Roy's house the next morning for him to take us to the train station. Dan recalled fondly of riding with my brother, Tom, for a short distance honking at us to just do a crazy thing to make people aware we were just married. From that point on Richard and Dan began discussing Florida, our families, what they had done in the Air Force, etc. We indeed found our common bond and it opened a fond memory for discussion. But in doing so, it also awakened some old wounds for Shirley and me.

When Shirley and I met at Carson-Newman as 19- and 18-year-olds, respectively we couldn't have been more opposite in culture, background and personality. I had just graduated from Leilehua High School, Wahiawa, Hawaii, as my dad was stationed there in my high school years as an Army Chaplain. Shirley had graduated from Auburndale High School, Auburndale, Florida, and her dad had been the town drunk in Alabama. I had middle class parents and had the privilege of living in officer housing on the Army base. Shirley was raised in a shack with an outhouse and the deep poverty of the Deep South and recalls hiding in a ditch from the fear of their drunken dad. Shirley's Mom was strong willed and picked cotton and worked in the orange canning plant to have biscuits and flour water flavored gravy for meals during the worst of their times. Shirley had a church, Lena Vista Baptist Church that took her under their wings as a young girl. Her Mom's strong will raised her, her sister, her brother and half-brother with a determination of survival. After some separation, her father came to know the Lord and rejoined the family although the bitterness of the hard years wreaked havoc on the relationship between him and Shirley's mother. During high school a friend, Vernon, advised Shirley of a bank that offered full scholarships to those who wanted to pursue God's calling. Shirley felt that call. She made her own dresses and clothes and off to Carson-Newman she came to rise above her past and live out what God had for her future.

In contrast, I went to Carson-Newman with the goal of entering the chaplaincy just as my dad had done. God had other plans and sent a wonderful counselor, Dr. Joe Chapman, to advise me to use my college years pursuing a teaching degree and wait until seminary for my theological training. My mother was an active leader in the church. With my dad a soldier's chaplain, he was in the field most the time and started his career serving in Korea at the conclusion of that Conflict. Given that, my Mom was a strong-willed disciplinarian for us three boys. We were in Hawaii when it became a State and my Mom became Hawaii's first State Baptist Women's Missionary Union President. She was clear in what she wanted for us and how we were to behave. And, her calling was to support my dad in his service.

Shirley and I met three years before my graduation. With her scholarship and my parents paying my tuition, with the understanding there would be no marriage until after graduation, our courtship served as a harsh battlefield of preparation. Once the passion had to face the realities of commitment by some hard questions, we began to ask ourselves questions, we found ourselves much too immature to find all the answers. At graduation the scholarship was over, the tuition was paid, but we had no money, no car, no home, didn't know how we were going to get to seminary and Uncle Sam was eager to send young men to Vietnam. We had a wedding ahead of us and her parents were too poor to pay for it and we didn't have the funds to pull it off, much less have a honeymoon. We were scared! But then God!

He opened the door for us to teach in a small Baptist school in Charleston, South Carolina, a pastor to loan us the money to put a down payment on a car and the Home Mission Board to let us serve as Summer Missionaries in Ohio until we could get to South Carolina. I got a deferment as a teacher and then as a seminary student a year later. Vietnam was not a fear for me or God's call for me; remember Dr. Chapman! We saw God's hand in all this, yet our first 10 years were tough as we were both so immature and strong willed. We both had strong-willed mothers we loved and adored. We both brought our strong wills into our marriage, which often resulted in conflicts, doubts about our marriage and saw our union often cracking. We didn't doubt God brought us together and miracles were happening but, at the same time, we began to doubt our love for each other. We didn't agree on roles in family, on raising the children, on how to plan together, etc. We had a dominance issue. I became overbearing, domineering, angry and loud. She became quiet and there would be days of silence.

The 11th year of our marriage a friend loaned Shirley the book *"Me? Obey Him?"* by Elizabeth Rice Handford. At the time her husband was pastor of First Baptist Church, Greenville, South Carolina. Shirley changed and it changed me! We came to understand that neither of us was to dominate, but to give to each other. The more she gave to me, the more I wanted to please her. We finally came to fully grasp that marriage is as the book suggested a 90%/10% relationship with each trying to give the 90%. We found ourselves giving to each other emotionally, lovingly, and spiritually and the old spark of seeing one's young bride as a beautiful woman can still be seen at age 75.

But on the morning following our wedding, we only had innocent eyes blinded by the belief that it was over. Shirley's sister jumped in and helped with the wedding, my mom gave assistance and though the wedding didn't live up to anyone's expectations and was stressful beyond words, we found relief that we'd be on the train soon. We had no idea what our future held, nor did we really fully understand each other.

As breakfast was winding down, Nehemiah returned to the microphone.

"Ladies and Gentlemen, as you complete your breakfast allow me to give you your instructions. To our guests who received our invitation to vacation with us, you are asked to finish that last cup of coffee and proceed to the foyer where we have several hostesses awaiting you with instructions and packages for your stay with us and the events we have planned for you. Those who have come as a part of the cruise, please remain in your seats."

"Well, Richard and Dan, I guess this means we will see you later. It was good to see you again and sorry we had such a short time together. I trust your vacation will be all it is anticipated to be." With that, Shirley and I awaited our instructions. Soon a hostess came by with an envelope for us. By this time, there was only one couple left at each table. Each couple apparently had guests brought in to share breakfast, but while a surprise, I was a bit disappointed it was only for such a short time. I wondered why we weren't going to share the vacation with them. I do know they brought back memories I wasn't anticipating, and ponder if it had anything to do with our forthcoming plans.

We opened our envelope and read, "Dear Dr. and Mrs. Meyer, this next 12 days will be a miracle of your dreams but only you will come to appreciate their true meaning. Please accompany your hostess to the limousine. Don't worry about packing, which has been done for you during breakfast." We were delighted and noticed the same sense at each table. I wonder if we were all going to the same place.

We got up from the table and walked to the door, following our hostess. She escorted us to the car awaiting us. As the car left the resort, we noticed it traveled on West as though going to Auburndale. Why are we going to Auburndale? Soon we arrived at Lena Vista Baptist Church, the very church in which we were married. The chauffeur opened the door for us and something rather astonishing appeared. Shirley got out but it wasn't Shirley. Rather it wasn't the present Shirley, I mean the 75-year-old Shirley. She was the 21-year-old beautiful brunette I was about to take down the aisle to be married. Out from the doors of Fellowship Hall came Dorothy, Shirley's sister and my mom and dad. Shirley, yelled, "Calvin," as though extremely overwhelmed. Looking over my hands and body, I was no longer the 320 pound 76-year-old, I was the slimmer 21 year old version of myself. Mom and Dad looked as they did on our wedding day as did Dorothy. Oh, my! We were about to experience another Miracle of Time as we did earlier in Hawaii.

Mom said, "Calvin, you come with us and Shirley will be going with Dorothy." Confused? You best believe I was!

Mom continued, "Calvin, we're going to spend the afternoon just enjoying your last day with us as a single son. Dorothy and I finished up the auditorium this morning. The florist arrived with the flowers and the cake is being delivered this afternoon. The photographer will be arriving an hour early."

This can't be. Our wedding was an utter mess. Shirley and I had $300 we saved from pinching pennies from the money we saved in working in the college cafeteria and we knew Shirley's family didn't have the funds to put on the wedding. Our florist had a death in the family and we had to get by with wild flowers picked along the highway. Dorothy did buy us a cake. But all we could arrange was the cheapest photographer who would do a few black and white pictures for us. Shirley's white wedding dress stained in storage, it was such a horrible nightmare. Mom and Dorothy didn't coordinate any of this and by the time our wedding night arrived Shirley and I were a total mess of stress. There was so much anticipation that we had to have a church wedding no one could afford. We were both ill physically and emotionally wishing we had simply eloped. I wasn't sure I wanted to repeat this.

Well anyway Mom and Dad took me back to the hotel in which they were staying and rather than the Mom and Pop motel we arranged for them, they were now staying in a nicer Holiday Inn near Winter Haven.

"Where is Danny, Tom and Susan?" I asked. "Oh, they are at Sue's house." Sue was the wife of Shirley's brother, Roy." They're having fun with Richard and Judy, their cousins. Keep in mind we're living in some dimension that isn't today. Susan is my adopted sister, one we lost years ago to mental illness.

Dad got my suitcase out of the car, which was given him at the church. "Well, it's going on 1:00, we need to get some lunch and start thinking about getting ready for the wedding," Mom surprised me. I should have surmised this from the earlier conversation, but all of this was stoning me out. "What wedding?" I asked. "Your wedding!" Mom said responding as though I had lost my mind.
We got back in the car and drove over to Sue and Roy's house, picking up Dan, Tom and Susan. Sue was home, but not Roy. She, too, looked as she did in 1965. "Good seeing you, Sue." I didn't know what to say. They were all acting as if this was normal. The family loaded in the car, we headed down the highway toward Lakeland and stopped at a nice place called "The Crab House." I don't remember its being there, but, oh, well. It was a rather nice restaurant and we appeared to have plenty of time. This was not at all like the day of our wedding. Mom and Dad wanted to go to Clearwater Beach and I got sunburned! It only added to the misery of our wedding. But today, I'm with family and just enjoying their presence in the calmness of a nice meal.

It wasn't long before Mom got a little panicky.

"My goodness it getting later than I thought. We've got to all rush back and get ready for the Wedding. Calvin your suit is hanging in the motel where you left it."

Where I left it? This isn't how it went! I left it in the motel but not in the one where Mom and Dad were staying. Oh, this is a different scenario, one of my dreams, my fantasy, I'm not sure what! We rushed back to the motel. As in reality, I was sharing a room with Danny and Tommy, although Dan was a child and Tom a teenager. There was my tuxedo suit, one I had wanted to wear but couldn't afford. It was nearing 5:30 pm and Mom knocked on the door encouraging all to rush on.

We got into the car and drove on to the church. Dad had his suit but this time was carrying his chaplain's robe. Mom wore the red dress she had originally chosen for the wedding. Upon arriving at the church, I noted the parking lot with several cars. I remembered we didn't expect a crowd as someone forgot to tell us it was the night of the high school graduation. We expected only a few family friends but not many of Shirley's high school friends. Auburndale is a close-knit community and families support each other. The high school is the center of community life. We walked into the church and I noticed a nice size group beginning to gather. Dad and I went to the back of the church into the pastor's office in preparation for my appearing before the processional. Needless to say, I was as nervous as our original date.

The photographer appeared and asked if he could take a few pictures of me and Dad and shared he had already taken a few of Shirley in her wedding gown.

"You've got a beautiful bride," he shared. "Yes, I know I do." Time seemed to trudge along ever so slowly. The wedding was to start at 7:00 pm, but it felt like it would never arrive. Then a knock on the door and in walked Rodney, one of my groomsmen who agreed to drive from his home in Jacksonville, to be in the wedding. Then I remembered, Tom was my best man and Danny served as my other groomsman. This was as we had originally planned. I was so embarrassed in our original wedding as I asked Rodney to be there, but I had no funds to help defray his cost or even give him a nice gift. The music started playing.

"Well, it's time for us to go out and meet the bride," Dad shared, with that wonderful grin of his.

Dad, led out as I followed and then Tom, Rodney and Danny. But, oh, wow! The auditorium was packed! Shirley's high school friends had showed up. I looked around the church and the floral arrangements were as Shirley had so desired, but again we had no funds. Then the processional began, and down the aisle came Judy, our niece, strewing flowers as our flower girl with Richard, our nephew, bearing the rings. Then came the bridesmaids, all from Shirley's high school class wearing the green and yellow dresses she had picked originally from a Bride's Magazine. My goodness where did the funds come from for that? Then, all the sudden bells in my head began to ring as I saw my bride! This time in a gorgeous white wedding dress that clearly wasn't one off the clearance rack! This wasn't the poor man's wedding that stressed us out and for which we felt such embarrassment in attempting to coordinate with no funds. One we regretted the rest of our married life. This was our dream wedding. It was a miracle!

Evelyn Hodge was there, as she was originally and sang "the Lord's Prayer." It was as awesome as ever. I couldn't keep my eyes off Shirley. She was the bride straight out of the bridal magazine as was this wedding. Soon the "I do's" and "You may kiss your bride" followed by "I present to you Mr. and Mrs. Calvin Meyer." I don't know how but I was indeed not only physically 21-years- old again but my emotions and heart were, as well.

After the wedding, our reception was in Fellowship Hall, as was the original. I must say, our original reception was perhaps the only highlight of our ceremony. This time Fellowship Hall was much more professionally decorated, with flowers, lighting, tables and to our delight someone had provided a Wedding meal of delicacies that would fit the most expensive plans. I don't know who paid for it, I didn't dare ask. This whole thing was a dream and miracle beyond our wildest imagination. The cake was several tiers high, not just the simple three-tiered Walmart cake of our original wedding and the Hall was literally full of guests. After a few pictures and guests were served, Dorothy, Roy, Rodney and some of Shirley's high school friends gave us words of encouragement. Then it came time for Shirley to change out of her Wedding gown and into to her dress for out departure. But I dearly love the lavender dress she wore at our original wedding and wouldn't change a thing about it. To my delight that's exactly how she came out. She was, indeed, my princess, my bride! Roy soon came up and gave me the keys to his Chevrolet, just as it was the original night of our wedding and we as we drove off for our first night.

I don't remember much about the morning after the wedding, only that we had to return the car to Roy and he took us to the train station. I knew we had just a moment to say our goodbyes to Mom and Dad and, as for the rest of the Wedding Party, they were gone after the wedding. And so it was this time. But this time, the goodbyes were much sweeter and for some reason we didn't experience the bitterness, hurt and disappointment of our original wedding. Then, it was "I'm so glad that nightmare is over." This time, there was a joy and sadness that it was over. It left us with sweet memories. I knew this was such a dream and we'd never see Mom and Dad again, or for that matter Roy or Shirley's family. I do know our future was so uncertain back in 1965 and our wedding proved such a dastardly thing start to it.

Roy drove us to the Old Seaboard Airline Train Station in Lakeland. Though long abandoned now, it was as it was in 1965. In my coat pocket were the tickets for the Atlantic Coastline Champion taking us to connect with Southern Railroad and our honeymoon in Gatlinburg, Tennessee. But the honeymoon didn't hold any more sweetness than our wedding. Shirley was sick from the birth control pills and given we were committed to the Home Mission Board for three months as Summer Missionaries to Ohio, we had no idea what our first weeks held for us. I do remember the Mission Board cut our planned Honeymoon short by two days by requiring us to report to Columbus early for orientation. It meant a two-day-only honeymoon in Gatlinburg with a sick wife.

Eagerly awaiting the train, I stood on the platform looking for the turning light and train whistle. Seeing the light down the tracks, the Public Address then announced:

"Atlantic Coast Champion arriving on Track #3 in five minutes with connection in Jacksonville to Atlanta, Charleston and points north. Please make your way to the platform."

I hadn't heard those sounds in years. With Amtrak you simply were told Train #52 arriving in so many minutes, etc. I so wanted to relive this trip but with a healthy bride and so hopeful our first few weeks of the summer would be so much sweeter. I do recall that when we finally got to Columbus, it was announced that the boys and girls would be separated into dorms for orientation as they held it at a Baptist Campground. Talk about frustration!

Soon the purple and white of the engine came breezing by as the train's brakes took hold and soon came to a stop. I took my lovely and we boarded the car to our left and sat on the left side.

"Are you feeling all right?" I asked Shirley." "Sure, fine."

She did indeed appear bright and cheerful. The engine did the traditional one toot to announce departure and off we went. I couldn't keep my eyes off my beauty. We headed to Jacksonville where we'd change trains for Atlanta and then on to Chattanooga and Knoxville. At Knoxville, we'd catch a Greyhound to Gatlinburg. Keep in mind, Pigeon Forge and Gatlinburg were in no way the tourist attractions they had become 40 years later.

I do recall that one of the things that overwhelmed Shirley's illness was our buying a grape drink and pastry for supper in Jacksonville. We were so poor we didn't have funds for a meal either on the train or in the station. We were trying to save our money, or as much of as we could, for our time in Gatlinburg. When we got to Jacksonville, we had about an hour's layover. This time we went to the station restaurant and this time my billfold was full of $20 bills. We had a nice meal. Once on the Southern Palm, we headed to Atlanta and early the next morning found the train backing into Chattanooga. It wasn't many years after our being there that the famed Chattanooga Station closed as an active train station and became the Chattanooga Choo Choo and city center with a hotel, shops and restaurant.

Finally, by mid-morning we arrived in Knoxville, and just two blocks over was the Greyhound station where we caught the bus to Gatlinburg. Another last time experience, as Greyhound now goes nowhere near there. Gatlinburg today is in no way the quaint little tourist town it was in 1965 with "Mom and Pop" motels and craft shops. But once again, Shirley and I walked from the bus station to Huff's Motel for our two days of Honeymoon. For whatever reason, Shirley was NOT sick this time. Thinking back to reality, we had only 14 days before the cruise ship docked. We're in a different world now and we're into Day 5 of our dream and miracle of this side trip.

The things I remember about Gatlinburg was the trip up the ski lift and our picture being taken on top. The thing Shirley and I remember most was getting up the morning after our arrival and going to the pancake house across The Street from our motel and ordering "Pigs in a Blanket." We had never heard of it and didn't know it was link sausage rolled up in pancakes. It was great. Shirley and I both enjoyed living our young years anew. This time from the wisdom of years later, but in the bodies of our youth. Talk about strange! Most of our time originally was Shirley just wanting to stay in bed and getting over her nausea, but this time we were both eager to enjoy the crafts shops.

Our two days went quickly as they did originally but we had a train to catch to Columbus. Now a week had passed since our side trip has begun and we had but one week left to see what was ahead of us. This time we caught the Southern out of Knoxville to Cincinnati and the New York Central to Columbus. We were dreading Columbus, knowing we were in for days of Orientation, separated, if it held true to our first summer as newlyweds.

Finally arriving in Columbus, we got off the train and headed toward the station. There waiting at the door was a group of students and a person in his 30's with a sign reading, "Cal and Shirley Meyer." We were excited. They were expecting us! It seems that was the case when we originally arrived. But it was also the case when we were first told we would be separated for two weeks for orientation.

"Hi, I'm Cal and this is my bride, Shirley." "Good meeting you Cal and Shirley. I'm Bill Collier, State Director of Missions. You are the last to arrive. The others arrived a bit earlier on earlier trains and we knew you would be arriving so we waited on you." We have a shuttle that will be taking us to dinner and a retreat north of town."

Nothing changed I thought. At least now I'm prepared for it. If I recall back in 1965, we spent the first two weeks apart and then were sent to our first assignment but, for us, it came with a hitch. Bob Slagle, the Area Missionary, to whom we were assigned, somehow didn't get the message that he had a newly married couple assigned to him. He had only planned for a group a girls and a group of boys and thus had living arrangements planned accordingly. That meant not just our first two weeks being married would be apart but for the foreseeable future, if not all summer. On top of that Shirley continued her very negative reaction to the birth control pills and was constantly nauseated. After our orientation, we were assigned with a team to North Olmstead, Ohio, for the purpose of Church Survey to start a new church and then from there to paint a church and teach Bible School near Cleveland. The only problem, it was in teams of girls and boys. I recall that in my rather strong frustration telling Brother Slagle he needed to let us get return tickets for Florida as we weren't staying. He made other arrangements but they weren't well planned. We didn't get to do a lot of Bible Schools but were forced to do a lot of church surveying in summer heat. Families had not made plans for us but accommodated us. One bivocational pastor was a church planter and accordingly the Home Mission Board subsidized his income but it had a time limit. As the church grew it was supposed to pick up the cost. The problem was the church didn't grow to pick up his salary. There he was losing salary and stuck with housing and feeding us. It made for some awkward moments.

We did have some good moments, *i.e.,* we held Bible School in a mobile home Park of new mobile homes near East Liverpool, Ohio. We were given a used mobile home for a week as our quarters. We were with the rest of the team once in surveying for the new church in North Olmstead, Ohio. We got to meet some nice couples our age in surveying for a church. But we felt most of the summer was wasted time, that we were simply being tolerated as no one anticipated us, nor had given thought to our service. You put that on top of a wedding we couldn't afford with expectations it was to be a normal wedding, it was nothing short of a miracle we made it past our first three months!
Finally arriving at the retreat dining hall, we were escorted into the hall where awaiting us was the entire group of Summer Missionaries for the entire state, about 150 students. The hall was rather large and before entering an aged gentleman came up to us and said:

"Cal and Shirley?" Rather surprised, as I don't recall him from our past. "I'm Bob Odom!"

Oh, my! He was in his late 80's. In real life I would be in my 70's. But in 1965 Shirley and I were but 21 year olds. Bill had to be in his late 30's if not his early 40's. Shocked, I didn't quite know what to say.

Bob encouraged us to follow him to a table he reserved just for the three of us and two others. We got to the table. "Hello, I'm sure you don't remember me. I'm Gary and this is Sarah. We're the Mackles. You stayed with us back in 1965." Oh! Not, the pastor who was called upon to take us in during the time of his financial burden and stress. All of them had certainly aged, yet there we sat looking as young as we did back in 1965. I was truly lost about how to react. In the time past I wasn't that fond of either. I felt both were in part the cause of our misery for the summer. I wasn't sure even how to make small talk. But thank goodness they did it for me.

Bob continued. "Cal, we're here as a part of your miracle. I know you know this is not a normal circumstance. We are as we are but you as you were past, two newlyweds. God has a reason for this reunion. Tonight is a night to enjoy the fellowship with your teammates. A fellowship you missed when you came in 1965. But tomorrow I'm taking you on a trip to your past once again."

"I'm eager to see what that means. But at the point, I'm not sure anything can surprise me. I'm glad to be here."

I then turned to Gary. "Gary, I look back and still have such a sense of remorse we were such a burden on you. We were so young and, yes, a bit immature. What ever happened to your church and you?"
"Cal, this is one of the places you'll stop and see tomorrow. Sarah and I stayed in the ministry for the next 45 years having pastored several churches. You know I was trying to help start that little church in East Liverpool. You stayed in the mobile home during the Bible School but when it was over you were sent to Cleveland to stay with a pastor in Cleveland."

"Yes, I remember. We didn't do much as he was sharing a church with a Seventh Day Adventist Group. He really didn't have much for us to do except join him in Bible Study with some of his people. We went to another group after that, who joined us with the team for a few days to help repair and paint a church, but then we were sent back to you to finish up the last two to three weeks of the summer. You sent us out each day for surveying."

I hope I didn't come across rudely but I do remember how punishing those days were. Gary would take us out about 9:00 am and pretty well dump us into a community. Pick us up for lunch and take us back around 2:00 pm and leave us until 5:00 pm. Though only five hours or so a day, it was grueling in the August Ohio heat without water or bathroom. I saw my bride suffering and I just hurt for her. But she was a warrior through it all. None-the-less, I wasn't a happy camper. But I had to remember we were "missionaries."

"Cal, I know that was hard on you and Shirley. I could tell it was difficult for you and I knew the whole experience was challenging for you. But, all was not lost, as you will see tomorrow."

The rest of the evening was a delightful evening with music, praise, a good meal and the charge from the State Evangelism and Mission director. After the meal, Shirley and I were expecting to be told to go to the different boys and girls dorms as happened in 1965. But that was not the case.

As we got up, thinking we needed to find our luggage and our dorm assignment, Bob said, "Cal, you and Shirley will be joining me in the main building where we have a private room for you. Tomorrow morning, we need to be up early. We'll get a quick bite to eat on our way, as we have three stops to make around the State and have quite a bit of traveling to do. We won't be returning here."

"Okay, we'll look forward to it. What time do you want us to meet you, and where?"

"7:00 am in the Main Lobby." Bob responded.

We awakened, got up early, and eager to meet Bob.

"Are you ready for a long day?" I didn't know just how far Bob intended to take us but we were, indeed, looking forward to it. On our way out of town we stopped at a Howard Johnson's. By our time in life now, Howard Johnson Restaurants had long gone. But they were family restaurants and very popular in 1965. Noting we were in a bit of a hurry, we tried to order simply *i.e.,* some coffee, an egg, biscuit and sausage.

Going on 8:30 am Bob suggested "We best be going, I've got the bill, you're my guests. We're first going to North Olmstead where there's something I want you to see." That was the place Bob was Director of Missions.

"Bob wasn't that the place where you were Director of Missions?"

"Yes, it was. It was where I met you and Shirley. It is where it began for you two that summer."

"Oh, do I well remember that!" I said softly to myself.

"Bob, how long were you there?"

"I stayed as Director of Mission in North Olmstead for about 15 years and then had an opportunity to work with the Ohio State Baptist Convention as their State Missions Director. We stayed there most of my career then moved on to Atlanta to join my kids and family as I retired."

On the way we stopped at Westerville, Ohio.

"Cal, do you remember this little town?"

"No, I can't say I do."

"Do you remember the Garage Bible Study I assigned to you and Shirley upon leaving North Olmstead?"

"Oh, yes, I wasn't quite sure why. As I recall the lady in whose garage we met was a sweet volunteer, but basically was a church member volunteering her garage, but counted on us to lead the Bible Study.

However, she had gone out and invited several of her neighborhood kids to join us. I recall we had about six or eight kids each morning for the week."

"That's right," Bob reiterated.

I also recall the Bible Study went on for only about an hour and half. There were materials Bob's office had sent, as well as supplies. The lady's home in which we held the study provided us an upstairs bedroom. She personally provided refreshments for the study. We figured that was a last-minute scheduled event, since Bob had to find something for us quick. Remember he wasn't expecting us. We got up each morning and prepared the garage for the activity, which met from 9:00 am until about 10:30 am. After clean-up, our hostess had a sandwich lunch for us. In the afternoon we prepared for the next day. In the evenings, young couples from the church came to take us to their homes for dinner. It was five days of an easy process but I confess we didn't give a lot of thought to it as we didn't consider it anything significant in terms of what we really accomplished.

Bob, turned off the Interstate and down into the town and soon we were driving into a residential street. I didn't recognize it. Bob soon stopped the car across the street from the house we had held the Bible Study.

"Cal and Shirley, do you remember that house?"

The dormer gave it away as I do recall that was the nice bedroom our host gave us for the week. But I wondered why we were being taken to see this house and why it was so significant.
A few minutes later he drove us on down the street to a church and on the front is the name, "Calvary Baptist Church."

"Cal, what I want you to see is that Calvary Baptist Church sponsored that Bible Study in which you and Shirley taught those six to eight kids." In this day of 1965, it isn't a big church, but in later years, it will grow into a church of over 500 in Sunday School. Do you know who had the vision to see this church become a bright light to this community? It was the grandson of the lady with whom you stayed. He was in your garage Bible Study each morning and at the end of the week he gave his life to the Lord. Later he was called to preach, went to college and then to seminary and later came back to this church to lead it forward in reaching this community, beyond expectation. There was a point the church wasn't sure it would make it until he came with a vision."

Tears whelping up in both Shirley's and my eyes, we felt so humbled. We had nothing we could say.

"Well, we need to travel on," Bob said, after touching our hearts and I wasn't sure I needed to or wanted to go further.

We got back onto the Interstate and headed north toward North Olmstead. We had about a four-hour drive ahead of us.

"Bob, what you just did has shown us yet another miracle. God uses the unusual, the unexpected, the simplest means to do marvelous things!"

"I know and we're not done yet!"

Nearing North Olmstead, we stopped for lunch and shared. "Bob, you know I've done a lot in my life and knew God has blest me in so many ways and I've considered the most obvious as his blessing, but I must admit, seeing the least obvious appears to have often surpassed my greatest expectations of how He has blest me. I believe I'm guilty of having taken Him for granted."

After lunch, Bob encouraged us to get back into the car.

"We have one last stop today. It's only about 20 minutes from here."

We soon came upon an empty lot. Bob stopped the car.

"This is the lot that in 1965 was the site for the new Olmstead Baptist Church."

I wondered why he was showing us an empty lot. Then he added.

"Shirley, you may not recall but you knocked on the door of the Barnett's from Georgia. They had just moved into the area. You were there doing a Church Survey and secured the information from them. I'm not sure if you remember their response to you, but they did. They later shared it was you who answered their prayer. They we eager to find Baptist work in the area and when you shared you were there doing a survey in hopes of starting a Baptist Church, they knew it was God who answered their prayer. What you did not know is that they became our first Charter Members of the church and for the first few weeks we held a Bible Study in their home. That lot soon became a good size church and eventually housed a congregation of almost 600 members."

Shirley was without words, as was I. We both thought the summer was such a waste. Finally, Bob sprang yet one more word of surprise.

"I have tickets for the late afternoon B & O Train for the two of you. It will take you to Washington where you will transfer to the Atlantic Coastline and on to Florida where you began this journey. Before running you to the train station I have one more stop. It's at the home of Jane and Todd Robinson. I'm not sure you remember their names but they remember you. They are present members of Olmstead Baptist Church. You will see them as they presently are not as they were in 1965. That is part of this miracle."

"I don't understand. How were they important to us?"

"Cal, do you remember the day Gary came to you and Shirley one late afternoon when you were doing church survey in and around East Liverpool. Without notice he took you to a home of young couples for dinner. You and Shirley were hot, dirty and tired and he failed to give you notice or time to clean up."

"Yes, I remember that very well. It was a rather awkward situation. But I remember when we arrived all three couples were dressed up with coats, ties and the ladies in dresses, while Shirley and I were sweaty, in tennis shoes, and just plain dirty from the dust and walking in the dirt. They had made plans for us to all go out to dinner then to some event. They saw the embarrassment on our faces. But, to our amazement, the men took off their coats and ties, the ladies took off their shoes and the hostess fixed a simple meal. They made us feel so at ease and we so enjoyed the fellowship with them. I never understood Gary's reasoning for that."

"Cal, Gary wasn't aware of their plans and he waited a bit late to get you but God had a plan. That night when you arrived they didn't know who you were or what summer missionaries did. When they saw how tired you were, how human you were and, yes, dirty, it impressed them. It told them you were for real and truly there to do the Lord's work. Those three couples became the backbone of the church Gary was trying to build in that community. The Bible School you had held earlier opened doors for children to come and those couples became teachers in that church. Even though you came at a tough time for Gary, God used it to develop a foundation from which a church did grow and to this day is a thriving church."

We soon arrived at the home of the Robinsons who welcomed us and invited us in for coffee and some of Jane's homemade apple strudel.

As we entered their homes, giving hugs I shared "Jane, it is so nice seeing you again after these many years." Of course they looked aged but as this miracle has occurred, we were as if we were in 1965. They didn't appear confused.

Jane added, "We understand, through Bob, that this is an experience no one can explain, so we will just enjoy it with you. But you two do look handsome and great cleaned up."

We understood the humor and laughed with her. I can't explain the dimensions that have been crossed through this as we've entered into the past while visiting members from it who have aged with it, while we didn't. Nor, has the environment we entered aged; it was as it were 1965.

"Well, tell us about your lives." I asked Todd.

"Well, we lived in East Liverpool most of our lives and became very active in the church there, but as I grew toward retirement our children moved here to North Olmstead and we decided to move here as well. Bob told us that Shirley was instrumental in finding the Barnett's who were the first Charter members."

"Yes, they were and you know, I must add, that the evening we had with you on that hot late July evening was one of the most delightful days of our summer back in 1965. We've talked about it often. We never knew what happened with any of our efforts that summer, but Bob has been kind enough to show it to us and this has been a complete miracle for us. Seeing you has just been the total confirmation that all of this was real. What a great God we serve!"

"Well, I need to rush you two to the train station. Your train arrives at 5:00 pm. We've got to get to Cleveland, which is about 30 minutes away depending on traffic," Bob inserted as he began rising from his seat.

I remember that day going to the train station. Shirley and I were both so eager to get on the train back in 1965 after a long hot summer. We had awaiting us our new start in Charleston, South Carolina. We were going to be teachers at Remount Baptist School. The pastor of the church had arranged a church family to take us in until we could rent an apartment. He also arranged to help us buy our first car, with a co-sign on a loan for a new 1966 Volkswagen. The only problem was that it was coming directly from the factory in Germany and we had hopes it would be there waiting for us. It wasn't. Oh, well, we were on our own and going to be able to support ourselves, so we thought, without dependency of living from home to home on the gracefulness of others.

We got to the station about 30 minutes early. Bob helped me get my luggage out of the trunk and walked with us to the station. It was still a station of those days, large, bold, built in the early 1900's. I expressed our appreciation, shook hands and he gave us our tickets. To my surprise he gave us three sets of tickets, Cleveland to Washington D.C., Washington D.C. to Charleston, South Carolina, and Charleston to Orlando, Florida. It looks like we were going to have a brief stay over in Charleston.

The big old Yellow and White engine arrived. I thought we were going on the B&O, but instead we were boarding a C&O train. That was fine with me. I never got over the thrill of seeing those revolving lights come down the tracks as the engine pulled into the station.
Soon the public address announcer came over the system in the loud cavernous room of the station announcing the arrival of our train and the destination and connections it would be taking us. We climbed the steep steps, luggage in hand, walked down the coach corridor, and found our assigned seats. Then the ever so familiar "All Aboard!" from the conductor, the clanging of the steps being lifted into the car and the train whistle giving its toot to foretell of its forward motion. We began to slowly move to our future. What a thrill of exhilaration that

overcame me then and now, my bride by my side and our future in front of us!

From my calculations we had only five days to get back to Florida to catch up with the ship. This was not a part of our regular schedule but it was one exciting trip of miracles. I couldn't help but begin to reflect on what we witnessed the past two days and the miracles God chose to show us. I also couldn't help but reflect on the state of our culture in the future we were about to return to. It was a joy to see what blessings came to the churches in which we had only a very small hand in seeding. But then I looked at my career and just like that summer felt my 43 years in education and ministry were often insignificant. Just eight years down the road from the summer of 1965, in fact on January 22, 1973 to be exact, the U.S. Supreme Court unleased a wrath of murder on this country that scarred it forever. That scourge of death was called Roe vs. Wade Supreme Case, unleashing abortion such that by the time this original journey began some 90 million unborn souls have been brutally taken. It has divided the country politically and has championed women's right to murder their babies without any regard for the rights of the unborn, the very ones Jeremiah proclaimed God's declaration, "Before I formed you in the womb I knew you, before you were born, I set you apart; I appointed you as a prophet to the nations" (Jeremiah 1:5 - NIV).

I truly believe this was the beginning of the end for the United States of America. But, you know, God predicted this back in Genesis. **Genesis 3:16** to the woman He said, "I will make your pains in childbearing very severe; with painful labor **you** will give birth to children. Your desire will be for your husband, and he **will** rule over **you**." When Adam and Eve partook of the one tree God forbade them to eat, they unleashed a consequence upon all mankind. When God said "Your desire will be for your husband, and he will rule over you," He was saying that, to this point you were partners in what I created for you, but now, as woman, you have stolen that partnership and will from hence forth seek to compete with him and that conflict will be such that it will always deny the partnership I once gave you. It is what I would call the curse of the Tree of Knowledge at the Garden of Eden. However, the blessing of the Tree at Calvary is that the cross would restore that partnership in Christ. But we are seeing the consequence of evil souls as they now seek to serve self. It leads to the murder of the innocent. And it is leading to the murder of a nation.

Recently in reading my devotions from the book of Psalms, I saw what I perceive as God's response to a nation that needs to gain a new perspective. **First – God's Judgement = Psalm 1:6 "The way of the wicked leads to destruction."** A famous singer once proclaimed that a national plague was a time God gave us to love one another. I concur with that, but at the same time, isn't it time to reflect on our lives? Our nation has been at war with God. I can't help but remember when the Governor of New York lit up the Freedom Tower in New York City to celebrate their new law of late-term abortion. Did that not become the modern version of our Tower of Babel? As shared above, since Roe vs Wade, over 90 million babies have been murdered in the US. Add to that is 90 million couples who took part in that act of murder by having that child and committing it, NOT to life, but to death. That was an additional 180 million people committing those acts of murder. Then you take the 90 million acts of murder by the doctors/nurses who committed the abortion itself, which adds to a total of 360 million acts of murder of the heart and of the act itself. Yet there is NO declaration of an Epidemic. There is NO sense that our country needs to be restored from it by an infusion of trillions of dollars to cure this disease of the heart as it has other national emergencies. I truly believe God will judge us as a nation for this. We must turn our eyes upward and forward.

Second-God's Timing = Psalm 2:12 "…for His wrath can flare up in a moment. Blessed are all who take refuge in him." I've been reminded by all of the great preachers on TV recently that we don't have control of eternity, God does. Steve Gaines, pastor of Bellevue Baptist Church, Memphis, reminded us that Jesus said that His "coming was eminent." What a call to live faithfully, not fearfully. We don't know when Christ will return, but if anything we need to look at our hearts and ask if we are ready to meet Him in the air?

Third-God's Cure = Psalm 6:1-4, a repentan heart by a repentant nation, **"Lord, do not rebuke me in your anger or discipline me in your wrath. Have mercy on me, Lord, for I am faint; heal me, Lord for my bones are in agony. My soul is in deep anguish. Turn, Lord, and deliver me; save me because of your unfailing love."** Unless we understand the cure to this eternal disease (sin) we have as a nation is going to be found on our knees, we will never find the peace we all seek. We must stop the war against God, and repent.

Fourth-God's Promise = Psalm 6:9 "The Lord has heard my cry for mercy; The Lord accepts my prayer." What can you add to that? There will be a healing for the believer. John's Gospel says it as clear as it can be, John 3:16 "For God so loved the World that He gave His only begotten son that whoever believes in Him will not perish but have everlasting life." That's our peace and our cure as a nation!
I don't think, back in 1965, any of us ever imagined such a degradation of the national soul and rejection of God would occur within the next 50-plus years. God Help Us!!!!!

Oh, well, we're on the train heading to Charleston and to who knows what in the miracle dream. I just feel so at peace as we pass by the little towns and through the country side. However, given it is winter, night has fallen upon us and all we're seeing are the city lights as we pass the small towns. I've often wondered what thoughts pass through the minds of those waiting in their cars as we pass them. I know my thoughts have often been a wish to be on that train taking me somewhere. Trains always seem to offer me a future. I visualized the next destination as a place of hope and destiny. Such as it was, back in 1965 when we got on the train in Cleveland, the one we're experiencing though some miracle now. To put this in real life perspective, this side trip on our "Cruise of Miracles" started back on November 11, when we left the ship and decided to go into Denali. We then ended up with all the miracles there on the mountain, flying then to Florida and now this train trip. We are to end this by rejoining the ship on November 26. Thus, we have only three days left before rejoining the ship. I'm not sure, as time has gone so quickly. Let me pull my ticket out and check our itinerary.

"Arrive Washington *NOV. 20*, arrive Charleston, SC *NOV. 21, arrive Orlando, Fl. NOV. 25.*" That's what's posted on our tickets. Hum, that means we have at least a three-day layover in Charleston. I wonder why? We're just in our 20's if we keep these same transformed bodies given us in this miracle.

The C&O continued to travel on through the night heading toward D.C. I loved the feel of the sway of the train as it rolled down the tracks and every so often hearing the train whistle as it crossed intersections and came into stations. We were scheduled to arrive in D.C. around 10:00 am. With a transfer to the Atlantic Coastline departing around 7:30 pm and arriving in Charleston around 4:30 am the next morning. My, what are we going to do in Charleston at 4:30 in the morning? I fell off to sleep. Neither Shirley nor I were hungry. Our day with Bob was full. Being in the car that long with all the events and surprises he had awaiting us rather exhausted us. The comfort of the train helped create a natural ease into sleep. I must admit I went into a deep sleep. I can't say I dreamed as this entire trip is a dream. I was a bit anxious about what awaited us the next morning.

"Excuse me," it was Shirley. She had awakened before me and had gone to the ladies' room to freshen up. She was returning and needed to get past me to her seat by the window. I don't know how she got past me without awakening me when she left. Yep, she was still the 21-year-old beauty, my bride. I went to the men's room, shaved and freshened up. When I returned to our seats, I realized we were about an hour-and-half outside of Washington.

"Let's go and get some breakfast in the Diner Car," I suggested. I do remember I always loved the Texas sized French Toast. We headed to the Diner only to find they were rather full, but had two seats left. The waiter indicated the Diner would be closing in 30 minutes. That only gave us a short time to order and eat. So I had to ask if they had any French toast ready or could get it ready. He checked and assured us they could. To our delight we got our French toast and coffee. By 9:00 am they closed the dining room down to new customers, but let those of us still eating to remain until we finished our meal. It was wonderful! Around 9:15 am, we headed back to our seats.

Shortly the sights of Washington's suburbs came into view and the number of tracks grew. All of the other trains traveling into D.C. both local and long distance were filling the tracks beside us.

"Washington, D.C. in five minutes. All will de-board the train at that point. Please secure your luggage. You will exit at the rear of the car," the conductor announced as he walked through the car picking up the ticket stubs he left on the top of our seat. It was exciting as the train slowed and we passed all the other trains, different colors, different names, some diesel, and some electric, different designs, as we began to pull into the station. Soon the concrete platform with metal shed covering it, was beside us. Slower, slower and soon we were at a complete stop. Hearing the conductor open the door, lowering the steps, I got our small luggage from the overhead, with our large suitcase in the back of the car to be picked up as we left the car. I wasn't ready for this part of the trip to be over. But here we were with about nine hours to waste. Shirley went ahead of me and soon we came to the door, the conductor and porter stood on the platform to take our luggage as I handed it to them and we stepped down off the train.

Once on the platform, we looked to see the escalator, quite a bit down from the platform, to take us up to the main terminal in Union Station. In 1965 luggage didn't have wheels. They hadn't been invented yet. It was all carried by handle. We had three cases, two small and one large. I let Shirley carry one small one and her purse while I carried the larger one and the other small one.

"We've got to find a locker to put these in because I can't lug these around all day." Sure enough there were lockers in the main terminal with coin slots. Upon arrival into the main terminal, Union Station was as it had always been, simply a train station. In later years it had become a shopping mall with restaurants, stores, a theater and metro station. In 1965 it was a huge waiting room with ticket booths and a few restaurants in this large beautiful early 19th Century cathedral sized building. We had to make a choice, use the day to wait or use it to see D.C. It was most unusual for us to venture out into the unknown back in 1965. This time, in living this miracle, we had the funds and the youth to want to see D.C., as we once did with my parents back in 1965. We put our luggage into the lockers. I wanted to see the Capitol and the White House. We first checked bus schedules, which were available at the main entrance. We found that for 25 cents each we could ride the bus to the Capitol. To our delight we found ourselves able to get to both locations. In 1965 you could get a free tour if willing to wait for an hour or so. There were street vendors to buy a quick lunch and we made a day of it.

But I must share that one incident that surprised us. As we walked to the White House we noticed anti-war protesters. This was the time our country was divided over the Vietnam War. With my dad an Army Chaplain, I always resented the treatment our soldiers received back home. They served their country. But I truly believe our divide over Vietnam was indeed the prelude to the cultural divide that was about to define the country for the foreseeable future. A divide that would slowly but assuredly turn our eyes from God. Indeed, over the next 50-plus years, America has taken a downward spiral morally and spiritually. We've lost our way and as shown in earlier comments, I can't help but believe our time as a nation is in its twilight years. None-the-less we must live faithfully. However, in 1965 we still lived with Hope. President Johnson had been thrust into leadership just two years earlier by the tragic assassination of President Kennedy.

Shirley and I came upon the gates of the White House just as they were organizing the next tour. It was going on 3:00 pm and the tour was to begin in 30 minutes. We were rather excited. We got in line. Finally, we were allowed through the gates, into the public foyer and a guide took us on into the areas for public viewing. I so wanted to see the Oval Office, but I understood the public wouldn't be allowed to go there. We got to see several of the rooms, all named by colors and told their history. I was impressed, but I wanted to see the Oval Office! I was hoping against hope it would happen.

Finally, it just came out. "Mam, can we see the Oval Office." "No, she replied, that is off limits. I believe the President is in today and thus for sure he will be needing it." With a smile we continued to step forward when out of the shadow of my eye a door opened and to our delight it was President Johnson, walking briskly with several men surrounding him.

"Sir," I said softly to him, "Can we see your office?" He stopped, looked a bit stunned. Came over to me. I continued.

"Sir, my wife and I recently married and we're traveling to a new home and jobs as school teachers in South Carolina. We appreciate you and would love to see your office."

"Sure, son. You bring your sweet wife along." He led Shirley and me to the Oval Office and spent some time sharing with us the mementos he had on his desk. I shared that my mom was born and raised in Ennis, Texas. He seemed thrilled he had another Texan in the room.

"Sir, my dad is an Army Chaplain and I want you to know we support you."

"Young man, I appreciate that more than you can imagine. What's your dad's name?"

"Sir, he's Chaplain Charles Meyer, now serving in France."

"We're proud of your Father's service," the President responded. With that he led us both out of the Oval Office and took us back to where we met him and he continued on his way. I couldn't believe the President gave us a personal office visit, but most importantly I couldn't believe I had the courage to encourage him.

God has a way of putting men in the right spot at the right time! I recall that in 1967, or so, Dad was sent to Belgium to become Post Chaplain after France asked the Americans to leave France. Dad was still only a Captain due to an efficiency evaluation by a colonel several years earlier that caused him to be passed over for promotion, but at the same time being assigned positions normally held by men of higher rank. Finally, the General asked why Dad wasn't Major and Dad told him the situation, which the General found unfair to my mad. The General flew to the Pentagon and brought back Dad's promotion to Major. Again, God put the right man in the right spot at the right time. God has a way of doing that.

I have no idea if my words had any real meaning to the President but I can only hope by a miracle, any encouraging word we give reaches the heart of the one to whom we give it.

Looking at our watches, we realized time had passed and we needed to get back to Union Station. Our train, the Atlantic Coastline, was departing at 7:30 pm and arriving in Charleston around 5:00 am. Given the Atlantic Coastline was coming out of New York, I figured they'd have the Diner Car still open, so we decided to have dinner on the train. Might be a little expensive, but for some reason we had the money this time. We got back to the station around 5:15, leaving us about two hours before boarding the train. Unfortunately by 1965 the station was in disrepair as railway traffic was in steep decline. As a result of the Redevelopment Act of 1981, Union Station was closed and restored. It was reopened in 1988 as an active Amtrak, intercity rail service with shopping mall, food courts and other restaurant facilities. But in 1965 it was just an old decaying architecture of decay with long wooden station benches of the early 1900's. At best they had a few snack bars with some sandwiches, soft drinks and chips and maybe an old greasy spoon off to the side of the Grand Hall. It smelled of the railroad stations of the '50's. None-the-less, for rail fans like myself, it still had the romance of calling one to the joy of train travel. We got our luggage out of the lockers, checked our tickets and went by the ticket window to see from what track our train would be leaving. Then we found a place on one of those benches and just people-watched as we waited for the call to our train.

We sat there pondering what two old people, looking like 21-year-olds, would be doing in Charleston the next four days, an awful long time in one stop. Afterall we only lived in Charleston our first year out of college. It was our first year of marriage. We had just left Carson-

Newman, were hired to be teachers at Remount Baptist School. We dreamed of this all summer long. Our original trip from Cleveland took us to our new beginnings as husband and wife. Now here we were experiencing it all over again. I've often asked myself if I knew what my future held, would I change anything. Well, guess what? I get to answer that question as I'm 75 years old, but through some miracle I'm living and looking at life as if I were as a 21-year-old. How many people get to do that? I've often compared life to a great train journey that makes many stops along the way. You get off, make your mark, or your mistakes, meet people, then get back on and go to the next station. All of it is a trip to your final destination, Home!

As I look at my life, I wonder which stops I made that I wish I had simply stayed on the train, or once off rather wished I had waited for another train? There was no mistake about it, I had to get on the final train taking me Home. But I had choices along the way. Oh, I could write about some of the magnificent accomplishments I thought I achieved. But, you know, many of those achievements often were followed by deep pits of sorrow due to misfortunes that entered our lives, either by my own failings, or those of circumstances that surrounded us. My life was neither a charted straight line going in a specific direction, or always upward nor downward, but it was one of waves, going up and down. It had its peaks and its valleys. When I measure my life by its success and its misfortunes, I find the blessings always outweigh the misfortunes. I ended my career some might claim successfully and indeed Shirley and I ended it more financially secure than we dreamed it would be along the way. But there's a part of me that keeps asking, "Just what did I give in my career that was significant?"

This trip has taught me that I may never know how my life impacted others, either for the positive, or, God forbid, for the negative. There were things said and done, some noticed and some unnoticed, that may have had impacts I could never imagine. I do know that God took my failings and first forgave them and, in all cases, used them to teach me and move me on to the next challenge and opportunity. Even in my deepest valleys, He was with me and got us, Shirley and me, out of them. He miraculously opened doors for me to advance in my education, advance in my career, reach lives for him, save us physically from deadly diseases and serious car accidents and kept me out of war. I've had a full life and although I don't necessarily want to die, I am ready for Heaven. I want to see Mom and Dad again. I want to leave this world that is so evil it is bent on self-destruction. I just fear leaving Shirley behind or her leaving me behind. She has been perhaps God's greatest gift to me, besides the Cross.

Well, I've contemplated to the point of passing so much time that our train is being called. Normally, when I hear the train called, I have an air of exhilaration overcome me. Just getting on the train going somewhere, anywhere, is a sense of freedom. But on this day in 1965 we were so eager to see where our home would be for the next year. We did not yet know where we'd live or if our new car had arrived, but that was part of the adventure. School was behind us. We were married. Our future was ahead of us. It was kind of strange as we were reliving this in our young 1965 bodies but had already lived our future. We knew what was ahead, yet the excitement was no less real as though we had choices facing us. That feeling was a miracle in and of itself. However, as a 73-year-old in real life, there are moments I still squeeze my bride's cheeks and see her yet as my 21-year-old.

Luggage in hand, moving down the escalator to the train, I noted that although train travel had declined, Union Station still was bustling with passengers, rushing to their various trains. This was not only a long-distance station, but still an intercity station. However, you could tell the trains themselves were aged and not quite as well-maintained as they once were. It was obvious the railways were wanting to eliminate the burden of passenger service, given so many were not making money. But as we walked to our car, it was still delightful to see our conductor in his black suit, golden buttons, conductor cap assigning us seats and helping us up the steps into our car. The smell of the car is still unique and never goes away from one's memory. It is uniquely railroad. We found our seats, giving Shirley the window seat as I always did, and awaiting to hear the wonderful sound I've loved through the years, as almost a hymn, "All Aboard," followed by the engineer's tooting the whistle and that signals the first roll of the train down the tracks.

We weren't on the train long before we asked if dinner was still being served. As it turned out, they made the main switch over from electric to diesel engine in Washington, thus shutting down the electricity on the train during the switch over. It seems the lateness of the layover and the decline of passenger service eliminated the dinner service for the evening. However, they did have a Club Car which offered sandwiches and snacks. Once the train was on the roll and we were heading out of the tunnels of D.C., we gave our tickets to the conductor. Finally, the conductor made the announcement the Club Car was open. It was going on 8:00 pm and we were famished. We apparently weren't the only hungry people. In 1965 the Club Car was different than modern day Club Cars. There were individual seats, rather bench seats surrounding a table. But the Food was about the same, as well as the prices. We were able to buy a couple of sandwiches, cokes, a bag of chips and a couple of candy bars. Not very nourishing, but it would fill two hungry stomachs. We sat in two overlarge chairs with two small individual round tables in front of us. The Club Car was also the smoking car. Keep in mind, smoking in 1965 was allowed everywhere. However, in the coach car, people generally sat in the rear of the car if they wanted to smoke. We ate our sandwiches but pretty much wanted to get back to our seats, the smoke was getting to us. I had forgotten the old days of railroading. It had its good and bad moments.

As we got back in our seats we simply reclined back, pulling our foot rests up. Leaving Washington, we saw the lights behind us and moved on into the darkness of night. With our train arriving 5:00 am, we knew the evening would be short. It wouldn't be long before the conductor would be coming by to awaken us. I wandered if anyone would meet us at the train station.

It, indeed, wasn't long, it seemed as only a few moments, when the Conductor came by, with the car lights still off, he announced.

"Charleston, next stop. Please secure your belongings and prepare to exit to the rear of the car."

Sure enough it was 4:45 am and we had, indeed, slept through the night. I do remember pulling into the Charleston station our first time. But as I recall it was small and not a very busy place. Looking around, there were about three or four others getting off with us. This stop will be the same as the Charleston of 1965. I wondered who would be expecting us. The train slowed and then came to a stop. We had arrived.

Stepping off the train, we looked around and to our surprise there was no one. The other passengers had been greeted by their families and were proceeding to their cars. But we again looked rather puzzled. Had we read our itinerary wrong? We supposed to have at least three days here. This is rather awkward. The train pulled out and even in 1965, being in the part of town of the train depot during a darkness, be it night or early morning, is a bit eerie. The depot was closing as it was apparent no other trains, north or south, are due for a while. It was a bit chilly; this is November. The station master came out.

"You folks waiting one someone."

"Well, we don't know. We're guests of a cruise line who made plans for us to visit Charleston before returning to port in three days. Unfortunately, they didn't tell us if someone would be by to pick us up."

"Well, I'll be here a few more moments. I can get you a cab to take you some place, if need be."

"Thanks, that's very kind. We'll give it few more moments and see if anyone comes by."

This is strange. The cruise lines have never left us in this type of a fix before. They've always been first rate. Where would we go if we wanted too? This is 1965, we don't know what motels are available, who to call. Mind you we were just two young marrieds new to town in 1965, knowing only the pastor who hired us and no one else. At 5:00 am, in fact a little past, who would be awake?   Where can we go?

We continued to sit. Soon the Station Master came out again.

"Young Folks, I am sorry, but I've got to lock up." With that he secured the building and headed to his car at the end of the station. After he pulled out, I noticed what seems like a little new mint green VW Beetle in the lot next to his. It was hidden from view by the Station Master's car. At first, I just sat there. No one was left. Why the one car? I nudged Shirley and pointed to the car. We both were unsure what to do. It was getting colder. Finally, I said, "Let's go look over that car."

I don't know why, but we didn't have anything else to do. There was an outside phone booth but who would we call. I went to the car, and stuck just below the windshield wiper on the driver's side was a brown envelope addressed, **"Cal and Shirley Meyer."**

We opened the envelope and in it there was a card that read:

"Welcome to Charleston. Glad you finally found the car. We knew you would. Miracles do happen. Key is in the glove compartment along with a letter. Carlos"

What a delight and relief. Now what? Well, we got into the car. It smelled just like our little new mint green, actually called "Bahama

Blue," 1965 VW Beatle. But I haven't driven stick shift in so long. I'm not sure I can do it. Putting our luggage in the front luggage compartment, remembering the motor is in the back, we also put some of the luggage in the rear seat. We started up the little air-cooled engine and then looked at each other. "Where are we going?" I asked.

The car had a full tank of gas and to my delight there was an Eastern US Map and South Carolina Map. In 1965 the interstates were not finished. I know I-40 between North Carolina and Tennessee wasn't. We tried in 1968 when traveling with our friends the Lees from their home in Louisville to visit our parents in South Carolina and Florida respectively. That was the time we had our cat Missy with us and in the middle of the mountains she was whining and letting us know she wasn't happy. We unfortunately did not have her in a carrier. Our friend Jan suggested we put some petroleum jelly on Missy's nose as she had heard it would calm her down by her attempting to lick it off. Shirley searched her purse. It was midnight, we're on a non-interstate, two-lane mountainous road somewhere between Tennessee and North Carolina and Shirley can't see what she reaching for her in her purse. She pulls out what she believes is the petroleum jelly, spreads a little on Missy's nose, only to find a rather subdued cat become a wild mountain lion, climbing, screaming, all over my head, shoulders, jumping over the seats and none of us knowing what to do, except drive off the road and let the wild thing loose. Jan, Tom and Shirley could protect themselves with their sweaters, but I was raw meat in the claws of a cat gone wild, while trying to drive a car down a mountain. Finally, finding a space in the crawl space of the back windows, Missy went back there, spitting and hissing. We left her alone!

We said, "SHIRLEY, what did you put on that cat?" She responded excitedly, "I don't know!"

She then looked in the top of her purse to find the Mentholatum she had just spread on Missy's nose. We all said nothing, just felt glad we were still alive. The cat finally went to sleep, the nightmare was over.

We thought about several potentials of where we might want to go. But this is November and Thanksgiving is just around the corner. In fact, according to the 1965 calendar, November 25 is Thanksgiving, the very day we are to be back in Florida. I wonder why our scheduled return is on Thanksgiving. Today being Monday, we have three days to fulfill whatever reason we stopped here. However, we're one day off the 2016 calendar as the 25th is Friday, the day we are to arrive in Florida. I wonder if that is significant.

You know one of the memories I've missed all along our later married lives was the family celebration with my Mom and Dad back in the '70's after they returned from Dad's last military deployment to Germany. Ten years after we were married, we found ourselves living in Florida, with Mom and Dad having just returned from being stationed in Frankfurt, Germany as a Chaplain at the Army Hospital. Dad miraculously survived a tumor on his prostate that almost took his life in 1970, thinking it would not only end his life, but certainly his military career. Instead, he recovered, but with the limitation of needing to be on hemodialysis and with the medical prediction his life would end within seven years. Typically, the Army would dismiss a person of such poor health but instead, through God's Grace, they gave him his last three years to allow him to complete his 20 years on active duty and be granted full retirement. To that end, they bought a home in Columbia, South Carolina, and retired there. In 1975, I decided I wanted to spend the last few years near my dad and, thus, made the decision to resign my teaching position in Florida, my bivocational church and accept a teaching position in Columbia. Those last few years with my dad were important to us. At Thanksgiving and Christmas time, the entire family gathered to spend the day with them. I'll never forget those days. At Thanksgiving, it was arrive in plenty of time to watch the Macy's Thanksgiving Day Parade with Dad in their sunroom. Mom always spent the morning getting the meal ready and I loved her Pineapple Spiced Tea, which we enjoyed prior to the afternoon meal. About the 1:00 p.m. the family would arrive, my brother Dan, his fiancé, Jan, and my brother Tom and his family. Shortly after they arrived, we'd sit down for dinner. And what a dinner it was!

Mom pretty much had the turkey carved, but gave Dad the honorary privilege of cutting a slice to pretend it was the first slice. To accompany it was her chilled shrimp cocktail, then her very moist dressing, sweet potato soufflé, cranberry sauce, green bean casserole, brown gravy, dinner rolls, and either potato salad or mashed potatoes. For dessert the choice of the traditional pumpkin or pecan pie topped with whipped cream. Needless to say, we were stuffed. But it was always so good to be there with the entire family.

In the afternoon, we take the kids and play a game of horse basketball on Mom's patio, followed with the men watching the late afternoon football game and the ladies finishing the dishes and retiring to the living room to discuss Christmas. Later in the evening, Tom's family would leave a bit early as they had traveled from out of town but the rest of us played a game of "21," or "Uno," with my aim to beat Dad. Somehow the family piled up on me and the game became "Beat Cal." About 9:30 p.m. with the kids falling asleep in their chairs or the floor, we'd head home, leaving with the sweet memories of the day knowing we'd repeat it in just a few weeks at Christmas. That became tradition long after Dad died and until Mom had her disastrous stroke which ultimately brought it all to an end. Dad, sadly, did die, as forewarned in 1977, from complications leading from the impact of the hemodialysis on his body.

Well, back to reality, I mean the reality of the moment, as much as you can call this reality. Here we sit in a new 1966 VW not knowing where to go, looking like two newlyweds in our 20's having just gotten off the train in Charleston, South Carolina, in 1965. Our reality is that we are in our 70's having been on a cruise, but by some miracle returned us to the bodies and time of 1965. In 1965 my parents were stationed in Europe, Shirley's parents lived in Florida, our children were not yet born, I had just completed my Bachelor's Degree at Carson-Newman and we were about to start our first job as teachers at Remount Baptist School. We were as confused as we've ever been. Here we sat early Monday morning, the train left us here and we had nowhere to go, but we had through Thursday to experience something. Why has the cruise line planned this part of the trip? Something was going to happen, but what?

It is Thanksgiving Week. School will be open through Wednesday at least that is the way most schools work, then close for Thanksgiving and the weekend. If I recall, we made the trip to Auburndale to spend Thanksgiving with Shirley's Mom and had Thanksgiving dinner at Shirley's sister house, in 1965. But we will be in Charleston this Thanksgiving, not Auburndale, that's how the cruise line planned it. Why?

I do know that one of our greatest regret is that we never had the privilege of hosting any great family gathering at our home. When Mom and Dad lived, it was Thanksgiving and Christmas at Mom's home. But as shared, that became such a wonderful memory we wouldn't have wanted to give that up. Later, after Shirley's dad passed, we often made it a point to spend some of our Christmas time to visit Granny, the name we called Shirley's mom, in Florida. Regretfully, that was often a trip the family sort of resented. Granny lived in a rundown 1920ish home in a rundown part of Lakeland. Florida, even in December, is unseasonable warm and doesn't seem like Christmas. We knew that once Granny died, we'd regret those feelings and indeed we did. We later cherished the moments we had at Christmas with Granny, even in that small home in hot Florida. But given Granny's home couldn't facilitate a meal for all, Dorothy, Shirley's sister, would host the family. It was not just our family, but the entire family, including Shirley's brother and his large family. Jim, Dorothy's husband, generally grilled, and all the ladies brought dishes, including Shirley and Granny. These were the days that Dorothy and Shirley were truly sisters, before Dorothy converted to being a Jehovah

Witness and family relationships were broken. Oh, if we could have one more moment as a family with them and host a meal!

Well, it is clear we're still in the midst of traveling, but where? I feel it's time we need to find our way back home. Here we are early Monday morning in Charleston, sitting in our new car, having no clue where to go, or for that matter, where is home?

Chapter 14: Thanksgiving

Shirley and I looked at each other and felt somewhat apprehensive as what to do. I took the car key with the intent to putting it in the ignition but not really knowing where we might go but then suddenly realized that as I grabbed the key, there were two keys. It was the key to the car and another was a house key. However, I had no clue to what the key might open. The only house we knew was the apartment we rented when we lived in Charleston in 1965. I asked Shirley to open the glove compartment to see if there were any other instructions. She found the sales papers to the car. On it was "Calvin F. and Shirley M. Meyer, 134 Remount Lane Road, Apt. A, North Charleston, South Carolina." That was our apartment. Well, it seems we have the key for a purpose but I no longer remember the way. Keep in mind this was right at 50 years ago since we actually lived in North Charleston. However, we decided to pull out of the train station and perhaps we might find a gas station with a city map. Surely the cruise line wouldn't leave us this empty handed. In 1965, gas station still had free maps. Sure enough just down the block from the station was a Diner that was opening for breakfast. We were hungry and decided to try it, by now it was nearing 6:30 am anyway.

We drove in, we were the first customers, and the coffee was fresh.

"Good Morning," came a welcoming word from the waitress.

"Good Morning, we just got off the train and are new here. You wouldn't be able to tell me how to find a city map." Carlos had already left us a South Carolina Map and Eastern U.S. Map.

"Yeah, just around the corner is a Gulf station, he probably has one, but he doesn't open until 7:00 a.m. However, let me see if I have a loose one lying around. What are you looking for?"

"We're looking for Remount Lane near Remount Baptist Church."

"Remount Road is on the Northside of Charleston. You do need a map."

We went ahead and ordered a typical breakfast of eggs, toast and bacon. The sun began to come up. I know I didn't want to find it in the dark. It was so good to experience good old South Carolinian hospitality. After eating, our waitress came with our ticket.

"Oh, I found a city map. It's not the newest, but it should get you there."

I opened it and asked the waitress if she could point where on the map we were now located and thus I'd find my way to Remount Lane. After looking over the map, it didn't seem that complex. We weren't far from the main highway leading out of town and once heading west we had a few turns to our right and we'd be right in the community.

Driving our new VW seemed awkward. I still hadn't quite conquered the stick shift. That was always my bane through the years and thank goodness for automatic transmission. But I do recall the utter joy of getting our new long-awaited little Bahama Blue VW. It still had its new car smell. It was our first car and thus something really special. We made our way to Remount Lane and then to our delight there was our apartment, 134, which we recognized this many years later. It was a small brick, one floor apartment, connected to a row of apartments. A simple one bedroom, living room apartment, but it was our first home in marriage. Ours was the first apartment, thus Apartment A. Our parking slot was the very first one. I remember parking in it as we came home from our teaching at Remount Baptist School. Our mailbox was by the street and still has the numbers 134, just as it did in 1965. Oh, this is 1965, we've been transported in time.

Just for fun, not really expecting anything, I suggested to Shirley that she go and check the mail. She opened the box and to our delight and complete surprise was a letter from Dorothy. Opening it, it read:

Dear Shirley:

> Jim and I have talked about it and have been in contact with Roy and Sue. We all accept your invitation to meet you at Myrtle Beach for Thanksgiving. We so appreciate you renting a cabin large enough to entertain the entire family. Granny will be riding with us. We plan on arriving sometime between 3:00 pm and 7:00 pm Wednesday, November 23. We have the address. Jim and Roy have indicated they are sure they can find it. If I'm correct, it is just outside the Myrtle Beach Air Force Base. We are surprised you were able to find it during the holidays, but we are so looking forward to being with you.
>
> **See you Wednesday!**
>
> **Love,**
> **Dorothy**

Shirley screamed with excitement and then it struck us. We don't even know where this cabin is, or how the reservations were made. What about the food and is this cabin going to fit 13 of us? There is no way Shirley will be able to prepare a Thanksgiving meal for this many in the time we have. Not only that, we don't have time to buy the food, much less drive to Myrtle Beach and prepare it. I mean we were overcome with fear and stress, lots of stress! All of this feeling and we haven't even opened the front door of the house.

As I recall the Air Force Base was still in operation in 1965, and in fact didn't close until 1993. I remember well the few times in the 50's our family, Mom and Dad, Dan, Tom, and I spent at the Air Force Base in guest housing during a Friday/Saturday weekend or early summer before Dad was sent to Korea. At that time Dad was stationed at Fort Jackson in Columbia, SC. But with Mom and Dad in New York in 1965, there is no way they can reserve one for us as they can't be there to check us in. I'm just surprised there is another cabin available just off the base and near the beach. The military guest housing often had to be reserved months in advance, particularly during holidays. I'm sure a small miracle had to happen for this particular cabin to be available. Not only that, who's paying for all of this? In 1965 we were two young newlyweds who earned a whopping $3,200 annually between us teaching school. We certainly didn't have the money then as we had just come off the summer mission field entirely broke, except for the small salary earned as missionaries during the summer. That was needed to finish covering our wedding debts and put a very small down payment on our new VW. Our minds were ablaze with downright anguish on just how this was all going to happen.

We moved to the door of the apartment and opened it. It was just as it was in 1965, a very small living room with a couch, a small kitchen across from it and a red Formica eating table on metal legs for two. Walking past the living room was our bedroom with bathroom to the right. This was our home and after living in dorm rooms for the past four years, it was a delight. It was ours, the home of Mr. and Mrs. Meyer. But there was no way we were going to fix a Thanksgiving meal for 13 in that small kitchen and transport it to Myrtle Beach.

After walking through the apartment, seeing our old clothes and remembering our time there, we thought of one of our sinful pitfalls, Cherry 'O Cream Cheese Pie. It was like a cheese cake but with the creaminess of a pie, topped with a can of cherries and cherry sauce on top. It was one of Shirley's first mastery of cooking as a wife. She learned to fix it well. She got the recipe from Doris Daniels, our good married friends at college. We loved it and Shirley fixed it as often as she could. We found that in the first few months we really began to put on the pounds! But back to our major issue, Thanksgiving.

Suddenly, I noticed a large brown envelope sitting on the counter with "TO: CAL AND SHIRLEY MEYER" written across the center. We opened it, out fell some keys. Inside was a letter from Carlos, from the cruise lines. Also included was a sheet with Room Reservations for Cabin #7 on Majestic Cove Road, Myrtle Beach, South Carolina, and a Map directing us to the cabin. Our fears began to subside. We knew something extraordinary had taken place. It was still Monday and we had tomorrow, Tuesday, to figure things out before leaving for Myrtle Beach on Wednesday. But wait a moment, school is still in session. Shirley and I are teachers! We have only 30 minutes to get to campus. But I had to read the letter from Carlos.

Dear Mr. and Mrs. Meyer:

I am confident by now you feel rather perplexed having received the letter from Dorothy Rewis and being notified the family would be meeting you in Myrtle Beach. Let me rest your minds. All of this has been taken care by your brothers and sisters in Christ from the Dove Cruise Line. It is our further gift to you. Noting the family will arrive Wednesday afternoon, the care takers of the cabin have set up the various rooms for the family. This cabin has four bedrooms and three baths. There is a bedroom for the two of you, Mr. and Mrs. Rewis, and one for Mr. and Mrs. Meadows. There is also roll out beds for the smaller children to be in the room with their parents and a fourth bunk room for the older children. You will see it when you arrive. On Thanksgiving morning, a catering crew will arrive around 9:00 am to serve all of you a small breakfast and then around 1:00 pm, the same catering crew will provide the full Thanksgiving meal. We simply want this to be a wonderful family Thanksgiving. I'm sure later in the afternoon you will want to visit the beach and Myrtle Beach. The forecast seems to suggest it will be cool.

Finally, I need to remind you that you have a train to catch around 5:30 a.m. Friday morning in Charleston to take you on to Florida. Enclosed are your updated train tickets. You will need to leave the cabin around 3:00 am. Just leave the car and keys in the parking spot where you found it. The family has been notified of your early departure but assured they can stay in the cabin until check out time, noon on Friday. Don't worry about clean up as the care takers have taken that responsibility.

Do have a blessed time.

See you on the MH MKaddesh.
Carlos

We didn't have time to soak it all in. All I knew is that if we are the Cal and Shirley Meyer of 1965 we had to get to school as this is the students' last two days before Thanksgiving holidays. I remember that, typically, students either went to noon on Wednesday or the entire day. If they got out at noon, we'd have just enough time to drive to Myrtle Beach before the family arrived.

This has already been a full morning. Shirley reminded me we were still in our traveling clothes and needed to get into our teaching clothes. In 1965 that meant Shirley needed to get into a dress and I, a coat and tie. I so remember that in those days we weren't at the level of casual as teachers are in the decade of 2010. Keeping in mind, Shirley and I are somewhat miraculously transformed into our 1965 bodies. As I reminded Shirley, as we reached our 70's, those were the days we were "Young and Beautiful." Those days do pass by quickly! After a change of clothes, we rushed to the car and headed toward Remount Baptist School. I must admit the years have long ago caused me to forget the way. But being in a hurry I had to count on finding the church soon. If I recalled it wasn't far. If we stayed on Remount Lane, it ran into Remount Road and once there the church was about a block or two to our right. I do remember the steeple on the church, which was in front of the school. My class was in an old WWII barracks building left on the site before the church was built. The church kept it and it became one of the classroom buildings for the school. My seventh-grade class was on 2nd floor. But what about lessons, I didn't have anything prepared. Shirley taught her first grade class in a Sunday School classroom in the church building. You know through the years I've had wonderful memories of my one year at Remount Baptist School.

I remember Leroy, my problem child, but one I loved dearly and he became my star student. In those days you could still paddle students if they misbehaved. Such was the case with Leroy. Leroy was always finding ways to test the rules, tease the girls and create mischief. Even though Grade 7, there was a childish innocence not experienced in later years as students were infected by a culture that stole that innocence. I could warn Leroy and warn him. It mattered not where I drew the line, he always enjoyed crossing it. That at times resulted in not only a denial of privileges but when it involved other students in a way I considered that became hurtful, I paddled. However, I always noticed a remorse in Leroy and an innocence that showed he was teachable and moldable. At the end of the year after we decided to go to Seminary and had turned in my resignation, Leroy's parents had Shirley and me over for dinner. Leroy was a military "brat" as we sometimes called them. You see I was one, with my dad, a Chaplain in the army. I understood it meant my dad would be in the field much of the time and it was my mom who became both Mom and Dad. Leroy craved a father's love, leadership and companionship over him. I came to understand that in many ways Leroy was acting out to get my attention and become his father figure in the absence of his dad. That night while at their home, I shall never forget Leroy's mom informed me that I was Leroy's favorite teacher. That touched me so deeply and all through the years I've remembered and cherished that moment.

Miraculously my instincts took me right to the church. It was going on 8:00 am. Typically, we'd arrive a bit earlier as class began at 8:00 am. We walked to our classrooms and to our surprise it was as familiar as it had been in 1965. We walked into our rooms and Shirley conveyed that it was as though we belonged. We followed our typical day of taking roll, glancing over our lesson plans and delving right into our lessons. It was all very normal as though we hadn't missed a beat. That, in itself, was yet another miracle. It was as though time indeed had not changed for us and to our delight our lessons came to mind with our materials all prepared. We spent the day loving and again cherishing these wonderful kids, our first responsibilities as newlyweds. We appreciated it so much more. Seeing Mr. Freund our principal and the staff was unusual as we knew Mr. Freund died a few years after we left with a brain hemorrhage. It was again wonderful to work with Ms. Kneece, Tommy and Willie Beaty and Dr. Russell, our pastor. Oh, I miss those days, my days of youth and the sense of significance I felt being a teacher. The day ended as per normal.

Shirley and I got into our little VW and headed home, rather our apartment. We had had a very full day from arriving on the train so early in the morning to receiving the letters from Dorothy and Carlos, to teaching school. I didn't realize you could cram so much into one day. We were exhausted. We yet had Tuesday to teach again, as well as Wednesday morning. Then Wednesday afternoon we would head to Myrtle Beach to be with the family. You know we hadn't given much thought to the fact this was November and we had been teaching at Remount Baptist School since September. A lot had happened in reality, back in 1965. As I recall we had made a trip to Florida shortly after we arrived to go and pick up the rest of our belongings at Shirley's home. When we originally arrived, we didn't have a car and several of the church members loaned us their second car to get around. I do recall a sweet lady by the name of Judy loaned us her Chevrolet Nova to drive to Florida. At the time I-95 was not completed and much of the trip was down Highway 17. So many sweet folks took us in. Rhetta and Herb Gilliam became our dearest friends. They were fellow church members about our age. They, too, loaned us their car until we were able to buy our VW. Herb was quite a character. He'd arrive blowing his trumpet coming down the walkway. He taught at the local Hanahan High School and offered to introduce me to his principal for a position the following year. The salary would have been almost double what we were earning at Remount. But I knew my destiny was Seminary. We made no secret that our time at the school was simply a transition to Seminary.

You know that all came about in a very unexplainable way. I had wanted to go Seminary as soon as Shirley graduated at Carson-Newman. However, I graduated in 1965 and Shirley was in the class of 1966. For whatever reason, Shirley had the impression that upon her marriage she would lose her full scholarship to Carson-Newman. Besides that, there were no jobs in Jefferson County for history teachers and we didn't have a car. Vietnam was in full swing and upon my graduation I became immediately available for the draft if I didn't get a teaching, ministerial or family deferment. I still remember Dr. Russell coming to interview us before my graduation. Most amazing is that Shirley had not finished her degree, she had no teacher education training and was not certified. In 1965 none of those were required to teach in a private school. To that end, Shirley became a First Grade teacher and I a Seventh Grade Teacher. We saw all of that as a miracle from God. I received my military draft deferment and we were off to South Carolina following our summer of missions. What made this even more a clear miracle, is we found Shirley wouldn't have lost her scholarship after all. She had misunderstood, but by that time we were committed to Remount. Not only that, there simply wasn't anything open for me in teaching in the East Tennessee area. Had we stayed until Shirley finished her degree, I most likely would have ended up in Vietnam, as did several of my classmates. But what makes this even more beautiful is that some 22 years later, God opened the door for me to follow a dream of going into college teaching. I was an assistant professor at Hannibal-Lagrange College and while there Shirley was able to finish her degree, the completion of her dream. As a faculty member my family was allowed to pursue their education free. Church friends, a deferment, Shirley's being a teacher, wonderful students, a home, a new car, what more can you say, it was all a miracle of God's grace and leading. He was in control of our lives and you know I'm not sure we realized the magnificence of that miracle until we looked back on it years later.

Tuesday morning came early and again we had school today. It was clearly a bit more normal than yesterday. The kids, as they always have, had their minds on the Thanksgiving holidays. We tried to do things normally but it was a lot of extra time on the playing field letting them use up some of that extra energy. I recall several of my school experiences used this day to have field events. We hadn't gotten that far at Remount. But you know that, as I was enjoying returning to my 1965 days, I couldn't help but recognize that as I grew older so did these kids. When as a 75-year-old, these kids would be 62 years old! I often wondered what became of them. Which ones became teachers, politicians, doctors, nurses, business men and maybe ministers? I guess I'll never know until perhaps in Heaven.

The day went quickly and what a joy just to be a part of these young lives again. Never in my wildest imagination did I dream this was the launching pad of my 43-year career in education moving from teacher, to principal, to professor to dean.

Shirley and I returned to our apartment ever so thankful for these two days and looking forward to tomorrow and Myrtle Beach. On Wednesday morning we got up, repacked our car with anticipating we'd be leaving for Myrtle Beach as quickly as school was closed. Upon arriving at school, we were informed that after an abbreviated time in our classrooms we were to report to the Fellowship Hall of the church to enjoy a special meal prepared by the ladies of the church. I had developed some academic competition games in math, spelling and social studies. We always enjoyed competing boys *vs* girls. You can imagine the girls always seem to win. They took it a bit more seriously. We took a few minutes to plan how we would decorate the room for Christmas and I organized the class into groups, with each a given responsibility. One of the tasks I recall so fondly was putting huge sheets of newsprint paper on the wall, shine a Christmas picture from the overhead and have the students either color or water paint the picture on the paper. Well, we had pretty well used up the morning and it was time to head to Fellowship Hall. There was sufficient room for most of the school. We had about 200 students and staff total. Upon entering we found the ladies had the eating table decorated with all kinds of Thanksgiving/Fall displays. They wisely separated us by grade levels. First through Third, we fed 45 minutes earlier and now it was time for Fourth though Seventh grades. They had two lines and each student walked through a serving line and back to our designated table, which were labeled. The fare was typical Thanksgiving: turkey, dressing, mashed potatoes, green beans and pumpkin pie. You know that never got old. It was just so great to have a meal with my kids and a bit sad, as I knew this was the last time I'd be with them during this miracle event of our returning to this moment in time. I was asked to give the blessing. I had to be careful noting I knew who I was in real time, but at this moment I was but a 22- year-old in my first teaching job. I bowed my head and prayed:

Dear Father:

We have much for which we are thankful. I give thanks for the miracle in our lives and for these precious students. May they grow in your love and peace. May they always find you sweeter each day. I pray as their days pass they will remember this sweet moment that we sit together in thanksgiving. I give you praise allowing me to be here at this time. Now we thank you for this food and

the love of these sweet ladies who prepared it. May hearts live each day in thanksgiving.

We pray this in your Beloved Name.
In Jesus Name we pray.
Amen.

After our meal, it was going on 11:30 am. We made our way back to our classrooms. The students gathered their belongings, and cleaned up our room. I always made it a practice to move desks in order, have the student organize their materials, pick up the trash, put supplies back in their places and then I'd say a closing day's prayer, upon which the closing bell soon rang and the school day was over. This day I had to give each a hug as they left. I couldn't help but have tears in my eyes. It was the end of this miracle with my kids and I knew that in reality my life and career had walked its path and life was not before me, but vastly behind me. I'm not sure I was ready to reenter the real world! There was a thought I'd like to start again, but neither nature nor God's calling would allow that. Besides I'd have an eternity in Heaven to walk with these kids again, but with new bodies and I'm sure a bit older in appearance.

Well, it was a time to head out to Myrtle Beach. We had about a two hour drive up Highway 17. Myrtle Beach is about 100 miles from Charleston. Myrtle Beach was a memorable place for us, as shared, this is where we had a few trips to the Myrtle Beach Air Force Base spending a day or two there before Dad was sent to Korea back in the '50's. Later, upon his retirement, we'd travel to Columbia during the summer, where Mom and Dad retired, from our home in Florida. Almost every time we made the trip Mom planned a day at Myrtle Beach. With Dad's terminal situation of his kidneys failing, he simply enjoyed walking the beach and picking up unique shells. One of my favorite pictures of my dad, one I cherish in our photo albums, is him standing on the beach looking out over the ocean. I look upon that now as a rather prophetic moment. For you see Dad retired from the Army in 1973 with a death sentence. He had an incurable kidney disease that would take his life. He was given only about four years to live. Even though going through dialysis, the pressure on his system would inevitably weaken his heart to the point of death. That's exactly what and when his last days in April 1977 occurred. But in that moment at the beach, I now look on that picture and see my Dad contemplating his future. He knew where He was going and never for a moment did I see anything but peace in his eyes.

Losing my dad at the young age of 57, my memories of him are frozen in time. I never saw him grow old. At the same time, he missed so much of my life--my graduation with my doctorate from the University of South Carolina, the development of our children and being a major part of their lives as their grandfather, my path from being a teacher to a principal to a Dean and my pastoral years, wishing I had him to share his wisdom on how to be a pastor. But I do remember a man of faith, a tearful soul when he saw one of his children go astray and a man who shared such a partnership with his wife to the extent his call into the Chaplaincy became Mom's call. Her support, gave him priority to be free to be a soldier's Chaplain. I cannot go to Myrtle Beach without taking the memories of Mom and Dad with me. Oh, how I wish they were there. However, being we are reliving our lives as a young couple in 1965, I am reminded that Mom and Dad are alive in this miracle event, but they aren't in South Carolina. In 1965 Dad was sent to France. Perhaps by some miracle we could still contact them.

I have so many questions I want to ask them, some of which include:

- Where was Dad's country church pastorate when he was a student at Carson-Newman?
- When and where did Mom and Dad meet?
- Where did we live in Chicago?
- How did we move from Chicago to Dallas?
- How did they take care of me when they were students at Moody Bible Institute?
- Why did Dad choose Dallas Theological Seminary for his theology training?
- What was the story about how Dad got his promotion to Major?
- When did Dad's relatives emigrate from Germany?
- Did Dad have any siblings?

- What was the name of the church in which I was first Baptized?

I'm sure there are a lot more questions, but these would be a good start. After your loved ones depart, you realize they left with so much information never known. As I've progressed in years, I now have a need for answers to questions never asked. Oh, well, that's now in the past.

We made our way toward Myrtle Beach, feeling the need to arrive ahead of the family. We got the directions left by Carlos. It was such a joy to drive our VW again. I'll never forget how thrilled we were to drive it for the first time in 1965. Being Thanksgiving, the roads were full of travelers. So many heading to Myrtle Beach. Shirley and I enjoyed the scenery along the way. I thought about how we would respond to the family. In 1965 family relations were harmonious, particularly given the fact that this was November and they had all attended our wedding in June. By this time in Dorothy's life, she was on a spiritual journey of finding different religions to answer the void within her. Sadly, she had tried the undenominational Church, the Methodist Church, the Baptist Church and in 1965 she became Catholic. Shirley so hoped she could influence her sister to remain Baptist. It was during this time that Jim, Dorothy's husband, became active in church. We never knew what Dorothy was seeking that she couldn't find. Clearly, she didn't take God's Word to heart. It seems she was seeking something in the institution of the church she just never found. She later became Jehovah Witness and that became her religion the rest of her life. Why, we'll never knew. It divided our family and turned Dorothy against Shirley. It changed her, but regretfully not toward the Truth of God's Word. To that end, when we see Dorothy this time, she will be Catholic and although we're living our past, Dorothy's life in real time will be without her knowing her future. If only we could change that future but to do so would be to see Dorothy saved and making Jesus Lord of her life. That, indeed, would be a miracle!

As for Roy, Shirley's brother, he was unsaved. He would find the Lord later in his life. He, at this time, was married to his high school sweetheart but within ten years they would divorce and Roy would marry another. Sue, Roy's wife, had grown up as Church of Christ and that became the family faith with their son Richard becoming a Church of Christ elder. Uniquely, we always maintained a good relationship with both of Roy's families, although knowing Roy and his second wife would suffer immeasurably by the tragic death of their oldest son in a motorcycle accident. This was going to be a delicate time with both families as they will only know us as we were in 1965, but we'll know their futures.

Following Carlos' directions, we began to enter the Myrtle Beach area and while it was as it was in 1965, not nearly as developed as it is of modern day, it was so refreshing to see the ocean, the tall grasses that line the sand dunes and the beautiful blue sky covering it all. I've always enjoyed just getting in the car and traveling. That has been a joy for Shirley and me when we simply got cabin fever or just needed to get fresh air. I've recently come to realize the peace and solitude was that we were experiencing God. To be out in God's creation is a great reminder of His love, His power and His beauty. No matter what calamity, what frustration, what sorrow, just being out in His creation is so soothing and peaceful. One feels like they are in the very presence of God. When I feel overwhelmed by the chaos of our culture, I think of "America the Beautiful from sea to shining sea." That's God, that's what He created by the mere action of saying it. But for the unrighteous eye, all they see are the negatives mankind has made of God's creation and then blame God for it. Thank You, God, we have been given eyes that truly see and in seeing it, seeing the God who created it!

We finally came to our street and turned the corner to the left onto Majestic Covenant Road. There was Cabin #7. It was a beauty. A typical two-story cabin one might find in the mountains or any area surrounded by beauty. Looking at our watches it was going on 4:00 p.m. We weren't sure when the family would arrive but we thought we needed to get settled and see if everything was in place. Opening the front door, we walked into a lovely living room with warm couches, rockers and a loveseat. The front porch also had rocking chairs across the length of the porch. Behind the seating area was a long, large magnificent maple dining table, decorated for Thanksgiving. The kitchen followed and was open to the entire area. Then to the left side was a set of stairs going up to the second floor. Once up the stairs we found a bathroom at the end of the hall on the right. There were three bedrooms, then at the top of the stairs was the master's with its own bathroom. Downstairs, across from the kitchen was a fourth bedroom, next to that was a huge closet and then small bunk room, with another bathroom to the back of the house. We got to counting and realized we'd have 14 of us crowded into that cabin. We decided we'd take the downstairs bedroom, assign Sue and Roy the master bedroom given, they would have their two-year-old Steven with them, then put Jim and Dorothy in the middle upstairs bedroom and Granny in the third bedroom. I hesitated on that but in 1965 she still had a lot of energy and could walk well. Besides that, it would put her next to the bathroom. We opened the closet and found a roll away bed which could be used for either Judy or Kathy, depending on who chose the couch. The bunk room had two bunks for four people. In that room, we put Gary, Eric, Richard and Wesley. What a crowd, but we could fit all of them in. The closet also had a small folding table, noting we weren't going to get everyone around the dining table. This was going to be some holiday!

Taking our suitcases to our bedroom, we went into the kitchen, finding only a few soft drinks and in the cabinet some snack foods but that was it. At first, we felt a bit of panic, then we noticed a note on the refrigeration. It read:

> **Dear Mr. and Mrs. Meyer:**
>
> **When your family arrives and you are ready for dinner, call us at 555-667-3312 and we'll bring the food to you.**
>
> **Sincerely,**
> **Hope**
> **Cabin Caretaker**

Searching for a phone, we found it on the end table next to the love seat. I mean Carlos and the cruise company thought of everything!

Having unpacked and feeling fairly secure our selection of rooms was on mark, we now waited for the family to arrive. It was going on 5:00 pm and shortly thereafter, Dot, Jim, Granny and the family began to arrive. It was clearly rather crowded with all six in one car. But in those days bench seats were the norm. Jim drove a 1965 Chevrolet Caprice. Dot, Jim and Eric sat in the front, with Gary, Kathy and Granny in the back. Right behind them was Roy and his family of six. Roy drove the very car he loaned us on the night of our wedding to go to our motel, before catching the train to our honeymoon site the next day. To our delight we got to see his 1964 Chevrolet Impala, indeed a very special car to us. But now the difficult part. What in the world were we going to talk about? We're coming back from the future, but looking like two newlyweds. In their time we had just gotten married in June and here it is November. How were we going to be able to explain the cabin, our leaving so early Friday morning and how they got invited? How could we avoid sharing anything about their futures? Is there anything we can do, or say, that would influence them to change their course?

As they all arrived, they were smitten by the beauty of the cabin.

"How in the world did you get this?" Jim asked.

"Oh, I'll share it when we all get settled and dinner ordered."

Before they unloaded their cars, I brought them into the cabin and showed them their individual rooms. Of course, the kids were thinking "Beach!" The girls sat on the front porch in the rocking chairs to talk, while Jim, Roy and I carried their luggage to their various rooms. Everyone wanted to see the entire cabin and, thus, all had to visit each other's rooms. The kids were delighted with their bunk room. Kathy and Judy didn't seem to mind they would be in the living room. Indeed, as large as the house was, it was going to be crowded. But, no less so than the days we spent at Dorothy's when she hosted a family gathering.

Once they got settled, I phoned Hope, the Care Taker, to bring dinner, then the three men joined the ladies on the porch.

Once again Jim asked how we were so fortunate to rent the cabin. I had to be honest, but only to the point of the reality of this time frame.

I started my explanation and found all were listening, including Shirley, who had that inquisitive look in her eyes wondering what I was going to say.

"Well, to be honest, we were chosen by the Dove Cruise Line to win a Thanksgiving cruise and that is the reason why we have to leave so early Friday morning. But don't worry, you have the cabin for the entire day Friday. The cruise company wanted to make it special by having all of you here so we could enjoy Thanksgiving together. On Friday we have to return to the ship, *via* train, to the port where our ship MH MKaddesh is docked. The cruise line made all the arrangements for this cabin."

I so hoped they didn't ask who really invited them as I couldn't tell them we were as surprised by their invitation as they were.

Jim and the others seem to accept it but we so hoped they didn't ask any other questions. The kids wanted to go to the beach, but Dot and Sue assured them we'd have plenty of time for that.

Hope soon arrived with all of the caterers. They opened the back of the van and started bringing in the food. Hope and her assistants set the table, brought the food into the kitchen from whence they began setting it on the table.

"I hope all are hungry as we figured that after the long travels you are ready to eat," Hope shared with such an angelic smile.

All agreed. On the table was a banquet of seafood. Anything from shrimp, to oysters, to flounder, to crab cakes, to cat fish, to coleslaw, hush puppies, French fries, and baked potatoes, and various seafood salad dishes. Tea and coffee, plus soft drinks, were available. Noting Shirley was not a seafood lover, they also brought a plate of prime rib. For dessert we had a selection of cheese cake, or fudge chocolate cookies with ice cream. I think we all worried that if we ate all that we wouldn't want Thanksgiving dinner!

I was so impressed that this was the chosen meal. It couldn't have been more appropriate, given that throughout time Jim and Dot were noted for the fish fries hosted at their house. Jim and Dot had bought a nice home on Kirkland Lake in Auburndale, Florida. Jim and the boys were always going out to fish. Over time they collected a freezer full of fish. The entire family was then invited to meet at their house for a fish fry. Unfortunately, Shirley and I never got to attend as we didn't live in Florida and with Dorothy turning Jehovah Witness, we were never invited.

"Dinner!" Hope called. All the adults and older kids gather round the huge dining table, with the smaller kids sitting at the smaller table.

Hope then turned and shared that they would return early Thursday morning to provide a selection of pastries for breakfast and then return around 2:00 pm to set up for the Thanksgiving dinner. She also shared that if the family stays through Friday night, she would provide meals for them. She wasn't sure if they would want to eat at the cabin or go out and enjoy the day at the beach and take in the highlights of Myrtle Beach. She motioned toward the phone, noting her phone number was on a card next to the phone.

"Once you finish eating, leave everything on the table, members of my team will be back later to clean up." What care Hope and her team were providing us!

Before dinner I asked that I say the blessing:

Dear Lord:

We come to You, ever so mindful for that which we have, to make this great thanksgiving. We thank You for our family, our safety in travel and the blessings You given us over the years. Help us never to forget You are the Creator of life and thus in You we have the security of having it

more abundantly. **We give praise for the meal we are about to partake and for the time we have together. In Your blessed Name, Jesus, we pray. Amen**

All the servings were in the center of the table. Before the adults ate, Dorothy and Sue took the kids plates, those sitting at the smaller table, and filled them. Then we all started serving ourselves with the plate nearest us. We sat as families, not in any particular order. During the meal we talked about our plans for the Thanksgiving Day. We decided to have breakfast, then go out to the beach before Thanksgiving dinner.

I kept wondering how we could witness to both Roy and Dorothy. Knowing the future, we realized the men of the family never stepped up as the spiritual leaders of their families. In both Dorothy's and Sue's cases, Jim and Roy were really oblivious to any discussion about church or faith. When could we find the opportunity to witness? That, clearly, had to be under the leadership of the Holy Spirit.

After dinner, the adults sat on the porch basically talking about old times when they lived in Alabama as kids. It was a rough life. They were poor and had to scrap for food. One of Shirley's favorite foods was "Red Eye Gravy." It was basically water flavored from droppings of whatever meat dish they had, primarily canned dried beef. They poured it over everything. Shirley reminded me that homemade biscuits were often the staple, meaning that's what they often had with a blessing of a small can of Corn Beef, if their dad brought it home. When I talk poor, I mean poor. Shirley's mom worked in the cotton fields to put food on the table and often did chores for the neighbors. To my surprise, Shirley said that while the neighbors paid her mom a mere few dollars, they would sell her food she had just processed for them, *i.e.,* churned butter, eggs, even knowing how poor they were. But, as I understand it, the family was always grateful for what they got, when they got it.

I can't imagine the level of poverty from which my bride had grown up. But she often said, "We were poor, but we didn't always realize it."

Now, here we sit, having just enjoyed a banquet and I hear them laugh and talk with pride over what they once didn't have and how they survived.

Then I heard it. My precious wife sharing:

"You know I thank God for what we didn't have as it showed me how blessed I was when God allowed me to go to college and have a future I know He has set before me."

At first none of the family joined in with a comment. I thought, "Well, that was a dud." But then Dorothy added:

"Shirley, I agree. I thank God for my family, my husband Jim, and for showing us how real He was in all that we endured, but always had family to take us in and loved us."

Dorothy was showing a spiritual side of herself I'd never seen. If only she would give up going to Jehovah Witness. I know the future is beyond our control, but if only we could find a way that both Dorothy and Jim would accept Jesus as their Savior. As for Sue and Roy, we knew the future would bear a lot of heartache due to wrong decisions but we also know both became saved. Even if life is a walk of faith and we face a lot of major storms, this life is but a grain of sand in our eternal life. We're only passing through. We know that when we get to Heaven, Sue and Roy will be there, but we're not so sure of Jim and Dorothy.

I could tell everyone was restless about tomorrow. There wasn't any time to go to the beach tonight and tomorrow would be a full day. Granny started it:

"Well, I think I'm going to bed."

Jim chimed in, "'Granny do you want me to help you up the stairs."

"You either help me or you'll have to carry me." Granny was always to the point."

Jim got up and guided Granny up the stairs. We were all a bit tired. The house hostess and her crew arrived to clean up dinner and get things ready for tomorrow. With that, we all realized today's travels had tired us out, as well as the wonderful dinner. The rest of the family headed toward their rooms. I helped the girls get out the roll-away bed and set up the couch. Once every one was settled, Shirley and I headed to our room. After brushing our teeth and getting into our pajamas, we hit the sack. Every night each of us said our own prayers. I suggested we pray for the family together tonight. We both shared our requests to the Lord but we were united on our having an opportunity to witness to them, especially Jim and Dorothy. We both went off to sleep, ever so amazed to be in this situation.

Morning came sooner than we anticipated. We were awakened by the noise in the kitchen. It seems Hope and the others came in the back door and set up breakfast. It had to be around 6:00 am. I know none of us would have gotten up that early otherwise. We stayed in bed and tried to stay until they were gone. I really could have used another two hours of sleep, but this was our only day with the family. After they left, around 7:00 am, Shirley and I took over the bathroom to get ready ahead of the others and make sure everything was set for breakfast. With our movement the girls soon awakened, followed by the boys and then we heard the families' upstairs stirring.

Around 8:00 am, everyone began to head downstairs and gathered in the living room. Granny was the last to arrive. The table was again set by Hope and her co-workers. The breakfast was a mixture of fruits, cheeses, beverages and pastries. She knew we needed to keep ourselves ready for the afternoon meal. I love cinnamon rolls, particularly the Cinnabons sold at airports. Sure enough there they were. Again, I suggest we have our blessing. I asked if anyone wanted to lead it. No one spoke up, so I asked Shirley to lead it:

Dear Lord:

> We come together ever so mindful we have a great opportunity before us, to love each other as a family and to give praise to You for all the rich blessings You have lovingly given us. Most of all, Lord, we pray that we always live the promise of the Cross, to share Your Good News wherever we go. Now, thank You for this food and bless our day.
>
> **In Jesus Holy Name we pray.**
> **Amen**

With that we helped ourselves to the breakfast set on the table and this time everyone had the choice of eating at the tables, or on the porch, or in the living room. After we enjoyed our breakfast, the kids yelled, "When are we going to the beach?"

We took the hint and got up, taking our dishes to the kitchen. After brushing our teeth and deciding we were all going to have to take our own cars, we agreed on joining each other on the South Beach. If I remember, it has a nice sized parking lot, a path to the beach and a picturesque shoreline. Shirley was thoughtful enough to grab a basket she found in the cabinets and load it up with left over pastries and a huge thermos of coffee. Knowing we'd eat about 4:00 pm, we knew we'd get hungry, but would also need some snacks before dinner. We really didn't anticipate seeing anything open on the beach itself. Remember this is November and even South Carolina gets cold then. The family was going to have all day Friday at Myrtle Beach while Shirley and I were on the train to Florida.

It was around 9:45 am when we arrived. There was a picnic area and we knew no one would dare go swimming today. It was walk, talk and pick up shells. We thought the kids would just enjoy playing in the sand. I guess we spent a couple of hours there all total, but we found ourselves just walking. However, during our walk I noticed Shirley nudge on over to Dorothy. Jim and Roy had gotten into a conversation and Sue and Granny were in another. It was a blessing to see that Shirley had some private time with Dorothy. Just maybe a miracle might happen.

"You know, Dorothy, I love you with all my heart."

"Shirley, I know you do. We've had a long hard life but I am so excited you and Calvin have gotten off to such a good start as husband and wife."

"Dorothy, do you know for sure that you have allowed Jesus to be the Master of your life?'

"I do believe in Jesus, but I'm searching for the right religion. I just keep hoping I'm choosing the right church."

"I know you have and I just trust you come to the reality it's not about the right church but the right relationship."

"What do you mean by that?'

"What I mean is that Jesus is a person, not an institution. Let Him guide you to the right church."

"Shirley, you know I'm Catholic and I believe I have the right church. Are you preaching to me because you're a Baptist?"

"No, never, I just know that in time this church or that church will disappoint you. You see a church is the body of believers in Christ, but we're still human and it is Christ upon whom we focus. He alone is the cornerstone and foundation of our faith. It isn't the institution of religion. If in the future you decide Catholicism is not what you anticipated, then I pray you will keep your heart open to the calling of Jesus."

"Okay I will, but for now I'm contented being Catholic, let's just enjoy being together as family."

Shirley had the sense she had gone as far as she could with this conversation but so hoped it planted a seed. However, having come from the future, we knew Dorothy would ultimately leave Catholicism and become entangled with the Jehovah Witness movement. I know we can't change the future but, oh, how by some miracle, Shirley's words impacted Dorothy and would in time to bring her home spiritually.

While the air was brisk, we enjoyed our time on the beach. But the chill of the breezes off the ocean made all of us realize we needed to head back to the cabin, or at least find some restaurant where we could get a cup of hot chocolate.

I yelled out so everyone could hear me. "Hey, gang, why don't we go up the road a bit, find a parking spot, and look for a restaurant for some hot chocolate!"

Needless to say, all agreed, and we headed out the parking lot and up the road. I suggested they follow me and I'd stop at a place with open stores. It was heading on 11:30 a.m. It wasn't long before we saw a major beach area with a lot of tourists walking around. Apparently, a lot of out-of-state families came to spend their Thanksgiving at Myrtle Beach. I drove into a parking lot surrounded by stores next to the beach with pathways to the water. As we drove in, I noticed a "Howard Johnson's Restaurant." It's been a long time since I've seen one of those! They went out of business within the decade. The family all arrived and we entered the restaurant, but we had a bit of a wait for 14 people. We had to wait for at least three tables to open up. It seems many had come for a late breakfast. We got one table for the seven adults, and two more for the children. Noting we wouldn't be having dinner until 4:00 p.m. some of the children indicated they were hungry. I'll admit I was, as well. However, we all warned the kids they needed to save room for the big Thanksgiving dinner. We all ordered something besides hot chocolate. I really just wanted some coffee, a piece of toast, an egg and bacon. Shirley ordered the same. Other family members had hamburgers or sandwiches of some kind, with colas. By the time the food arrived and we ate it, we realized it was going on 1:30 pm. However, the stores were beginning to bustle with patrons and we agreed to go our ways to the stores with a return to the cars between 2:30 and 3:00 p.m. at the very latest. Everyone saw the stores they wanted to go into. Shirley and I just mingled in an out of a few looking at shells and handicrafts, as well a beach clothes. We knew with our getting on the train the next morning at 5:30 a.m., there was no need to buy anything. After about 45 minutes, Shirley and I decided to sit on a bench in front of the stores and wait for the others to arrive. Granny stayed with us and did the same. We looked at brochures from the area, discovering there were several miniature golf courses, as well as a carnival area with rides. That was something the family would enjoy after Thanksgiving.

About 2:45 p.m. the family, having seen us sitting on the bench, began to gather to return to the cabin. We loaded the cars and headed back. When we arrived, we found Hope and her crew setting up Thanksgiving Dinner. It seems much of the food was already cooked but they were in the kitchen still preparing several of the dishes, like the Green Bean Casserole, the Sweet Potato Soufflé, etc.

Hope welcomed us, "Dinner will be ready by 4:00." That's what she originally promised. The time came for dinner. We gathered around the huge dining table and I suggested we hold hands and I'd give the blessing.

> **Dear Lord:**
>
> **Thanksgiving is such a precious time to think about family. We've so enjoyed our day with each other. We thank You for the time, love and fellowship of this family. We pray that as we consider our futures You will be in the center of our thoughts and dreams. Let us not forget our past and the wonderful memories it has given us. May we live each day as a day of thanksgiving for all You've given in blessings. Now, thank You for this food and most of all for Your love.**
>
> **In Jesus Name we pray.**
> **Amen**

All joined in with an "Amen." We all took our seats at the table and the children at their tables. Needless to say, this was a feast! Hope had prepared for us all the traditional dishes. I know when I think of Thanksgiving, I can't help but remember my mom and the spread she always laid out. I looked across the table and to my astonishment, the dishes looked so much like that which my mom fixed, including her Green Bean Casserole, the Shrimp Cocktail, the Sweet Potato Soufflé, the Huge Turkey and Honey-Glazed Ham. It was so similar I even had a thought Mom came from Heaven to prepare it. I looked over at Hope and she winked. Chills ran all over me.

I'm so glad we had this time with all of Shirley's family. I loved it, but it brought back so many memories of being with my mom and dad during this season. It was apparent Shirley's family all had so much to talk about and they included Granny and all their memories of their past. They talked of it, not with sorrow, but with appreciation for the sacrifices Granny made in raising them in such poverty and giving them of value system of sharing, bonding and sacrifice. I can honestly say no one could measure up to the extent Granny would sacrifice herself for her family. Working the Alabama cotton fields, and the Florida cannery just to be sure food was on the table and each had good school clothes and learned to make their own clothes. Roy took on a major support for the family and learned to be a carpenter, foregoing finishing his high school years. While their dad was in their early years an alcoholic, he got saved and attempted to be a part of the family in his last years. But through the years, Shirley never forgot those nights sitting on the front porch of their Alabama shanty, being told about the stars by her dad or the times he cut sugar cane for her. She loved him even though he was the center of their pain in their formative years. The evening went by quickly, as again we filled our stomachs to the point of misery. Sitting on the front porch, talking, was so much fun for the family as it was through their growing up years. No afternoons of watching football or taking in a movie. It was family togetherness that made this family. I wondered why the miracle of this trip to Myrtle Beach? This was clearly more for Shirley and her family. Was there some eternal purpose in this time together?

Well, night came soon enough and Shirley and I had to be up at 2:30 am to pack and get back to Charleston to catch our train. We again encouraged the family to stay the extra day. It was going on 8:30 pm and we needed to get to bed. Hope and her crew came in to clean up from the dinner. She again announced that the family could stay all day Friday and leave Saturday morning. She would provide meals if they wanted to eat in the Cabin and she told them how to close up and where to put the keys, which I had returned to her. Shirley hugged her sister, brother and the in-laws, as well as having a hard time letting go of Granny. We went off to bed, but could hear the family just enjoying the evening, long after we went to our room.

Chapter 15: Florida and Homeward Bound

Having enjoyed our time with the family, I slept soundly and, boy, did the sound of the alarm clock startle me! I have always hated being awakened by an alarm clock. Normally, when I know I have to get up early for a particular reason, my body clock kicks in and I typically begin to awaken two hours ahead of time. I spend those two hours snoozing, but about every 20 minutes check the clock to see how much longer I have to anticipate the alarm going off. I don't know why that happens, but when I'm in a deep sleep the alarm clock is needed to awaken me. Indeed, the alarm clock was needed this morning! We had gotten our showers before we went to bed, so it was a matter of simply getting ready, packing the car and heading out without awakening the family. We had two hours to get to the train station, so we had to leave no later than 3:15 am.

Packing our little VW, we looked back at the cabin sadly wishing we could stay on. Car packed, we started our new Bahama Blue Volkswagen and headed toward Charleston. Needless to say, it was dark but our hearts felt the light of His love as we had such a wonderful family time and our minds couldn't help but relive the last two days. The further I drove the early hours of the morning began to awaken me to the reality of what was ahead. I always loved train travel and getting back on the train has always been exhilarating to me. Then, of course, once we reached Orlando we were anticipating being met at the train station by Carlos, or some representative of the cruise line, to escort us to Port Canaveral, where the MH MKaddesh awaited us. It was Friday, November 25, and the ship is scheduled to depart at 11:00 pm tonight. This was going to be a long day. We anticipated arriving in Orlando at approximately 1:30 pm. By the time we unloaded and were taken to Port Canaveral, we anticipated being at port no later than 4:00 pm.

Well, the train station was in sight. The two hours passed quickly. It was going on 5:15 am. The train wasn't in yet. However, we parked the car in the same place we found it. We unloaded it and locked the keys in the glove compartment. It was hard to leave our little new VW behind. It held so many memories for us. We felt as though we were leaving our past behind and we weren't sure that's what we wanted to do.

As we entered the station, we noticed a change. The sign over the ticket window said, "Amtrak." We came in on the Atlantic Coastline and Amtrak didn't go into effect until 1971. This is 1965, or is it? We went to the restrooms and as I looked into the mirror I was stunned. I was no longer the young 22-year-old. I had returned to my present age of 75. Shirley came out of the ladies' room looking as though she had seen a ghost. She, too, discovered that by some miracle we had returned to our present-day age. Our clothes were as they were before we had changed into our younger selves. You know it matters not whether we are 22 or 75, Shirley is still my gorgeous bride and our lives have been full.

Another couple was there awaiting the train. They were about our age. We didn't say much but they looked somewhat familiar. Well, I just heard the train whistle and the announcement came over the Public Address.

"Ladies and Gentlemen, Amtrak Train #97, the Silver Meteor, is arriving. Please proceed to the train platform for boarding." It was indeed coming into the station. You could feel the swish as the cars passed, then came to a stop. We boarded the train, looking to get some sleep given we've been up since 2:30 am and still rather sleepy.

The couple we noticed boarding with us were seated just in front of us. I couldn't get them off my mind. Who are they? They look so very familiar. I clearly wasn't going to sleep until I found out. The train whistle blew, signaling we were about to leave the station. Sure enough the train began moving slowly. Once the train was under way, I leaned over and spoke to the husband.

"Sir, I'm so sorry to bother you, but you look so very familiar. Are you from Charleston?

"Yes, we've been here for years. I'm Herb and this is my wife…."

I interrupted, "and Rhetta."

Stunned, Herb turned to me and said, "And you are?"

"I'm Cal, Cal Meyer" upon which Rhetta stood and looked as surprised as we were. She pointed to Shirley.

"And you're Shirley."

Neither of us could get over it. The last we saw of Herb and Rhetta was back in 1965. They loaned us their car until we were able to buy our new VW. Herb was the one who always came to see us blowing his trumpet. We loved them.

"Oh, my, this is some kind of miracle," I sputtered.

Knowing the club car would open around 6:00 a.m. I suggested we go for some breakfast when it opened. So much for getting some sleep. Well, it did open, but not until 6:30 a.m. Meaning we did get to shut our eyes for about 30 minutes. Soon I heard,

"Cal, you and Shirley want to join us in the club car?" It was Herb, we apparently had fallen into a light sleep.

We headed to the club car. I loved Amtrak's cinnamon rolls and hot chocolate. We thought about going to the diner, but they would be busy with ushering patrons in and out. In the club car we could stay as long as wanted.

The girls found us a booth while Herb and I ordered our food at the counter. We sat and, again, weren't sure where to start. I really wanted to hear what they had been doing all these years

"Tell me about your family and your careers since 1965. How long did you keep the car you so graciously loaned us?"

"Oh, we sold the car within the year. If you recall it was about nine or ten years old when we loaned it to you. You remember it was a '50's Hudson."

"Yes, I do remember. We loved driving that. It was a classic, even then. Did you continue to drive for Greyhound during the summers?"

"I drove for another two summers but with the interstates developing, air travel becoming competitive, Greyhound began to change. I saw a deterioration in service and routes. As you know they began to shut down all the small-town stops. Thus, they were beginning to lay off summer drivers. I saw the handwriting on the wall, and I quit around 1967."

"Do you and Rhetta have children?"

With that I saw a tear in Rhetta's eye.

"No, we later wanted to, but we had some rough edges in our marriage after you guys left South Carolina. We began to leave the church and I regret to say we began social drinking. It killed our marriage. No church, no commitment to the Lord and a life filled with everything, except God. During that time, Rhetta and I began finding a distance between us. We decided to divorce and even separated. I continued to work at the high school as band director, but even that began to fail me, all due to my drinking."

Rhetta joined in. "We were lost and both of us were lonely. We knew we had gone astray, but we couldn't seem to find our way back. I went to work as an office administrative assistant in a real estate firm. Then one night I got a call from Herb. You could tell he was impaired. He was at a local bar and said he wanted to die."

Herb opened up. "That was the lowest point in my life. I wanted to give up. But then in a miracle, God sent us another friend we had met before our separation. He, too, had followed the path that almost destroyed us. However, his wife, a committed believer, encouraged him to go to their church's revival. It was a smaller Baptist Church in Mt. Pleasant. Anyway, he went, and the Holy Spirit spoke to him. He and his wife grew closer, they both became active in their church and he's a new person. I knew he had what I wanted."

Rhetta excited joined back in. "They talked us into going to church one Sunday morning. We were reluctant but we wanted their friendship. We went to Sunday School and then to worship. The choir was tremendous but then pastor spoke on the topic, "Finding Your Way." He shared how so many lose their way and the only answer was returning to God. We knew God had sent us that friend and to that church that morning. At the invitation, Herb was out of his seat before I knew he was going forward. Weeping bitterly, he almost ran to that pastor. I joined him."

Then Herb shared, "We asked to set up a conference with the pastor and indeed that next day we met with him. At that point Herb and I joined hands and made a commitment to return home, God's home. We've never looked back and have spent the rest of our lives active in the church. The church in Mt. Pleasant grew into a larger church and it wasn't long before we found ourselves teaching the high school class and, later, I became a deacon."

"What about your career?" I asked.

"Well, as you know I was the Band Director at Hanahan High while you and Shirley worked at Remount Baptist."

"Yeah, I know. You tried to get me to apply at Hanahan, where my salary would have increased from $3,000 to $5,000 annually. But you know, back then that extra $2,000 would have meant a lot. However, my calling was to seminary."

"I resigned, as shared earlier, about two years after you all left. I had lost my way. Rather, we had lost our way spiritually. That was the same time I quit driving for Greyhound during the summers. Rhetta moved out into a small apartment. She went to work for a Real Estate Company. I believe I already mentioned that."

"So, what did you do?"

"Oh, I meandered from job to job. Drove a truck for a while, went to work at Walmart. Just anything I could find. I wasn't happy and drinking was my passion. After about a year and a half I hit that low point when my friend invited me to Mt. Pleasant Baptist. I called Rhetta and asked if she wanted to go with me. I needed her strength to get us there."

"That's where our lives changed. Rhetta and I came back together, and our love and marriage has never shaken since. Vocationally, I reapplied to the school district. They didn't have a high school position for me but there was a Middle School opening. I took it."

"That's great!" I assumed that's where Herb remained.

"That wasn't the end of my search but the beginning. Charleston Southern College was just beginning when you were here. Well, after a few years, they opened their master's program and I went back and got my degree in elementary education, just in case the Lord wanted me at the elementary level. I stayed at the middle school, but several years passed again and I decided to get my doctorate in Educational Leadership at the University of South Carolina. They had a residency program during the summers." Around 1982, I finished my doctorate."

"Herb you won't believe this, but I almost followed the same path. I got my master's degree in elementary education at Spalding University in 1973 and ended up in Columbia working in middle school. I started my doctorate there in Curriculum and Instruction and receive my degree in 1979. What a small world!"

Rhetta heard this and her face lit up. "Cal this is a miracle. Both you and Herb followed very similar routes."

"Yeah, I know. Upon completion of my degree, I became principal of Richland Northeast High School in Columba."

"Cal, you won't believe this, but I entered the District Office in Charleston as Coordinator of District Fine Arts Programs. Then, I became Associate Superintendent. However, it wasn't long before

Charleston Southern had an opening in the Educational Leadership program and I've finished my career there."

"Herb after leaving the principalship I entered higher education, teaching at Liberty University and Marshall University and went into higher ed. administration toward the end of my career."

We were both a bit overcome about how our two careers followed such a similar path.

"Cal, what brought you back to Charleston after all these years?"

"You wouldn't believe me, if I told you. The cruise company paid for a trip to Myrtle Beach. But we found it wasn't present day."

Herb looked inquisitive, if not doubting my words.

I continued, "The Company rented a log cabin for all of Shirley's family to visit us. It was just off the Base on Majestic Cove Road. We were only a short distance from the beach. It was a wonderful time with the family, but we so hoped our time together would, in time, change destinies. You see Shirley's sister became a Jehovah Witness and now doesn't believe Jesus is who the Bible claims He is. Simply, she's lost. We were hoping we'd have one last opportunity to witness to her."

"Cal the Base closed in 1991 and redeveloped into commercial use. How did you rent a cabin just off the Base?"

How was I going to explain our existence back in 1965 as just before we boarded the train in present day and sound credible?

"Yes, I know, but all I can say is we were experiencing a miracle. We found Majestic Cove Road just off where the Base used to be."

I hadn't told a lie but needed to move on and Herb rather accepted it.

"Well, one afternoon Shirley had some private time with Dorothy, her sister, and witnessed to her posing some serious questions to her. We don't know if it had an impact, but we so pray it was a seed that would open her heart to the Holy Spirit's yearning."

"Cal, where did you say the cabin was located? Rhetta and I have been to Myrtle Beach numerous times through the years and until now have never seen a Majestic Cove Road on or near Myrtle Beach. Nor have we seen it on a map. We would have loved finding a cabin near the beach like that. The base was basically right on the ocean. We haven't seen such a location, even after the Base closed. Oh, well, it is perhaps a new construction as Myrtle Beach is expanding exponentially."

I nodded, not verbally responding. But Herb made a point. The cabin wasn't new construction and if the Base was on the ocean, the cabin couldn't have been off Base. Given I was not in the military in 1965, I would have never had permission to use housing on Base. Had we just experienced an even larger miracle? Could this have been a dream or were our days at Myrtle Beach a surreal experience that was supernatural in time, events and people. It was real to us just as this train trip. How would we ever know? If it was a supernatural event, then was Shirley's witness a natural, real, event that might have changed destinies? Regardless, Shirley and I experienced something miraculous.

We had no way of explaining this, so I attempted to change the subject.

"Herb, what brings and Rhetta on this train?"

"We're heading to Port Canaveral for a cruise. We're going on a cruise destined for New York, we were told. We've never been on a cruise, so this will be our first. It's only a short trip but it will give us a feel for cruising just in case we want to do it again."

"Oh, what ship?"

"It's a ship we've never seen on any advertisements and a cruise line with which we've never been told about. It's Dove Cruise Lines and the ship is the MH MKaddesh. We understand it came out of San

Francisco, went to Hawaii, Alaska and through the Panama Canal, before coming to Florida."

I was speechless.

"Herb, that's the very ship we've been on and are now traveling back to for departure tonight. We were on the ship but got off in Alaska to pursue other adventures. The cruise line was so accommodating and sponsored all of this for us. Now we're going back to catch the last leg of the trip. It's a great and beautiful ship. Unlike any we've sailed on. I don't believe this. Yet another miracle. I'm sure once on board, we'll see each other."

I think that announcement was so shocking neither Herb nor I could think of any more to say. Shirley was similarly overwhelmed. After another cup of coffee, we all headed back to our car and seats. It was getting late morning and we were all a bit tired from the early morning need to board the train. Besides that, I'm not sure any of us could handle any more surprises.

We sat back and enjoyed the morning views of the Georgia countryside. After our time with Herb and Rhetta we noticed we had long passed Savannah and nearing Jacksonville. I've always enjoyed train travel. To me it was calming to my soul. The last time we rode the train through Georgia was on the Amtrak Auto Train following a brief vacation in Florida. That was quite a different experience than the one we're riding now. It was a double decker with one car devoted as a viewing car. Our car was on the train with us, and meals were provided with our ticket. The train makes no stops along the way to Washington, D.C. The train we're now experiencing is the Amtrak Meteor. On this track once rode the Seaboard Airline Meteor and the Atlantic Coastline Champion. It was the Champion that took us from Washington, D.C. to Charleston back in 1965. Prior to tracks being fused, one could sit back and be mesmerized by the clicking and clacking of the train passing over those tracks. It would often put you to sleep. Just the sway and movement of the train has a calming effect. I clearly felt at peace as we attempted to consume all the revelations of the morning. We had only about four hours left before arriving in Orlando. I momentarily felt a sense of sadness this part of our journey was coming to an end.

Reliving so much of our past was not only revealing, but there was a sense of finality to all of this. I started my life's journey on the train from Chicago to Dallas, Texas, as my mom and dad left Moody Bible Institute and headed to Dad's schooling at Dallas Theological Seminary, so my mother once told me. I was only a baby and, thus, did not recall that. I saw my dad leave Dallas, following seminary, to interview for his first pastorate in Fort Oglethorpe, Georgia. It was on the train that we left Jefferson City, Tennessee, back in 1954 to meet my dad in New York City following his graduation from the Army's Chaplain School. It was on the train I left Seattle and headed to Carson-Newman. It was the train my bride and I rode from Lakeland, Florida, to Columbus, Ohio, to work in summer missions the first summer just days following our marriage. It was now the train taking us to our final destination. The train provides a synoptic of my whole life. It indeed saddens me to see it end this day. I don't know what life has yet for me, but my past has clearly been full of blessings, and this trip was such a reminder of that. There is such a sense of closure to my book of life. My heart awakened from my melancholy as I realized we were heading back to the MH MKaddesh and getting ready to enjoy the rest of our cruise.

Upon passing Savannah and heading toward Hinesville, I couldn't help but think of the dramatic change in life my dad experienced while stationed at Fort Stewart, Georgia. In 1969, having just returned from being stationed in Holland, my dad was diagnosed with a growth on his prostate. It wasn't just a growth, but a tumor the size of a softball. Concerned about his future in the military, Dad let it go unattended until almost too late. Upon collapsing after Christmas, he was rushed to Walter Reed Hospital where it was diagnosed as a fatal situation. The family was told to expect him not to survive the operation that would take out the tumor. To our delight and surprise, he did survive but with the prediction he would not live more than seven years due to the loss of one kidney and damage to the other organs by use of a catheter. In those days, a catheter required three days of dialysis each week. The whole process was a three-hour ordeal each time and, over time, weakened his heart. In 1977 he passed away just as predicted, but he had a great final three years to his career. The Army let him stay in with an assignment to be the Hospital Chaplain at the Army Hospital in Frankfort, Germany. Even in that, we saw miracle upon miracle. Life with the Lord is just that, miracle upon miracle.

Oh, well, here I go reflecting again. When on a train one can't help but contemplate life given the total peace in the ride and passing God's creation. It was going on lunch time and with the train reaching Orlando by 1:30 pm, I didn't feel like going to the diner for lunch. We knew that upon arrival at the ship we'd have a full buffet awaiting us. However, I never tire of cinnamon rolls. Shirley and I went to the Club Car for a bottle of tea and a cinnamon roll. We figured that would hold us until we reached the ship. The afternoon Florida sun was beaming over the train. We knew we were in Florida when passing all the trees covered in Spanish moss. Passing town upon town was becoming more common. Upon reaching Deland, just past Daytona Beach, we weren't too far from the station in Orlando, at most 45 minutes, or so. I had a sudden sadness creep over me as our ride was nearing the end. I don't know why but it seemed like such a finality. However, I must confess I never reached my destination on a train that I didn't want to stay on and keep going.

Finally, we came through Orlando and knowing the station was just ahead, Shirley and I gathered our things.

"Orlando, next stop. Please exit at the end of the car," the conductor announced as he passed through the car and picked up our seat tickets.

We rolled into the station and, upon stopping, we exited the trains as did Herb and Rhetta. That seemed so strange.

"Well, we're here," I said to Herb. "Look forward to seeing you on the ship."

I looked up and there stood Carlos, awaiting us.

"Hi, Carlos, what a treat!"

"Welcome back. I trust you had an adventure, a blessing and some miracles," Carlos responded with that awesome grin.

"Follow me," and he took us to the limo awaiting us.

We noticed Herb and Rhetta were also welcomed by a steward from the ship and they too were led to a waiting limo.

I must admit I was a bit tired and eager to get on the ship and some food. We weren't to be on the ship until between 4:00 and 5:00 pm, but with the Orlando traffic that was about right to get to Cape Canaveral. I'm just glad I didn't have to drive it. By the time Carlos got all our luggage into the car and drove out of the parking lot, it was going on 2:00 pm. And, sure enough, the Orlando traffic.

I rather regretted the drive noting that we were hitting the go-home traffic. Today, being the day after Thanksgiving, a major part of the traffic would more than likely be shoppers or those going to the various attractions, like Universal City or Disney World. I recall a very similar drive when we flew to Florida to attend the funeral of Shirley's brother, Roy. It was sad in the respect the most of Shirley's family was lost and we were burying the one sibling who loved her so dearly. However, it was not all sad in that Roy had recently professed his acceptance of Christ as his Savior. It was a time the family came together but we found that, even though family, we had so little in common, faith wise. A miracle happened in Roy's life, but one was needed in the life of Dorothy, Shirley's sister, as well. Oh, well, I need to refocus as this trip has been about miracles, not death. There is still time.

Chapter 16: Last Leg

Carlos moved me out of my sense of melancholy. "We're just about five minutes away from the Pier. When we get there, I'll take care of your luggage and take it to your room. Once I let you out, go through check-in so they know you have returned to the ship. Give me about 30 minutes to park and get your luggage to your room. The main buffet is open if you want to get a bite to eat. As you know, we don't leave port until 11:00 pm, as so many are returning to the ship between now and then."

I was wondering if many had side trips as we did. I do know they were taking on new passengers, *i.e.,* Herb and Rhetta. I had assumed that all those who boarded originally would be on the ship, but it appears many of those passengers may have departed the ship along the way.

We came in view of the MH MKaddesh and, as I was when we first saw it, we were simply awed by its size and gleaming white presence. Upon our arriving at the Port, it all seemed as though we were just beginning our trip rather than making the last leg of it. It had been a while since we left the ship and so much has happened. We had no regrets of leaving it in Alaska and flying back to Florida. While I would have enjoyed going through the Panama Canal, I don't think it would have been as unbelievably awesome as the journey we've made reliving our past. We made our way to check-in. It was just a matter of formality, as they still had our original check-in forms, and it was a simple matter of rejoining the ship. We approached the Check-in counter and the Hostess behind the desk said:

"Welcome back, Dr. Meyer and Shirley. We're so glad to see you again."

How did she remember us? These folks either had outstanding memories or were angels from Heaven. The latter skipped through my mind as I felt so complimented, she had remembered us.

"Your room is still 4344 and, as you remember, the door opens simply by touch." Yep, that brought my memory back to our first day on ship.

The Hostess went on to say, "You're early enough to go to the Buffet, or any of the dining rooms. Just a reminder, we depart at 11:00 p.m. We will have a midnight Welcome Back celebration on top deck. We're encouraging all to attend. It will be an enlightening and joyous time. You're free to enter your cabin most any time, as Carlos has reported in, and your suitcases have been returned to your room."

This is the most unusual check-in I've had with any cruise taken. The courtesy, the quickness, the personal care was unlike any we ever experienced before. Given it was nearing 5:00 p.m. and we were losing sunlight we decided to go to the Buffet and have dinner. However, before going to the restaurant, we decided to take a brief walk around the upper deck to see the lights of the Florida landscape, knowing it was November and thus we could probably stay outside but for a short time. Even Florida can get a chill in late November.

We entered the restaurant named, "The Heaven's Abundance." It was as we remembered it before we left the ship. Even though a buffet, the food was as tasty as that found in the more formal dining rooms. I was struck by the memory of our very first cruise on the Star Princess. When I got to the buffet and saw foods of all varieties to meet all the culinary tastes of the various cultures, I couldn't imagine leaving that ship without gaining at least 10 pounds, which I did rather easily. Meats, vegetables, fruits, soups, salads and then came all the different deserts served at every lunch and dinner meal. Sometimes you felt you were being punished as you wanted to taste everything, but you just couldn't. Why would they put before you the impossible? What we enjoyed the most was that you had to share tables with other families, both on the Star Princess and MH MKaddesh. I was hungry for a good meal, but wasn't sure I wanted to stuff myself, given we weren't departing until 11:00 pm. There would be plenty of time to return to the restaurant. But as always, sight and smell overwhelm your senses and, once you taste, you're done for. The thought is always, I'll sample this and that," and before you know it you haven't eaten a four-course meal, but rather an eight course one, instead.

After getting our plates we searched for a table. So many of the passengers had already returned. We looked around and thought we saw in the distance Dot and Jim, Shirley's sister and brother-in-law. But it couldn't be, as we just left them in South Carolina. Oops! That was a trip back in time to 1965, not today. We began to dismiss our thoughts, as this couple seemed so much older now. Wait a minute they would have aged, as we have. I looked again and they had disappeared into the crowd. We found another couple who had a table for four and we asked if we could join them.

"Hi, may we join you?" I asked.

"Certainly, help yourself."

Sitting down with our plates, I excused myself to go and get some tea for Shirley and myself. As I returned, I noticed that there was some familiarity with the couple we were joining. They were about our age.

I introduced we, "I'm Cal Meyer and this is my wife, Shirley."

"Glad to meet you, we're the Lovings. I'm Bernard and this is my wife, Marilyn."

The Lovings, I thought. We knew such a couple years ago. But we clearly hadn't recognized each other by our appearances today.

"Lovings? Where are you from?

"We've lived in Columbia, South Carolina, all our lives."

Then it hit me, is this the Bernard and Marilyn that were in our Sunday School class at Rosewood Baptist Church!
"What church did you attend?"

"We belonged to Rosewood Baptist Church all of our lives."

"Bernard, I'm Cal, do you remember? I was your Sunday School Teacher."

Both Shirley and Marilyn looked up and we all were amazed by the surprise of being together after all these years.

"Bernard, do you remember the class socials at our house?"

"Yes, I do, they were fun, along with the Friday night volleyball games at the church."

I had forgotten that. I loved those times together with our young families. Needless to say, we began comparing notes about our lives and how God had blessed us. We were saddened to hear that the church had begun to lose membership over the years. Bernard shared that members of the church decided in 1996 to designate a prayer room in honor of my dad with a plaque on the door, stating his name and the honor bestowed by establishing this special room for prayer. I couldn't think of a greater honor to my dad.

After we left Rosewood back in the '70's, we lost contact with the church and the members, including those who had been our Sunday School class members. I'm not sure why many others all moved on. I became a high school principal and ended my time in South Carolina as a pastor and consultant with the State's Department of Education. Our career paths were just so different, not to mention the pastor and church staff soon left. We never crossed paths with the Lovings since we left. I wonder why now? Perhaps, it was to share the honor given my dad.

"Bernard, how long have you been on the ship?"

"We just got on. We've always wanted to go on a voyage, and we received a letter inviting us to join the ship today."

I considered it a bit strange that so many new passengers were joining the ship, particularly given this is the last leg of the trip. It was also more than a coincidence that we just happened to share a table with the Lovings. Miracles continue to happen!

After our chat with the Lovings, we excused ourselves and headed to our room to unpack and have a brief rest. I didn't realize I was so tired. After all we had been on the train since early morning. While enjoyable, I was a bit worn out. We got to our room and remembered that we only had to touch the door, and sure enough it opened. However, we were a bit shocked not to see our suitcases present. Carlos promised us they would be here. We checked the closets and, nope, no suitcases, but astonishingly all our clothes were hung, and drawers were full. We surmised Carlos took the suitcases for storage. It was going on 7:00 pm and realizing we had a midnight, top deck celebration, we lay back on our beds and before I knew it, it was going on 9:00 pm. I was tired and clearly dozed off. I got up and awakened Shirley.

"Hon, if we want to see the ship leave Cape Canaveral, we need to get up. I'd like to walk around and get reacquainted with the ship."

We both washed our faces and headed to the upper deck. They were setting up the sound system and arranging the stage area and some seating. I needed a cup of coffee, so we went back into the buffet area, and I got coffee and Shirley got some tea. It was dark outside, and the lights of the port and surrounding areas were shining. I could hardly wait until we left port. I was eager to have another peaceful couple of days out to sea before we landed in New York.

Nothing had been said about what next after New York. I assumed they would fly us back home, but it just was not noticed on the itinerary nor had anyone shared with us that information. Oh, well, they took care of us to this point we just need to trust them the rest of the way. I suggested we go back out on deck for me to sip my coffee. We tried it but even Florida is cold the end of the November, particularly with the ocean breeze flowing around us. We decided to return to the restaurant and just watch our departure from there. I really didn't want to walk the ship; we could do that tomorrow. As we sat down, I looked at the couple two tables down. I had to look again as I was most certain I saw Dorothy and Jim. I motioned to Shirley to see if she noticed them. But just as she looked, they got up from the table and left the restaurant.

We wondered if we should get up and follow them. But we realized it had to be a case of mistaken identity. Why would they be on this ship? Why didn't we know? Well putting that aside, we continue to sip coffee and I couldn't help it, but I had to help myself to a piece of pie. Arriving at the dessert bar I saw every imaginable dessert possible. Cakes, pudding, pie, etc. flavors unimaginable and decorated in every form possible. I just wanted a piece of pie but now I have to make a monumental decision. I'm pretty sure with Thanksgiving behind us, I wasn't in the mood for either pumpkin or pecan pie. I just wanted some simple chocolate pie. Anyway, I saw this absolutely mouth-watering lemon meringue, beckoning to me. I got back to our seats with Shirley seeing my pie and wanting some, too.

As we ate our pie, I began to hear music coming from the speakers around the room. I listened closely and I wasn't sure, but I thought I was hearing an orchestral version of "Soon and Very Soon" by Andrae Crouch. I had heard it sung by Andrae Crouch but putting it to an orchestra was beautiful. Other songs followed like, "When We All Get to Heaven," etc. It was peaceful and inspiring. We had about an hour before departure and then, the upper deck program at Midnight. The night was as clear as I've ever seen it, with the stars brighter than most nights.

It wasn't long before my mind meandered back to my mom and dad and the nights on the Army Transport ship Huey J. Gaffey, as we crossed the Pacific toward Hawaii, Dad's next assignment. I also fondly recall that as we left port in San Francisco the Army Band played "Anchors Away." That song was like a farewell to the States. When we made that trip back in 1957, Hawaii was not yet a state. We had no idea what was ahead.

"Ladies and Gentlemen, the Captain and crew welcome you back on the MH MKaddesh. We will be departing in 45 minutes. Just a reminder that, at Midnight, we will be having a special program on Deck 1. Please dress warmly as we'll be facing a cool ocean breeze. We are happy to have you on board as we join together in this final part of the journey."

I had almost forgotten that this ship is labeled backwards. The top deck is #1 and then, the numbers go higher as you go to the lower sections of the ship. Not sure why they did that. I'll have to ask.
"Let's go out on the deck. I want to see our departure," I motioned to Shirley as we got up and started moving.

Thank goodness we had our hoodies. I watched the pier as the crew finished moving supplies onto the ship. I didn't see many still boarding as I believe all were to be on board by 10:30 pm. A few crew members and officers were moving about. However, I did notice what looked like a military band move on to the dock. That was strange. This is not a military ship! They were in white uniforms, including caps. Ah, they began releasing the ropes that held the ship to the dock. The deck began to fill as other passengers joined us. In fact, the deck was becoming rather full. Finally, the ship's horn blew, announcing our departure. I looked at my watch and it was 11:00 pm. At that time the band began to play "Anchors Away." It was beautiful and sentimental. It was a reminder we were leaving on a fantastic journey, almost as though we were leaving for the unknown. Of course, I stood there with tears pouring. It was as though Mom and Dad were standing right there beside me!

Chapter 17: Beyond Imagination

I couldn't hold back the tears. This seems so final. I can't help but think of how large the Huey J. Gaffey appeared in 1957, but comparatively speaking, the MH MKaddesh was absolutely beyond anything I could have dreamed in 1957. I can't forget the wonder of it all, then and now. It was so comforting to know I was under the care of Mom and Dad. We were without home as we were traveling to a foreign land, Hawaii. At the time Hawaii was still a territory. Our first few weeks on Oahu would be spent in a motel until Dad could secure quarters. It was Christmas time. We celebrated Christmas with a small tree sitting on a coffee table and out the door was the canal passing our motel on one side and Waikiki on the other. I'll admit, it was strange. There was a deep sense of wanting to go home, but, then again, our home was where we were at the time. Oh, I'll admit going down to the beach, attending a luau and seeing Hawaii for the first time was a tremendous adventure. But it was Christmas time. Christmas on a warm day, with palm trees and Hula girls just didn't feel like home at all. I was about to get an even bigger surprise. After visiting his post, Schofield Barracks, Dad arrived with the news. He couldn't get on-base quarters until the summer, but in the meantime, he was able to secure a rental house in Wahiawa, Hawaii, the local community just off the Base. Upon partially moving in, with most of our furniture still in storage, I was told I had to walk to my new school, Leilehua High School, just about a mile down the road. I wasn't looking forward to that. I do remember my first few days at school. I was an entering second semester freshman. I quickly realized I was in the minority. I was a Haole. Simply, I was not a native of the island. Given I didn't live on base, I didn't get to ride the military bus that took the military kids to school. Most of my classmates were Japanese, Filipino, Hawaiian or Chinese. It took a little time to assimilate into the culture. I would later come to realize it was one of the best experiences in my life and rather molded my appreciation for the cosmopolitan environment. I wouldn't have traded it for the world, but at the time, it was a bit intimidating.

For one semester, I walked that mile to and from school. I found that in time I'd have many school friends and would be involved in a lot of school activities, including the ROTC Drill Team, where I was the only Haole. I now look back on my high school years with a yearning to return, as Hawaii did become home. But then again, the Hawaii of 1957 was completely different from the Hawaii of today. The military, sugar cane and pineapples were the main economic power of the islands. Today it is tourism, with the others fading away. Sugar cane has all but vanished from the islands, as has pineapple. I'm rather saddened over that. Particularly, given the fact, working in the pineapple fields one summer helped me save money for college. Today, Hawaii is often referred to as Paradise. I guess it's all in one's perspective. For me, it was simply home for a few years.

Well, so much for reminiscing over the past. As we made our distance from the land, we settled into the fact we were on our own at sea. All our friends and family, we were slowly leaving behind. This seemed so eerily final.

"Ladies and Gentlemen, please make your way to the upper deck for our departure ceremony."

Given we were already there, we simply made our way toward the stage. The music began to play. They were playing an orchestral rendition of "Heaven Came Down and Glory Filled My Soul." It was beautiful. As we made our way to some empty seats, we noticed Herb and Rhetta approaching the stage. I was about to wave to them to come join us, but then to the left I noticed Dorothy and Jim. It couldn't be! I nudged Shirley and pointed. She had no caution and began yelling.

"Dorothy! Dorothy!" Waving at them they began coming our way. Shirley was exuberant. She ran over and hugged Dorothy before they even reached the two seats we were holding for them.

Shirley was almost too excited to talk.

"Dorothy, when did you and Jim join the ship?"

"We just got on at Cape Canaveral. We received a letter from the cruise line inviting us to join them on this trip."

About this time, the music began to silence, and a gentleman on stage began to speak.

"Ladies and Gentlemen, Welcome to the MH MKaddesh. We're here to celebrate Heaven."

Heaven? While indeed a thoughtful way to talk about the beauty of the night, with the stars shining so brightly, I couldn't help but ponder why this topic for a departure ceremony. Typically, such a program is to introduce the coming voyage with a celebration of music and food.

I looked at the speaker and he looked so familiar. He was familiar, it was Pastor David Jeremiah, the pastor of Shadow Mountain Community Church in San Diego. I love his TV program "Turning Point." He wrote a book on "Revealing the Mysteries of Heaven." I read it and was so inspired. I wonder if this will be the spiritual emphasis of this trip. The first leg we talked about being Saintly. He continued to speak.

"Now let me introduce you to those who will lead us in the joy of music, friends you know well. The Gaithers and their Homecoming singers." Sure enough they had a wonderful Gospel program called "A Gaither Homecoming." Typically, the singers were Gospel music stars from all over the country. Oh, the music was beautiful and included several of the Gaither favorites and some favorite hymns. Given it was going on midnight, we knew the time was late but somehow, even though a long busy day, most of us began to feel rejuvenated. Following the music program, Dr. Jeremiah stood to the podium and spoke.

"Ladies and Gentlemen, knowing the hour, I want to take a few minutes to introduce you to Heaven, which will be the theme of this cruise."

Having read John 14:3 where Jesus spoke in the Upper Room on the night before His death, "I go to prepare a place for you." He continued:

"Along our journey in this life, we have been consumed by all that is required of us to make it through each day, through the many opportunities we face, as well as the challenges. It is regretful we put our eternity in the hidden corner of our priority and thinking. But, Ladies and Gentlemen, I want to assure you that your time on this earth has but one purpose, to give you the opportunity to decide where you want to spend your eternity. By being on this ship, it has and will become obvious, all of you have made the right choice. Tonight in the brevity of this moment, let me assure you Heaven is a place. A real place. A place as solid and real as where you are presently standing. In this last leg of this cruise you will have encounters that will make Heaven even more real to you. With that thought, let me wish you a blessed evening and cruise."

We were led in prayer and dismissed to whatever we chose to do. I know we needed time with Dorothy and Jim, but with it being so late, we knew all we could do is get reacquainted and plan for being with them later.

Shirley leaned over to Dorothy, "Dorothy, we really need to talk."

"Sure, why don't we meet in the morning for breakfast, say 8:00 am?"

I really wanted to talk with them but it was so late and my mind was boggled with weariness. Early morning, long train trip, getting onto the ship, waiting for departure and the program were all exciting, but if I don't get to bed soon, I felt like I'm going to collapse on my face. I was tempted to go to the restaurant for a cup of coffee.

We made it to our room and every ounce of my energy was gone. I barely got into my pajamas and hit the bed before I was gone. With the roll of the ship my mind went into deep sleep. Usually when I go into this type of sleep, I have very detailed dreams and when I awake, I have difficulty determining if it was real, or a dream. This night I had such a dream.

I dreamed I was asked to speak at a large university in a town with which I was not familiar. Shirley was with me and having time to review my speech before presentation, I decided I needed a cup of coffee. I left to get us both a cup, but I couldn't find a coffee room or small canteen. I stepped outside and saw a coffee shop just across the way. I looked at my watch and realized I had about 45 minutes before speaking. I thought I could make it. I headed toward the coffee shop. It was about two blocks, just off campus. I made my way there. Upon securing my coffee I stepped outside and realized I was a bit confused. I made a turn right, rather than left, as I should have. I walked further realizing none of this seemed familiar. I turned the next corner and thought I'd surely see the University from there. I was lost and the more I tried to find my way, the more lost I became. I was in a panic and knew I was about to miss my appointment at the University. How embarrassing! Finally, a car drove up and asked me if they could help. It was Dorothy and Jim. I was delighted but couldn't figure out why they were there. Jim yelled "Cal, you lost?" I explained my predicament. Jim said, "Come on, we'll take you." I ran to the car and we were off. As we drove, I realized we weren't heading to the University. I said, "Jim, I don't believe this is the way." He responded, "Shirley is there waiting on you." I didn't know where we were going but for some reason Jim and Dorothy did. I awoke and felt a bit unnerved. I felt at one point this has some reality to it, but I don't know why.

I got up and realized we needed to get ready to meet Jim and Dorothy. I, at first, thought about telling them of my dream but realized it would be of no interest and they might find it a bit weird. We were eager to get to the buffet and meet with them.

We made our way to breakfast where Dot and Jim were waiting on us. We were able to secure a table near the window. I always loved looking out over the ocean during a meal while on other cruises. It was just so surreal. A cruise provides the best atmosphere for feeling so at peace. I could go on a cruise annually. We've met folks who leave one cruise in time to join another. Not sure I'm that big of a fan, but I do love the comfort of one. I mean everything is taken care of. Food is available almost 24/7, beds are made with even a little piece of chocolate on the pillow, entertainment throughout the day, and great devotional speakers when on a Christian cruise. I suppose cruising is my most cherished way to vacation and travel, other than riding a train.

After putting sweaters on our seats to reserve our table, the four of us went to the buffet to load our plates with eggs, bacon, toast, or everything else. You almost feel guilty for eating so much. It has been said that a normal person gains 10 pounds on a seven-day cruise. I believe it. Well, our real eagerness was not the food, but the conversation. To my delight Dorothy asked if I'd say the blessing. That was a shock, given we hadn't heard her pray or ask for it in 40 years, or so.

I gave the blessing thanking God for bringing us together, the food and asking His guidance in our conversation. We really didn't know what to say, how to start the conversation, or even where to begin. Keep in mind, before we got on the ship, we had been miraculously transformed to our younger selves in 1965 and had Thanksgiving with them just before leaving to return to the ship. At that time Dorothy was very much involved in her Catholic religion, before forsaking it and becoming a Jehovah Witness. We were also very concerned that we might reflect back on Thanksgiving that just happened a few days ago, representing over 50 years past in our lives. Where do we begin?

"Dorothy, what a shock to see you on board," Shirley initiated the conversation.

"I know, it was a last-minute invitation and plan. Dove Cruise Line contacted us just about a week ago and invited us to join this cruise."

Shirley responded, "Do you mean over Thanksgiving?"

Dorothy came back with "Yes."

This is rather surreal in that in our miracle of going back to 1965, they were with us at Thanksgiving.

Dorothy continued. "The whole week leading up to Thanksgiving, we had this strange sense of something about to happen and don't ask me why, but we felt it involved you and Calvin. Shirley, I don't know when or where but I heard your voice say 'Do you know if Jesus is Master of your life?'"

Shirley remembered saying that just last week, but it didn't impact Dorothy's heart. Last week we were miraculously back to our 1965 lives shortly after we had gotten married. In front of Dorothy was not only her Catholicism but her later becoming Jehovah Witness. Yet in reality that question struck her. Another miracle that was transported in thought, not only over miles, but over years?

"Shirley, that question has haunted me over the years. I know every time I changed religions I was ignoring that question. I continued to get involved in religions, but not with the Lord. Then Jim had his heart attack and that question began to overwhelm me. For years I was the sickly one, but after Jim's heart failure, I saw him begin to deteriorate."

Jim looked and nodded, but kept silent. After Dorothy had begun her life of chasing different religions, Jim gave up spiritually. He at one time was a vibrant Sunday school leader in his church. Now if anything he had become an agnostic. We watched Dorothy's family sink into total darkness spiritually. They were either Jehovah Witness or nothing. Dorothy and Jim had a very compelling charisma with their family. They were close to the children and multiple grandchildren, through the multiple marriages of their sons. There were always multiple family gatherings and fish fries. Dorothy even made a move to steal the hearts of our children and sadly, she became successful to the point of our losing our children spiritually. She was very convincing that our faith was one of intolerance and hatred while she repeatedly attacked us. With our children marrying spouses outside of our faith, it was an easy sell. They all seemed to find us as common enemies who couldn't accept anything outside the Bible as truth.

Thank goodness after all of our children had personal failures, they began to realize Dorothy didn't have the answer and we were the parents who raised them and hadn't changed. For a while it was a bitter walk. But times did change things. We had a lot of reasons to resent Dorothy and Jim, but deep in our hearts, we kept praying and hoping they would find their way.

Shirley asked, "What does that mean for you now?"

"Shirley I just want to share that Jim and I have found the Lord again and we know Whose we are."

Tears began to flow from Shirley, like nothing I've seen before.

"Ladies and Gentlemen, this is to remind you that a morning worship service will begin in 30 minutes in the **Heaven's Gate auditorium.**"

We weren't sure we wanted to leave. This was already such a miracle and homecoming celebration with Dot and Jim. However, we all knew that hearing Dr. Jeremiah was a gift we didn't want to miss.

Shirley began to rise and hugged Dorothy. Jim and I stood and the two sisters grabbed each other's arm and walked ahead of us. When we arrived, an orchestra was playing "Soon and Very Soon," "Blessed Assurance," "We're Marching to Zion," and a cadre of hymns as we entered the auditorium. The four of us found seats and soon a Sandi Patty came out and sang my favorite "We Shall Behold Him."

As a family we have such fond memories of Sandy Patty. We remember her parents introducing her as the little girl who had such an awesome voice, even as a child. At one of the concerts we attended and then as she became known, she performed a concert at what was then Columbia Bible College, in Columbia, South Carolina. It was an evening of such praise that Sandi Patty simply became one of our most loved singers. After she sang, Charles Billingsley came out and led us in a beautiful rendition of "We're Marching to Zion." I mean our souls were beginning to leap out in expressions we just couldn't contain.

Dr. Jeremiah stood and asked us to join him in reading 1 Thessalonians 4:17, which was posted on the stage screen, *"After that, we who are still alive and are left will be caught up together with them in the clouds to meet the Lord in the air. And so we will be with the Lord forever"* (NIV), Assuming that was the text for his message, we then heard a trumpet sound. At first, we weren't sure if it was planned or from just where the sound was coming. Dr. Jeremiah looked up as though equally surprised. We heard it again and then suddenly the doors flung open and a bright light began to shine through the windows outside the auditorium. We were stunned. No one seemed to understand what was taking place. We heard the trumpet again and this time we felt our bodies moving. I looked at Shirley and her at me. We looked at Dot and Jim and all of us had a sheen about us, as did everyone in the auditorium. Admittedly my initial response was a bit of fear, but then the most serene sense fell over me. We began to move upward but this time we were being transported through the ceilings of the ship as though they weren't there. We were several feet above the MKaddesh when we looked down and saw it floating on the water, but all the passengers were no longer on board.

As the sky opened there stood Jesus with His arms open wide. A sense of unknown calmness and peace fell upon all of us. This was the end! No, this was the beginning. There is only one time in my life when I felt such a total overwhelming sense of well-being, inward happiness and a total release of all the world's worries. I was in my office at Valley View Baptist Church when I felt such deep distress over my job as Minister of Education. Issues dominated all that was happening. I was feeling full of burden, concern and worry and an unexpected call came from a friend telling me to pray and share with Jesus "Lord I can't do this, but I know you can." At that moment I looked up and felt the presence of the Holy Spirit grab my shoulder and my total being was so released into such freedom and peace such as I had never felt before. I often said, following that moment, I had a three-day spiritual honeymoon. It was a miracle beyond belief only to be matched to that I am now joyously experiencing.

This was indeed the Cruise of Miracles. This cruise gave us insights into paths we traveled throughout our lives. It showed us friends we have long endeared and often pondered their outcomes. It brought us face to face with family, seeing dreams fulfilled. It gave us insight into the many opportunities God put before us and although we didn't always see the harvest, we planted and watered, but saw Him give the increase. It gave us a complete reality of the many ways He blessed us. Although this ends the story. In real life it will be but the beginning of an eternal story.

THE END

About the Author:

Dr. Calvin Meyer received his B.A. in History with emphasis in secondary education from Carson-Newman College, Jefferson City, Tennessee, in 1965. His first professional positions as a classroom teacher were in South Carolina, Michigan, Kentucky and Florida. During that time, he also completed his M.A. degree in elementary education at Spalding University, Louisville, Kentucky. In 1976, he was chosen to enter public school administration in Richland School District II, Columbia, South Carolina. As principal of a large high school, he was honored as the Outstanding School Administrator for South Carolina in 1982. Simultaneously upon entering school administration, he began his doctorate at the University of South Carolina, completing it in 1979. Upon serving two high schools as principal, he was appointed as an Educational Specialist for the South Carolina Department of Education, where he assisted in coordinating the statewide Performance Based Education program.

In 1987, Dr. Meyer received a faculty appointment with Hannibal-Lagrange Baptist College, Hannibal, Missouri. He eventually served in seven universities, being promoted to full-professor and receiving tenure. Progressing in higher education, he designed the curriculum and instruction doctorate for Marshall University, assisted in moving the entire master's program, with eleven areas of emphases, to an online format and wrote a fifth-grade math textbook used in up to 5000 schools.

Upon receiving tenure at Marshall University in 2006, he served as Program Director for the Graduate Elementary/Secondary Education Program. Dr. Meyer moved on to the chairmanship of the Middle Grades/Secondary Education Program at Morehead State University before being named Dean of the School of Education at a Georgia Board of Regents College.

Dr. Meyer is published nationally and is international in his presentations having been the invited guest of Beijing Normal

University and Beijing Institute of Education to address formative assessment. He is a former member of the Board of Regents of Liberty University, served on the Board of the National Association of Professors of Middle Level Education, Chaired the Special Interest Group for Middle Grades Education of the Association of Teacher Educators and as Chair of the Communications Committee. He received the "Online Faculty of the Game Award" for Marshall University in 2008.

Bivocationally, Dr. Meyer has pastored and served as Minister of Education in nine churches. Scholastically in this field, he holds a Master of Religious Education from Southwestern Baptist Theological Seminary and a Ph.D. in religion from Berean Christian College. As of the completion date of this book, Dr. Meyer and his wife, Shirley, had been married for 56 years and retired in East Tennessee.

Dr. Meyer went Home to live with Jesus on February 21, 2022, just days after he completed Cruise of Miracles.

www.ingramcontent.com/pod-product-compliance
Lightning Source LLC
Chambersburg PA
CBHW070543160426
43199CB00014B/2346